The Depression Cure

The six-step programme to beat depression without drugs

DR STEPHEN ILARDI

Vermilion
LONDON

14

Vermilion, an imprint of Ebury Publishing,
20 Vauxhall Bridge Road,
London SW1V 2SA

Vermilion is part of the Penguin Random House group of companies whose addresses can be found at global.penguinrandomhouse.com

First published in the USA by Da Capo Press, a member of the Perseus Book Group, in 2009

First published in the UK by Vermilion in 2010.
Updated edition published 2019.

www.penguin.co.uk

A CIP catalogue record for this book is available from the British Library

ISBN 9781785042515

Printed and bound in Great Britain by Clays Ltd, Elcograf S.p.A.

Penguin Random House is committed to a sustainable future for our business, our readers and our planet. This book is made from Forest Stewardship Council® certified paper.

Contents

PART THREE
MAKING THE CHANGE

Introduction

Depression is a devastating illness. It robs people of their energy, their sleep, their memory, their concentration, their vitality, their joy, their ability to love and work and play, and—sometimes—even their will to live. As a clinical psychologist, I've worked with hundreds of patients to help heal depression's debilitating effects, so I will never underestimate this treacherous foe. From the day I first walked onto a psychiatric unit at Duke Medical Center nearly three decades ago, I've devoted my career to fighting the disorder: I know it far too well to make any blanket promises of a one-size-fits-all cure.

Yet here's what I *can* say with complete confidence: Depression is beatable. And the six-step program outlined in *The Depression Cure* is the most promising treatment for depression I've ever witnessed in my years of clinical research and practice. Admittedly, this is a bold claim—one I never would have imagined making when I began developing the program.* But it's based on three important observations:

- The program—*Therapeutic Lifestyle Change* (TLC)—has proven remarkably effective in a preliminary treatment study at my university. Patients were randomly assigned to receive either TLC or treatment-as-usual in the community (mostly medication), and fewer than 25% of those in community-based treat-

* With the help of several talented graduate students.

ment got better.* But the response rate among TLC patients was over three times higher. In fact, *every single patient who put the full program into practice improved*, even though most had already failed to get well on antidepressant medications.

- All six components of the TLC program—omega-3 fatty acids, engaging activity, physical exercise, sunlight exposure, social connection, and enhanced sleep—have antidepressant properties. We know this from mountains of published research. But TLC is the only approach that combines these separate elements into an integrated package—a comprehensive, step-by-step program that's more potent than any single component on its own.
- Most important, TLC addresses the modern depression epidemic at its source: the fact that *human beings were never designed for the poorly nourished, sedentary, indoor, sleep-deprived, socially isolated, frenzied pace of 21st-century life*. The program provides a long-overdue, common-sense remedy for a contemporary First World lifestyle that's drifted dangerously off course.

In recent years, I've been invited to speak with thousands of people—patients, therapists, psychiatrists, students, and many others—about this lifestyle-based approach to healing depression. The question I'm most frequently asked is: Who might benefit from the program?

My reply: Everyone. This usually draws some laughter, as most people think I'm joking—a bit of ironic, self-mocking exaggeration. But I'm actually quite serious. At least four groups of people can

* "Getting better" was defined in the study as: experiencing at least a 50% reduction in depressive symptoms and no longer meeting diagnostic criteria for major depressive disorder by the end of treatment.

benefit from the TLC program, and together they include just about everyone.

- The program was initially designed to help those suffering from clinical depression—whether or not they're already receiving some other form of treatment. TLC is highly effective when used on its own, but the program can also be combined with antidepressant medication or traditional psychotherapy.
- Then again, you don't have to be diagnosed with full-blown depression to benefit from TLC. The protocol can also help those who are simply feeling blue or fighting milder symptoms of the disorder.
- Likewise, the program offers protection to anyone who wants to minimize the risk of depression in the future.
- And several years ago, psychologist Harriet Lerner—the best-selling author of influential books like *The Dance of Anger*—observed something else about the TLC program that I had never considered: Each step involves something that's good for us, no matter how well we may be doing already. As Harriet put it, "Your program isn't just about depression. It's something *everyone* can use to their benefit."

She's right, of course. There's a wealth of research on the physical and psychological benefits of the program's core elements: weight loss, increased energy, lower blood pressure, improved cardiac health, better immune function, reduced inflammation, greater mental clarity, and an enhanced sense of well-being. These are treatment "side effects" worth signing up for, and they represent another important reason for embracing the TLC program.

Despite the treatment's beneficial effects, it's still advisable to get a physical exam before you start putting the protocol into practice. In my own clinical research at the University of Kansas, I don't let anyone begin the full program until they've first seen a doctor. This policy may surprise you, but it's based on sound reasoning. For one thing, it's always a good idea to check with a physician before embarking on a new exercise program. The same goes for taking high-dose nutritional supplements or increasing sun exposure. Since these are all core elements of the TLC program, it's important to get the okay of your healthcare provider before you begin.

In addition, people occasionally write to ask me if they can stop taking their antidepressant medications once they begin putting the TLC program into practice. My advice is always short and simple: They *must* make any such medication-related decisions only in close consultation with their own prescribing physician. In fact, it can be dangerous to discontinue an antidepressant without close medical supervision, because in some cases difficult withdrawal symptoms—including a worsening of depression—can occur if the medication is stopped too abruptly.

Finally, depression can be triggered by many common medical conditions—diabetes, sleep apnea, thyroid disorder, heart disease, chronic infection, and hormonal imbalance, to name a few—and the disorder can be very difficult to treat effectively until such underlying medical problems are addressed. Several drugs also carry the potential to cause depression (ironically, even some common psychiatric drugs), and your doctor can help you consider this possibility, as well.

In the chapters that follow, I'll describe the Therapeutic Lifestyle Change program in clear, step-by-step detail. And I'll share the stories of those who've used the program to overcome depression and find their way to lasting recovery. My hope is that by putting TLC into practice in your own life—one step at a time—you, too, will begin living the depression cure.

PART ONE
UNDERSTANDING DEPRESSION

1
The Epidemic and the Cure

"I don't know what's wrong with me. All I want to do is close my eyes and never have to wake up again. It's like my whole life is slipping away, and there's nothing I can do about it. Everybody keeps telling me I just need to 'snap out of it.' Don't they know how cruel that is? I mean, do they think I want to be like this? Sometimes I just start crying and I don't even know what I'm crying about. People stare at me like I'm crazy, like: 'Look at that poor guy. That poor, pathetic . . .'" Phil's voice trailed off as he slumped forward in his chair and cradled his head in his hands.* He fixed his gaze on the office floor and whispered, "I'm sorry." He repeated the phrase over and over, like a mantra.

Even though I was all too familiar with the devastating effect of depression, I still found it difficult to picture what Phil had been like just a few months earlier, before his illness struck. Phil's wife, who phoned to set up his first appointment, described him as "a confident, fun-loving guy." He was someone who ran a successful business, enjoyed a strong marriage, and adored his two

* All names and other potentially indentifying information for each patient have been altered to preserve confidentiality.

kids. His wife said, "You would have looked at Phil and thought, 'Here's a guy who has it all.'" And yet there he was in my office, struck down by depression in the prime of his life. Over the span of a few short months, he had lost his energy, his memory, his sex drive, his confidence, his ability to sleep through the night, and his concentration. He could no longer function effectively at work. He had completely withdrawn from his friends and his family. Lately, he had even lost his will to live.

Like many of the patients I treat, Phil had been taking antidepressant medications for a few months before he came to see me. Unfortunately, the drugs hadn't helped very much—an outcome that's more common than most people realize. Although medications are certainly valuable in some cases, they work for fewer than half the depressed patients who try them. (And many quit taking their meds anyway due to difficult side effects like sexual dysfunction or weight gain.)

Even though antidepressant use has skyrocketed in recent years, the rate of depression in the US and UK hasn't declined: It's *increased.* According to the latest research, nearly one in three Americans—over ninety million people—will meet the criteria for major depression at some point in their lives. Ominously, the rate of depression has been on the rise for decades. It's roughly ten times higher today than it was just two generations ago. How can we be so much more vulnerable to depression now? What's changed?

It's clearly not a matter of genetics, since the collective gene pool simply can't change that quickly. It has to be something else. That something else, I believe, is lifestyle. Consider the following:

- Only one known group of Americans has escaped the modern depression epidemic: the Amish. Still clinging tenaciously to their eighteenth-century way of life, Amish communities have a rate of depression dramatically lower than that of the general population.
- In developing (third-world) countries, the lifetime rate of depression is often a fraction of that observed in the West. However, the prevalence of depression has begun to go up in those countries where people are shifting from more traditional to more Americanized lifestyles.
- The risk of depression has increased relentlessly in recent years across the entire industrialized world (such as the UK, Germany, Australia, New Zealand, and South Korea). It's not just an American phenomenon.
- Modern-day hunter-gatherer bands—such as the Kaluli people* of the New Guinea highlands—have been assessed by Western researchers for the presence of mental illness. Remarkably, *clinical depression is almost completely nonexistent among such groups*, whose way of life is similar to that of our remote ancestors. Despite living very hard lives—with none of the material comforts or medical advances we take for granted—they're largely immune from the plague of depressive illness that we see ruining lives all around us. (In perhaps the most telling example, anthropologist Edward Schieffelin lived among the Kaluli for nearly a decade and

* The Kaluli subsist on a combination of hunting, foraging, and gardening, so they are also sometimes referred to as horticulturalists.

carefully interviewed over two thousand men, women, and children regarding their experience of grief and depression; he found only one person who came close to meeting our full diagnostic criteria for depressive illness.)

Such cross-cultural studies make one thing quite clear: the more "modern" a society's way of life, the higher its rate of depression. It may seem baffling, but the explanation is simple: *The human body was never designed for the modern post-industrial environment.* Until about twelve thousand years ago—when people invented farming and began domesticating livestock—everyone on the planet made their living by hunting and foraging for food. People lived as hunter-gatherers for the vast majority of human history.

And our genes still reflect this history: They've changed very little since the days of our hunter-gatherer forebears. Our genes are still beautifully calibrated to that ancient environment, and they're still building—in effect—Stone Age bodies. Unfortunately, when Stone Age body meets modern environment, the health consequences can be disastrous.

Consider the obesity epidemic. A staggering 70% of American adults are now clinically overweight. Why? Because our appetites are still fine-tuned to the Stone Age. Our hunter-gatherer ancestors faced a fluctuating, seasonal food supply—with the prospect of hunger and starvation ever just around the corner. So it made sense for them to crave sweets, starches, and fats—the richest calorie sources available—and to binge whenever those rare, nutrient-rich foods happened to be on hand.

Our brains still harbor this ancient programming. We, too, find it virtually impossible to resist the urge to feast on calorie-rich foods. When we savor, say, a slice of cheesecake (a sweet, starchy, fatty trifecta), our Stone Age brains gleefully register the satisfaction of storing away many, many calories for a rainy day—no matter how much energy might already be tucked away in our fat reserves.

But over the past several decades, for the first time in human history, high-calorie foods have become available 24/7. Because the brain was never designed to regulate appetite in the face of such perpetual abundance, daily calorie consumption has gone through the roof. We see the food and our brains can't "just say no." To make matters worse, this nutritional bonanza has coincided with a sharp drop in the number of calories people burn each day, as conveniences like cars, electrical appliances, and television have gradually turned us into a nation of couch potatoes. The result? A modern epidemic that's explained by recent changes in lifestyle.

The Amish, duly famous for their resistance to lifestyle changes over the past two centuries, make the point quite powerfully. Their rate of obesity? A recent study puts it at a mere 4%. As for modern-day hunter-gatherers, their obesity level is approximately 0%.

But can the modern scourge of depression, like that of obesity, really be explained by changes in the way people live? A wealth of scientific evidence—from several converging lines of research—says it can. As we'll see in the next section, this evidence has important implications that may forever change the way we understand and treat depression.

THE ANTIDEPRESSANT LIFESTYLE

In many respects, Americans and Britons should be among the happiest people in the history of the world. Whether we look at rates of infant mortality, hunger, medical care, life expectancy, or material comforts, we are better off (on average) than the vast majority of people who have ever lived. Doesn't it follow, then, that we should also be among the least likely to get depressed? Shouldn't we, at the very least, have lower rates of depression than contemporary hunter-gatherers, whose lives are often much harder than our own? After all, they're much more likely than we are to experience tragic events like the death of a child, crippling illness, or violent assault—events that can serve as powerful triggers of depression.

Yet even as they suffer these disastrous events, hunter-gatherers rarely become clinically depressed. For some reason, they're much more resilient than we are. (It's a good thing, too, because if they *weren't*, the human species probably would have become extinct back in the days of our remote ancestors.)

But how are hunter-gatherers able to weather life's storms so effectively? That's the question I kept coming back to when I began wrestling with this mystery a few years ago. What emerged from my quest, after poring over hundreds of published studies in search of clues, was a finding so clear—and so obvious in hindsight—I was amazed no one had ever noticed it:* *The hunter-gatherer lifestyle is profoundly antidepressant.* As they go about their daily lives, hunter-gatherers naturally wind up doing many things that keep them from getting depressed. They do things that change the brain more powerfully than any medication.

For most of human history, everyone benefited from the antidepressant effect of these ancient lifestyle elements. As a result,

---

* At least, after reviewing the relevant scientific literature, I couldn't determine that anyone had noticed it. Science journalist Robert Wright does hint at the possibility, however, in his 1995 *Time* magazine article, "The Evolution of Despair."

people were able to cope with circumstances vastly more difficult than most of us ever face today. But over the past few hundred years, technological evolution has proceeded at a relentless pace, and many protective features of that ancient way of life have gradually disappeared. Accordingly, the rate of depression has begun to spiral out of control. Our Stone Age brains just weren't designed to handle the sedentary, isolated, indoor, sleep-deprived, fast-food-laden, stressed-out pace of twenty-first-century life.

In the chapters that follow, we'll look at the potent antidepressant effects of six major protective lifestyle elements that we all need to reclaim from our ancestors:

- Dietary omega-3 fatty acids
- Engaging activity
- Physical exercise
- Sunlight exposure
- Social support
- Sleep

These six elements form the core of a breakthrough treatment for depression, Therapeutic Lifestyle Change (TLC), developed by my clinical research team at the University of Kansas. TLC is a natural approach to healing depression, with no common side effects and no insurance forms to file. And in our preliminary research, TLC has yielded exceptional results—far superior to those typically observed with medication. Among our study patients, the rate of favorable response to TLC has been *over three times higher* than that of antidepressant "treatment as usual" in the community. And we've yet to see someone put the entire TLC protocol into practice without experiencing significant improvement.

Omega-3 Fatty Acids

Did you know your brain is mostly made up of fat? It sounds like a straight line from a stand-up comedy routine, but it's true—the human brain is about 60% fat by dry weight. Fat molecules (sometimes called *fatty acids*) play a crucial role in the construction of brain cells and the insulation of nerve fibers. Fortunately, the body is able to make many of the fat molecules the brain needs. But there are some forms that the body can't manufacture on its own; these fats can be obtained only from our diet. And among the most important dietary fats is a group called *omega-3* fatty acids—critical building blocks for brain structure and function.

Omega-3 fatty acids are found mainly in fish, wild game, nuts, seeds, and leafy vegetables, all things found in abundance in the hunter-gatherer diet. *Our distant ancestors ate five to ten times more omega-3 fat than we do.* In fact, omega-3s have gradually disappeared from the American diet over the past century.

In the days of our great-grandparents, for example, beef cattle fed on the free range, where they ate grasses and wild plant sources of omega-3. Remarkably, beef used to be good for us. Today's cattle, in contrast, are mostly grain-fed, and they have little beneficial omega-3 content. The same is true with our grain-fed, farm-raised fish (most of the fish now consumed in America).

Because the brain needs a steady supply of omega-3s to function properly, people who don't eat enough of these fats are at increased risk for many forms of mental illness, including depression. Across the globe, countries with the highest levels of omega-3 consumption typically have the lowest rates of depression.

Clinical researchers have even started using omega-3 supplements to treat depression, and the results so far have been highly encouraging. For example, British researchers recently studied a group of depressed patients who had failed to recover after taking antidepressant medication for eight weeks. All study patients stayed on their meds as prescribed, but some also took an omega-3 supplement. About 70% of those who received the supplement* went on to recover, compared with only 25% of patients who kept taking only the medication. This study—along with dozens of others like it—suggests that omega-3s may be among the most effective antidepressant substances ever discovered.

Engaging Activity

Depression is closely linked to a toxic thought process called *rumination*—the habit of dwelling on negative thoughts, turning them over and over in your mind. We've probably all ruminated at some point. It's a perfectly natural response to upsetting events. And when rumination lasts for only a short while, it can even be useful, helping us figure out what went wrong and how we might work to correct things in the future.

The problem comes when people start ruminating for long stretches of time, going over the same thoughts again and again and again. Such chronic rumination actually cranks up the intensity of our negative mood, making it unbearably painful.

---

* Study patients were randomly assigned to various omega-3 dosage levels. I've presented here the results for those who received the supplement at the dose recommended in the TLC protocol: 1,000 mg per day of the active omega-3 molecule.

Unfortunately, many depressed individuals spend literally hours ruminating every day.

The first time I introduced the concept of rumination to patients in a TLC group, it was as if a light went on for many people in the room. "I do that all the time!" one patient exclaimed. "And it definitely makes me feel worse." Someone else chimed in, "You mean there are people who *don't* ruminate all the time? I thought it was just something everyone did." Another smiled knowingly and said, "It's so cool that there's actually a *name* for it. But how do you *stop* ruminating?"

How, indeed? For one thing, people tend to ruminate when they have free time on their hands, when their minds aren't occupied with some reasonably engaging activity. Sitting stuck in traffic, watching a boring TV show, eating a meal alone, staring off into space . . . those are the times when rumination typically takes over. The biggest risk factor for rumination is simply spending time alone, something Britons now do all the time.

When you're actively interacting with another person, your mind just doesn't have a chance to dwell on repetitive negative thoughts. But, really, any sort of engaging activity can work to interrupt rumination. It can even be something simple.

Dana, a forty-something accountant in one of our TLC groups, told us the following story: "You guys had just covered rumination, and literally as I was driving out of the parking lot after group, I noticed I was doing it! The negative thoughts were right there, going around and around in my head. I mean, I had no idea I was doing it that often. Anyway, I pulled the car over and just sat there in the parking lot and thought about how I could stop it. All I could think of was to turn on the radio and find a good song to focus on instead, so that's what I did. And it worked. I didn't ruminate for the entire drive home. Before I learned about this, I would have just stewed in those negative thoughts and pulled into my garage feeling like crap, but now I think I know how to turn it around. It feels like I finally have some control."

In Chapter 5, we'll go over the link between rumination and depression in much greater detail. We'll also cover several key strategies for helping you break the rumination habit.

Physical Exercise

Hunter-gatherers are in remarkably good shape. They get hours of exercise every day, with a fitness routine rivaling that of elite athletes. They commonly walk five to ten miles each day just to find food and water, which they then have to haul back to the rest of the group. They erect their own dwellings and routinely handle logs weighing hundreds of pounds. They perform ritual dances that last for hours.

In effect, the hunter-gatherer life is an intense cross-training regimen—one that involves lots of lifting, carrying, sprinting, climbing, walking, and stretching on a daily basis. Modern life, on the other hand, is notoriously sedentary, and most Americans are woefully out of shape. Many can run no farther than the distance from the sofa to the refrigerator. This is unfortunate, because exercise is a remarkably potent antidepressant.

Researchers have compared aerobic exercise and Sertraline (a commonly prescribed antidepressant medication) head-to-head in the treatment of depression. Even at a low "dose" of exercise—thirty minutes of brisk walking three times a week—patients who worked out did just as well as those who took the medication. Strikingly, though, the patients on Sertraline were about three times more likely than exercisers to become depressed again over a ten-month follow-up period.

There are now over a hundred published studies documenting the antidepressant effects of exercise. Activities as varied as walking, biking, jogging, and weight lifting have all been found to be effective. It's also becoming clear just *how* they work. *Exercise changes the brain.* It increases the activity level of important brain chemicals such as dopamine and serotonin (the same neurochemical targeted by popular drugs like Sertraline and Prozac). Exercise also increases the brain's production of a key growth hormone called BDNF. Because levels of this hormone plummet in depression, some parts of the brain start to shrink over time, and learning and memory are impaired. But exercise reverses this trend, protecting the brain in a way nothing else can.

Chloe, a twenty-one-year-old college student with a shy smile, was a patient in one of our TLC treatment groups. Introducing herself at the first session, she told us, "I've struggled with depression—on and off—for pretty much my whole life."

Abandoned by her mother and raised by an alcoholic father who often left her to fend for herself, Chloe confessed that feelings of loneliness and sadness were constant fixtures of her childhood and adolescence. Things got even worse when she went off to college, where she fell into a debilitating episode of clinical depression. By the time she started treatment, she had stopped attending her classes and instead spent much of her time holed up alone in her apartment.

I spoke with Chloe early on in her treatment about the therapeutic value of exercise, but she said she'd never enjoyed working out. She also expressed a strong distaste for "the whole gym scene." I reassured her that our goal was to help her find some kind of physical activity she could enjoy. "I guess I used to like riding my bike as a kid," she recalled, "but I haven't done anything like that in years." With a little encouragement, she agreed to make a trip home to pick up her old bike and bring it back to campus. The following week, Chloe started going out for short rides, mostly just exploring the streets around her neighborhood. But before long she was pedaling all over town, often riding for over an hour each day.

Within a few weeks, Chloe began noticing a bit of improvement in her mood, her energy, and her sleep. Even though she was still depressed, this modest turn for the better seemed to spark a glimmer of hope. So, despite her continued symptoms, she kept on riding. And things slowly kept getting better. The following week, buoyed by her increased energy (a typical side effect of regular exercise), she worked up the courage to venture out shopping with some girls who lived next door in her apartment complex. Chloe found—much to her surprise—that she actually enjoyed herself. Soon, it was like a vicious cycle in reverse: exercise led to increased energy, which led to a better mood, which led to greater social activity, which led to more exercise (since she rode her bike to most social engagements), which led to increased energy, and so on.

The more we learn about the beneficial effects of physical activity, the more the following truth comes clearly into focus: *Exercise is medicine.* Literally. Just like a pill, it reliably changes brain function by altering the activity of key brain chemicals and hormones. This is a crucial point, but one that's often missed. For when people hear that depression is linked to a chemical imbalance, they usually conclude, "Well, if *that's* true, people with depression obviously need to take a drug—another chemical—to straighten out the imbalance." It's an understandable assumption, but it's dead wrong. Medication isn't the only way to correct brain abnormalities in depression. Physical exercise also brings about profound changes in the brain—changes that rival those seen with the most potent antidepressant medications.

In Chapter 6, I'll explain how you can start and maintain an exercise program to bring about these important benefits. You'll find a way to work out that doesn't feel like *work*—an exercise routine you can actually enjoy. After all, isn't that the best way to make sure you'll stick with it? And I can reassure you at the outset: Antidepressant exercise is much more doable than most people imagine, and it doesn't require an expensive gym membership. It can be as easy as going for a walk with a friend or taking a bike ride in the park. Physical activity is something we were designed to find enjoyable.

Sunlight Exposure

Millions of Americans and Europeans get depressed every year, almost like clockwork, during the dark, dreary months of winter. They suffer from a disorder aptly named SAD (for *seasonal affective disorder*)—a condition triggered by reduced light exposure during the short, cold, cloudy days that run from November through February or March (depending on where you live). Predictably, SAD hits people particularly hard in northern latitudes, where winter daylight is scarce (residents of New England, for example, are afflicted much more often than those living in Florida).

Although simply going outside on a sunny day can brighten your mood, an even deeper link exists between light exposure and depression—one involving the body's internal clock. As it turns out, the brain gauges the amount of light you get each day, and it uses that information to reset your body clock. Without enough light exposure, the body clock eventually gets out of sync, and when that happens, it throws off important *circadian rhythms* that regulate energy, sleep, appetite, and hormone levels. The disruption of these important biological rhythms can, in turn, trigger clinical depression.

Because natural sunlight is so much brighter than indoor lighting—over a hundred times brighter, on average—a half hour of sunlight is enough to reset your body clock. Even the natural light of a gray, cloudy day is several times brighter than the inside of most people's houses, and a few hours of exposure provide just enough light to keep circadian rhythms well regulated. But people who are inside from dawn to dusk often find their body clocks starting to malfunction.

Of course, thousands of years ago our ancestors were outside all day every day, so they always had enough light exposure to boost mood and prevent SAD. Likewise with modern-day hunter-gatherers. Even Americans of a few generations ago typically spent at least a few hours outside each day. For us, though, the situation is different. Increasingly, we just aren't bothering to go outside at all. And even if we wanted to, most of us don't have the luxury of spending hours at a time outside on a regular basis.

Fortunately, when getting enough sunlight isn't a realistic option (during the shorter days of winter, for example), you can use an elegant, high-tech solution that's effective in elevating mood and resetting the body's internal clock. In Chapter 7, we'll cover a range of options—both natural and high-tech—for getting adequate light exposure year-round and keeping mood and circadian rhythms in sync.

Social Support

Anthropologists who visit modern foraging tribes invariably notice something peculiar about their hosts' social lives: *Hunter-gatherers almost never spend time alone.* Even though the typical village consists of only fifty to two hundred people, it seems that just about every activity is a social occasion. Hunting, cooking, eating, playing, foraging, sleeping, grooming—they're all carried out in the company of close friends and loved ones. Loneliness and social isolation are virtually unknown.

The contrast with our way of life is profound. We often struggle to carve out the smallest blocks of face time with the very people we hold most dear. Not only do we spend much less time than previous generations interacting with our friends, neighbors, and extended family, but we're even less likely to connect with others in church or synagogue, or in civic groups like the Rotary Club or Scouts.

Sadly, many Americans now spend the bulk of their leisure time walled up in their homes, parked in front of a TV or computer screen—alone. They spend hours each week sitting in traffic—alone. They often eat alone. And now they can even go online and do their shopping alone.

In many cases, technology promotes our increasing social isolation. For example, until a few months ago, I used to enjoy bumping into my friends and neighbors at the local video rental store. But that doesn't happen anymore, now that I can stream films. And even on the university campus where I teach—a place where people are still forced to get out and walk in public—many are now oblivious to the social world around them as they march along to music on their phones. Sadly, our coolest new gadgets always seem to wind up cutting us off from each other.

As if we weren't becoming isolated enough, one of the great tragedies of depression is that it causes people to withdraw even further from the people around them.

Jane, a middle-aged divorcee with downcast eyes, was one of the more socially withdrawn patients we've ever treated in a TLC group. She used to shuffle unobtrusively in to each session, staring at her feet and speaking (only when spoken to) in a barely audible voice. Since depression had taken hold of her life the year before, she'd become increasingly reclusive, pulling away from her friends and loved ones, and even avoiding her adult children who lived in the area. But as my co-therapist and I learned more about Jane over the first few TLC sessions, it became clear that before her depression struck she'd been a vibrant, socially confident woman. A few weeks into treatment, we gently challenged her to think about friends or loved ones she might try to reconnect with, and she promised to "think about it." As fate would have it, her daughter contacted her shortly afterward to see if Jane might be willing to watch her two-year-old grandson every night after work that week. Reluctantly, she agreed.

After just a few days of this "grandson therapy," Jane noticed her mood starting to lift slightly and a little bit of her energy returning. The shift was subtle, but she said it felt like "somehow life wasn't quite so awful." So she took the fateful step of volunteering to watch her grandson the following week as well, and the improvement in her mood and energy slowly continued.

Jane was surprised by this clear connection between social contact and mood, but she couldn't deny her own experience. Gradually, with our encouragement, she started reaching out to reconnect with other people as well—an old friend, a neighbor, a coworker, a daughter. She said it felt like she was learning to reconnect with her old self in the process, to rediscover the person she used to be before depression robbed her of her social world. Inspired by her progress on this front, Jane grew determined to put other TLC elements into practice: She began getting regular exercise, taking an omega-3 supplement, and seeking out daily sunlight exposure. Over time, this process catalyzed further improvement—her sleep, her concentration, her appetite, and her confidence all slowly began to return. Fourteen weeks after she began treatment, Jane's depression was in full remission.

The research on this issue is clear: When it comes to depression, relationships matter. People who lack a supportive social network face an increased risk of becoming depressed, and of remaining depressed once an episode strikes. Fortunately, we can do a great deal to improve the quality and depth of our connections with others, and this can have a huge payoff in terms of fighting depression and reducing the risk of recurrence. In Chapter 8, I'll help you assess the strength of your social support networks, and provide a set of strategies for enhancing the quality of your connections with others.

Sleep

As you've likely discovered from your own experience, sleep and mood are intimately connected. After just a few nights of poor sleep, most people are noticeably less upbeat. Many of us start to get downright cranky. And when sleep deprivation continues for days or weeks at a time, it can interfere with our ability to think clearly. It can even bring about serious health consequences. Disrupted sleep is one of the most potent triggers of depression, and there's evidence that most episodes of mood disorder are preceded by at least several weeks of subpar slumber.

Not only can poor sleep cause depression, but depression can cause poor sleep. (Talk about a vicious cycle.) Fully 80% of depressed patients experience some form of sleep disturbance. While some have trouble drifting off at night, most have even greater difficulty *staying* asleep. Often, they'll find themselves wide awake in the middle of the night, tossing and turning until daybreak. Even worse, depression also affects sleep *quality,* depriving people of the deepest, most rejuvenating sleep phase (known as *slow-wave sleep).*

Despite its obvious importance, a good night's sleep is something many of us rarely get. It's a distinctly modern problem. Hunter-gatherers, whose sleep cycles are closely bound to the natural ebb and flow of darkness and daylight, have been observed to sleep about 10 hours a night. Even American adults of the nineteenth century averaged a good 9 hours. And now? American adults clock in at a paltry 6.7 hours per night. Not surprisingly, most of us walk around in a state of perpetual drowsiness, masked only by our collective caffeine habit (about 90% of Americans now consume it on a daily basis) and the widespread use of other stimulants.

Fortunately, as we'll cover in Chapter 9, you can take numerous steps to improve both the quality and quantity of your sleep. Not only can these strategies help improve mood and many other symptoms of depression, but they can also prevent the chronically disturbed sleep that so often ushers in an episode of full-blown depressive illness.

THERAPEUTIC LIFESTYLE CHANGE: AN IDEA WHOSE TIME HAS COME

The way we live can powerfully affect the way we feel. It's a simple observation, but one with profound implications when it comes to fighting depression. For as we've seen, six distinct lifestyle elements—ranging from exercise to nutrition (omega-3 fats) to social support to light exposure—can fight depression as effectively as any medication. They can even bring about important changes in the brain. Modern-day hunter-gatherers benefit from each of these lifestyle factors in abundance, and this explains why they rarely get depressed, despite leading very difficult lives. And although the world has changed a great deal since the days of our ancestors, these protective lifestyle elements were still present in American and British life—to a somewhat lesser extent—right up until the past century. In recent decades, though, they have steadily disappeared, and the rate of depression has skyrocketed in lockstep with their departure.

When I first began to put all this together a few years ago, I started encouraging my depressed patients—whom I treated at the time with a more traditional form of psychotherapy—to incorporate these antidepressant lifestyle elements into their daily routines. Not only did I find that most patients were surprisingly eager to make such lifestyle changes, but the clinical results were stunning. Even patients who had not responded to drugs or traditional therapy began recovering—*quickly*.

Such dramatic results took me by surprise. Sure, I thought a lifestyle-based strategy might be helpful in some cases of depression, but I had no idea just how powerful it would prove to be. I caught an early glimpse of its effectiveness, however, in the experience of the first patient I ever worked with on these principles of therapeutic lifestyle change.

A tall, soft-spoken man in his mid-forties, Bill had been severely depressed for over four years. Other than a few brief periods of remission, he had been continuously depressed since his early teens. When we started working together, he had already been on depression medication for well over a year with little meaningful improvement.

In one of our first sessions together, Bill casually mentioned that although he didn't exercise regularly, he'd noticed in the past that working out sometimes made him feel a little better, at least for a short while. Since I'd recently been immersed in the research literature on exercise and depression, I was intrigued by his comment and decided to push him a bit on the point. "Bill, would you be willing to try working out on a regular basis? Dozens of published studies show it can help with symptoms of depression." Although his energy level was pretty low, he agreed to try jogging three times a week, either outside or on the small treadmill stored in his basement. (Like most pieces of home exercise equipment, it had been gathering dust for years.)

At our next session, Bill reported a small but noticeable improvement in his ability to sleep through the night, and he attributed this to the exercise. The following week brought a noticeable upswing in his energy level. Encouraged by this development, I decided to see if he was willing to crank things up a notch on the lifestyle front. So we spent the next few sessions talking about the clinical benefits of omega-3 supplementation, the toxic effects of time spent alone ruminating, and the importance of getting adequate sunlight exposure, social support, and sleep. To his immense credit, Bill gradually began putting into practice every major therapeutic lifestyle element we discussed. And within two months, his depressive symptoms were gone. Completely gone. It was nothing short of remarkable.

It's now been over five years since we began working together, and Bill is still fully recovered—the first stretch of continuous recovery in his adult life. In fact, we still touch base by phone every so often for a quick checkup, and during our most recent conversation Bill told me, "Steve, these past four years have been by far the best of my life."

Many others like Bill—people who had given up hope of ever beating their depression—have overcome the dreaded illness as well. The great majority of patients in our clinical trials have escaped depression's grip, and the response rate to Therapeutic Lifestyle Change has been considerably higher than researchers typically see with antidepressant medication.

I realize this is a surprising claim. After all, depression is a serious illness—one that robs people of their vitality, their hope, their sleep, their play, their friends, their work, and sometimes even their very lives. Can this debilitating disorder really be fought more effectively with a set of basic lifestyle changes than with powerful antidepressant drugs?

It *is* hard to believe. But I've seen firsthand the dramatic improvements that typically follow in the wake of these simple changes, even among those who haven't responded to medication.

Despite the best efforts of mental health professionals, depression continues to destroy millions of lives each year. This simply cannot continue. As we begin to reclaim the natural antidepressant benefits of the life we were all designed for, I believe we can put an end to the modern depression epidemic once and for all.

2
Making Sense of Depression

Mysteriously and in ways that are totally remote from normal experience, the gray drizzle of horror induced by depression takes on the quality of physical pain. But it is not an immediately identifiable pain, like that of a broken limb. It may be more accurate to say that despair, owing to some evil trick played upon the sick brain by the inhabiting psyche, comes to resemble the diabolical discomfort of being imprisoned in a fiercely overheated room. And because no breeze stirs this caldron, because there is no escape from the smothering confinement, it is entirely natural that the victim begins to think ceaselessly of oblivion.

—William Styron, ***Darkness Visible***

Wendy, a thirty-four-year-old middle school teacher from Kansas City, enrolled in one of our Therapeutic Lifestyle Change groups a few years ago after struggling with depression for the better part of a year. Like many of the patients we've worked with, she said her friends and family didn't really understand the disorder that had her in its grip. During the group's first session, as we reviewed the hallmark symptoms of depression and the devastation the illness leaves in its wake, Wendy turned to me and said, "You guys—you psychiatrists or psychologists or whatever—really need to come up with a better name for this thing. *Depression* just doesn't cut it. I mean, everyone knows the word, so they think they get what it's all about. But most of them have no idea."

She has a point. Depression *is* a problematic word, the source of so much needless confusion and misunderstanding. Here's the problem: Depression has two very different meanings—depending on the context—and people mix them up all the time.

In casual, everyday conversation, depression serves as a good synonym for *sadness.* In this sense, it's simply a mood state we all experience from time to time, typically after we've brushed up against one of life's inevitable setbacks or disappointments. For example, I've heard people say they were depressed after watching their favorite team lose a big game, or even after ripping a hole in a good pair of blue jeans. Such "depression" doesn't last for long, and it rarely affects our ability to function.

In a clinical context, however, the word has a radically different meaning. It refers to a profoundly debilitating form of mental illness. (The precise diagnostic label is *major depressive disorder*, but most clinicians simply call it *depression* for short.) It's a syndrome that deprives people of their energy, sleep, concentration, joy, confidence, memory, sex drive—their ability to love and work and play. It can even rob them of their will to live. Over time, depression damages the brain and wreaks havoc on the body. It's a treacherous illness—a shudder-inducing foe that no one in their right mind would ever take lightly, certainly not if they understood the disorder's capacity to destroy life.

Unfortunately, despite an encouraging increase in public awareness in recent years, confusion about depression abounds. In short, people still confuse the two vastly different meanings of the word. That's why so many believe the disorder is no big deal, that those cut down by the illness are just making mountains out of molehills. As one of my unenlightened students put it in class a few years ago, "I've always assumed these people are just a bunch of slackers—whiners who simply need to suck it up and snap out of it."

Over the years, I've found that such harsh, critical judgments usually stem from ignorance. Fortunately, once people grasp the true nature of depression, they usually develop a strong sense of compassion for those who fall under the disorder's tragic sway. The same basic principle also applies to one's *own* experience of depression: Knowledge can serve as a powerful defense against the destructive impulse of self-blame.

So, although this is a book about strategies for treating depression, I think it's useful to pause first to reflect on what the disorder is all about, and to address the most important questions people commonly raise. How is depression diagnosed? What are its telltale symptoms? What causes people to get depressed? Doesn't stress play a big role? What about genetics? And is depression really just a matter of chemical imbalance? It is to these questions that we now turn.

THE SYMPTOMS AND THE DIAGNOSIS

In the often-mysterious world of mental health practice, diagnoses are made according to the criteria laid out in a reference book called the *Diagnostic and Statistical Manual of Mental Disorders.* Most of us in the field simply call it the *DSM,* for short. The book serves like a sort of diagnostic Bible, with a set of elaborate rules for deciding exactly who does and doesn't qualify to be diagnosed with any given disorder. When it comes to the diagnosis of depression (*major depressive episode* in technical diagnostic language), fortunately, the criteria are pretty straightforward.

First, the *DSM-5* lays out a set of nine core diagnostic symptoms:

1. Depressed mood
2. Loss of interest or pleasure in all (or nearly all) activities
3. A large increase or decrease in appetite/weight
4. Insomnia or hypersomnia (greatly increased sleep)
5. Slowing of physical movements, or severe agitation
6. Intense fatigue
7. Excessive feelings of guilt or worthlessness
8. Difficulty concentrating or making decisions
9. Frequent thoughts of death, or suicidality

A diagnosis requires at least *five** of these hallmark symptoms to be present most of the day, nearly every day, for two weeks or more. These core symptoms also have to cause functional impairment or severe distress. In addition, the *DSM* includes some common sense guidelines to help clinicians distinguish between authentic cases of depression and other syndromes that can mimic the disorder—such as poor thyroid function, chronic

* And at least one of these symptoms has to be either depressed mood or loss of interest/pleasure.

fatigue syndrome, or some forms of substance abuse.* Likewise, the *DSM* urges clinicians to delay making a diagnosis for up to two months when someone has suffered the death of a family member or close friend, as it's normal to experience at least some depressive symptoms—including sad mood, thoughts of death, and sleep disturbance—when we've just lost a loved one.†

Although the *DSM* does a pretty good job of laying out the most common symptoms of depression, it leaves much to be desired when it comes to conveying what the disorder actually *feels like.* For example, in talking with hundreds of patients over the years, I've been struck by how often they use the word *pain* to describe the experience. (The word is nowhere to be found in the diagnostic criteria.) Several have told me the emotional anguish of depression far outstrips anything they've endured in the way of physical pain. They say it's worse, by orders of magnitude, than the prolonged agony of natural childbirth, spinal injury, or passing a kidney stone.

Back when I was a rookie psychology intern at Duke Medical Center, one of my patients helped me gain a much-needed sense of perspective on the intense suffering depression entails. He said right before he was hospitalized, he spent an entire day curled up in a fetal position on the floor of his apartment, sobbing, with no energy to move and powerless to get up. But then he finally

* In essence, if the depressive symptoms can be explained by a medical illness or the effects of substance use (or withdrawal), the diagnosis needs to reflect that.

† However, if the bereaved individual is suicidal or suffers from major functional impairment, a depression diagnosis may be given after only two weeks.

noticed a little improvement in the evening. So he forced himself to get up and make a long-neglected trip to the grocery store. As he ambled up and down the aisles, he noticed a haggard man perched in a wheelchair near the checkout line. The man had visibly shriveled legs, and one of his arms had been amputated just below the shoulder. After passing him, many customers would glance back in pity. Taking in the scene, my patient began brooding: "I've been in agony for months, but no one else can see it. As far as they know, there's nothing to be concerned about and nothing to pity. But if they could actually see what I'm going through, they'd know that I'd give my right arm to be free from this depression, and I'd do it in a heartbeat. *I would give literally anything—even my limbs—just to escape this pain.*"

DEPRESSION ON THE BRAIN

As it turns out, some of the brain pathways that register physical pain serve double-duty by signaling emotional pain as well. These important neural hubs—with obscure Latin names such as *subgenual cingulate, thalamus*, *amygdala,* and *orbitofrontal cortex*—light up every time they detect something harmful happening to the body, and they don't always distinguish between physical and emotional sources of injury. As far as the brain is concerned, the experience of depression is very much like an excruciating physical sensation that never goes away. The illness brings relentless suffering, week after torturous week.

To make matters worse, depression also locks the brain into a gloomy, biased mode of thinking, shifting our perceptions in an extremely negative direction. Because it causes us to view things in the darkest possible terms, most depressed patients come to believe things will never get better. They genuinely believe their pain will never end, despite all the evidence to the contrary. That's why many eventually look to death in a desperate bid to escape their (seemingly endless) suffering. Each year, depression accounts for an estimated one million lives lost to suicide worldwide—a tragedy of unimaginable proportions.

The Stress Response

The toxic effects of depression on the brain are pervasive, going far beyond the function of pain circuits and biased thinking. It's impossible to truly understand the disorder—and equally impossible to treat it effectively—without factoring into the equation the myriad crucial events taking place in our gray matter. Although the neurological underpinnings of depression are astonishingly complex, involving dozens of neurotransmitters (brain chemicals), hundreds of specific brain regions, and billions of individual neurons, one of the most important discoveries on this front is remarkably intuitive: *a key trigger for depression is the brain's runaway stress response.*

Like death and taxes, stress is an unavoidable part of life. Most of us endure at least a few stressors every day: getting stuck in heavy traffic, quarreling with a family member, facing a tight deadline at work, opening an unexpectedly large bill—the list goes on and on. And when we face such strains, the brain springs into action with a clever set of adaptations that prepare us to rise to the occasion. But here's the thing: The brain's stress response system is ancient (in evolutionary terms). It's designed to help us deal with the sort of intense, short-term challenges faced by our remote ancestors. It's poorly suited to the stressors we face today.

When our hunter-gatherer forebears experienced stress, it often involved an immediate *fight-or-flight* response—evading a predator, fending off an attack from a hostile neighboring tribe, or scurrying for shelter in the face of an oncoming storm. In that ancient environment, *stress signaled the immediate need for vigorous physical activity.* And the brain's stress response is still calibrated to those ancestral conditions, mobilizing a cascade of physical reactions that quickly prepare the body for an intense burst of action.

For starters, when we're stressed, our bodies release potent hormones such as adrenaline and cortisol, which set in motion a host of other reactions. The liver dumps its stores of sugar into the bloodstream, providing booster fuel for the muscles. The lungs ramp up their intake of oxygen (another muscle fuel). The heart beats faster and stronger, sending more nutrient-rich blood throughout the body. And the immune system shifts into tissue repair mode to get ready for any injuries that might happen during a fight-or-flight encounter.

Bizarrely, when the stress response lasts into the night, it even prompts the brain to change the structure of our sleep. It shifts us out of the deep, restorative slumber the body needs and pushes us instead into a much shallower, restless, dream-filled sleep—not nearly as healthy for the body, but easier to wake up from in the case of encroaching danger.

Such changes are beautifully calibrated to an ancient world in which each stressor called for a robust physical response to a short-term threat. And even though the stress response can wreak havoc on the body if it ever lasts longer than a few days, ancestral life included several built-in safeguards to make sure that didn't happen. For example, intense physical exercise—once part of nearly every fight-or-flight encounter—provides direct feedback to the brain, prompting it to slam the brakes on its stress circuitry. (The basic message to the brain is: "A big burst of activity just took place, so there's no need to keep gearing up for more.") Likewise, the protective presence of loved ones—which our forebears experienced for the better part of each day—gives the brain a strong, primal signal that we're probably no longer in any immediate danger, so it ratchets down the stress response accordingly.

With such protective mechanisms in place, our hunter-gatherer ancestors were well-equipped to face the stressful events that came their way. They could instantly mobilize for activity in a crisis and just as quickly find their way back to a state of calm when the challenge had passed. How can we know? We can study modern-day hunter-gatherers, whose way of life is similar to that of our remote ancestors. And in one telling investigation, contemporary hunter-gatherers were found to have low levels of circulating stress hormones—considerably lower, on average, than those of the typical Brit or American.

Then again, modern life seems almost perversely designed to keep the brain's stress response in high gear, with a relentless procession of day-to-day pressures and hassles. However, while these routine, everyday strains certainly *can* usher in an episode of depression, they usually don't. Instead, the illness is most often triggered by the added stress of more painful, high-impact events—divorce, separation, job loss, sickness, failure, rejection, physical assault, or geographic relocation. For people who are vulnerable to depression (we'll take a careful look at who they are in the next section), such traumatic events can kick the brain's stress circuitry into such a high state of overdrive that it simply can't be turned off.

How, exactly, does the runaway stress response cause the full-blown syndrome of depression—with symptoms like social withdrawal and lethargy and loss of concentration and sleep disturbance? The short answer: It's complicated. Thousands of talented researchers from all over the world have been working for decades to fully unravel the causes of depressive illness. Every year, the picture comes a bit more clearly into focus. Two areas of the brain that play particularly important roles are the *frontal cortex,* which regulates mood and behavior, and the specialized neural circuits that coordinate sleep. We'll consider each in turn.

Frontal Assault

The frontal cortex is the outer part of the brain that sits right behind the eye sockets and forehead. It's the hub of conscious mental life, where the sense of self is made flesh. And, like many other regions of the brain, the frontal cortex is split down the middle. It's divided into separate-but-equal hemispheres (left and right) that play distinct, complementary roles in shaping our mood and behavior.

The frontal cortex is also richly interconnected with a little almond-shaped area deep in the brain called the *amygdala*—it's the brain's generator of strong emotions. The two hemispheres of the frontal cortex work with the amygdala to steer and direct our deepest feelings. When the left frontal hemisphere grows more active than the right, for example, our mood shifts in a positive direction and we experience a strong impulse to pursue our goals.* On the other hand, when the left hemisphere shuts down, mood takes a sharply negative turn, goal pursuit stops, and we become focused instead on avoiding harm. People who have suffered major damage to the left frontal cortex typically experience depressed mood, along with a profound decline in goal-directed activities. Frequently, they meet the full diagnostic criteria for depression.

As you may have guessed, the brain's runaway stress response—that important neurological trigger for depression—also causes a dramatic decrease in left frontal cortex activity. This, in turn, sends mood and activity levels plummeting.

Stress hormones like cortisol also have an important effect on another key function of the frontal cortex: memory. In the short-term, these stress hormones can enhance our ability to store new memories, increasing the odds that we'll learn from our stressful experiences and, with luck, put such knowledge to good use in the future. But when the stress response goes on for weeks at a time—as it typically does before an episode of depression—cortisol begins to exact a toxic toll on the memory circuits of the frontal cortex. These areas of the brain actually start *shrinking*, and mental function grows less efficient: concentration, memory, attention, and abstract reasoning are all affected. Not surprisingly, depressed patients often complain that their minds don't seem to work as well as they did before the onset of the illness.

---

* This is the case, at least, for those who are right-handed. Among lefties, the brain's hemispheres can be wired the other way around.

The Sleeping Brain

As we saw previously, when the brain's stress circuits are fully engaged, they can profoundly alter the structure of sleep. Specifically, there is a steady disappearance of the deep, restful form of slumber known as *slow-wave sleep*—the phase of sleep the brain needs to keep brain chemicals and hormones in balance, and to coordinate things such as tissue repair.

When laboratory rats are experimentally deprived of slow-wave sleep for several days at a time, their brains start to malfunction and they become seriously ill. Humans react in much the same way. After just a few nights of slow-wave sleep deprivation, most people report intense, aching fatigue. After a few more days, they begin to feel physically ill. They also start moving and speaking more slowly. Many people even complain of a sensation of physical pain (even though they can't quite tell where it's coming from). In this sleep-altered state, mood turns despondent, social interest disappears, thoughts turn negative, appetite becomes erratic, and concentration wanes. In other words, with the disappearance of slow-wave sleep, the core symptoms of depression quickly emerge.

RISK FACTORS

We've briefly touched on the fact that some people are much more vulnerable to depression than others. But what actually puts a person at risk? And what makes others resilient, allowing them to remain unaffected by the illness even in the face of unimaginably stressful circumstances? Let's briefly review some of the major known risk factors, as well as the things known to confer protection.

Genes. Much has been written in the popular press about the role of genes in depression. This prominent coverage has led some people to conclude—mistakenly—that the disorder is somehow "all genetic." Genes are far from the whole story. However, they certainly play an important role in determining who is at risk. We know this from several converging lines of evidence. For example, identical twins—with exactly the same genes—are much more similar in their susceptibility to depression than fraternal twins, who share only half their genes in common. Likewise, the biological (genetic) children of depressed parents are at greatly increased risk, but their adopted children generally are not. Based on such studies, geneticists have even been able to estimate how much of the risk for depression is directly linked to our genes. And the best studies have come back with a result of about 40%. In other words, faulty genes account for a little less than half the story of who gets depressed and who does not.

The most interesting link on this front comes from a stretch of DNA known as the *serotonin transporter gene.* As its name suggests, this gene affects the function of serotonin, a chemical messenger that plays a major role in shutting off the brain's stress response circuits and reducing anxiety. (As we'll see in Chapter 3, popular drugs like Sertraline, Efexor, and Prozac directly target serotonin function in the brain. Likewise, serotonin abnormality is what most people seem to have in mind when they refer to depression as a matter of "chemical imbalance.")

The serotonin transporter gene has a key region that comes in two varieties,* dubbed *long* and *short,* and people with short versions of the gene have less effective serotonin function. As a

* Technically, there are not two versions of the gene itself, but of a sequence of molecules (called the *promoter* region) that control the gene's functioning.

result, they're more prone to feeling anxious, and to suffering a runaway stress response. From early childhood, such individuals are frequently anxiety-prone, and they are also highly vulnerable to depression. In a large landmark study of New Zealanders, young adults with short copies of the gene were about two and a half times more likely than those with long copies to become depressed when faced with severe negative life events.

But of course, lots of people with no known genetic risk also become depressed. Because fewer than half of all cases of depression can be chalked up to genetic factors, it's clear that the environment—that is, all the things we *experience*—also plays a major role.

Child abuse. The experience of severe childhood trauma, for example, has a potentially devastating long-term effect, no matter what sort of genes a person was born with. Children who have suffered physical or sexual abuse are at much greater risk for depression—even later as adults—than those who have not. Tragically, such early trauma can leave an enduring imprint on the brain, placing its stress circuitry on a permanent state of hair-trigger alert, and making it very difficult to shut off once activated.

Social support. Some forms of experience can also *protect* us against depression. As we've seen, the human species is hardwired for extensive person-to-person contact, and the supportive presence of loved ones is a powerful signal from the environment that helps keep the brain's stress response in check. Several studies have shown that people with strong social support networks are relatively unlikely to become depressed. In fact, a British team of researchers found that simply having *one supportive confidant*—an emotionally close friend or family member—cut the risk of depression in half following a painful event like separation, divorce, or job loss.

When such support is absent, even owning a pet seems to provide at least some protection, since the comforting experience of close physical contact with any other animal—human or nonhuman—reduces activity in the brain's stress centers.

Not all social contact is beneficial, however. Sometimes, as Sartre complained, "hell is other people." Researchers have found, for example, that the presence of a harshly critical, emotionally abusive spouse renders a person more vulnerable to depression—even more so than if they had no meaningful social connection at all. Some relationships are so psychologically toxic that they can keep the brain's stress response networks in a perpetual state of overdrive, ever teetering on the edge of the depressive abyss.

Thoughts. Another big set of risk factors has to do with the way we *think* about things. That's because the way we react to events often shapes our feelings more than the events themselves. When something upsets us, it's natural to spend at least a little time reflecting on what went wrong, what we might have done differently, and what we could still do to make things better. But some people have an unhealthy tendency to brood on negative events. They spin them around and around in the mind's eye, torturing themselves for days on end with endless thoughts of "woulda, coulda, shoulda."

This kind of rumination is an effective way to keep the brain's stress circuits revved up, and people who dwell on their negative thoughts like this are especially prone to depression. On the other hand, learning how to short-circuit rumination—redirecting attention away from such thoughts so we can engage in more rewarding activities—is a highly effective tool for keeping the illness at bay.

Biological sex. Women get depressed about twice as often as men do. This is perplexing, and nobody knows for sure what makes women so much more vulnerable. But consider this: Boys and girls get depressed at roughly the same rate during childhood, and men and women also have about the same rate of depression in late adulthood. In other words, the male-female gap is there only during the prime reproductive years, when sex hormone levels are at their highest.

Researchers have found that estrogen and progesterone, major female reproductive hormones, have a large effect on mood and other depressive symptoms. Specifically, when estrogen and progesterone levels drop suddenly—as they do during the premenstrual period and also right after childbirth—mood and energy are also liable to plummet. Estrogen levels also swing wildly (with many sudden drops) during the years leading up to menopause, and this is a time of particularly high depression vulnerability for women.

Women with the highest overall estrogen levels may also be more vulnerable to the experience of anxiety,* and under some conditions, estrogen even helps to prime the brain's stress response. Among all known primate species (not just humans), females experience anxious arousal more readily than males do—a finding consistent with the role of estrogen and related hormones in promoting the stress response.

On the other hand, testosterone has been strongly linked to a sense of well-being and to high levels of activity. In other words, this male reproductive hormone is a natural mood booster. It

---

*At a first read, this might seem at odds with information in the preceding paragraph, but it's not: *sudden drops* in estrogen levels are linked with depressed mood, but *consistently low* levels of the hormone generally aren't.

also tends to suppress feelings of anxiety* and to blunt the perception of stress. It's probably no coincidence, then, that men are less vulnerable to depression than women precisely during those prime years of adolescence and adulthood when testosterone levels are at their highest.†

Lifestyle. As we saw in Chapter 1, people who exercise regularly are at much lower risk of depression than couch potatoes. Exercise changes the brain as powerfully as any medication, and it helps slam the brakes on the depressive stress response. Similar protection is found in other lifestyle factors. People who eat lots of fish and other sources of omega-3 fat have greatly reduced depression vulnerability. Likewise with those who are exposed every day to high levels of natural sunlight, and who get adequate sleep each night. And these four lifestyle factors, together with those we mentioned previously—pursuing social connection and engaging activities—are at the heart of the Therapeutic Lifestyle Change program, which allows us to reclaim key protective elements from the ancestral milieu.

THE GREATEST CHALLENGE

There's an old adage in psychology: *The best predictor of future behavior is past behavior.* In the case of depression, the saying is particularly apt. Consider this: Among Americans, the risk of

---

* This also helps explain why high-testosterone males are more likely to engage in foolish risk-taking behavior.

† Men produce up to forty times as much testosterone as women, although women's bodies are more sensitive to the hormone. Men's testosterone levels also peak during late adolescence and decline slowly into their thirties and forties—after which the pace of decline for most men picks up considerably.

future depression now stands at roughly 30%, but it rises to well over 50% among those who have been depressed before. And after three episodes of depression, the lifetime risk of relapse—getting depressed again—rises to a staggering 90%. Clearly, the best predictor of future depression is past depression.

But why should this be? Sadly, there's evidence that depression can leave a toxic imprint on the brain. It can etch its way into our neural circuitry—including the brain's stress response system—and make it much easier for the brain to fall back into another episode of depression down the road. This helps explain a puzzling fact: It normally takes a high level of life stress to trigger someone's *first* episode of depression, but later relapse episodes sometimes come totally out of the blue. It seems that once the brain has learned how to operate in depression mode, it can find its way back there with much less prompting.

Fortunately, though, we can heal from the damage of depression. All it takes is several months of complete recovery for much of the toxic imprint on the brain to be erased.* And in the chapters ahead, we'll address the many things you can do to promote such a healing process.

But first we need to consider the most important reason why the rate of depression relapse is so high: Our risk factors tend to remain stable over time. For example, with few exceptions,† our genes don't change. And while you might think that behavior can change like the wind, it actually stays surprisingly consistent for most people. Those who avoid exercise today will probably still be sedentary tomorrow—and next week, and next month, and next year, and the year after that, and so on. Likewise

* Technically, the toxic imprint on the brain is not actually erased—more like overwritten.

† These exceptions include radiation-induced genetic mutation.

are those who tend to ruminate, those who stay chronically sleep-deprived, those who fail to invest in social relationships, and those who eat too few omega-3 fats. Without a high level of motivation and commitment—and (in many cases) a little outside help*—most of us simply keep repeating the same unhelpful patterns of behavior, despite our good intentions to the contrary.

Over the past few years, I've had the privilege of working with many depressed patients who knew they needed to change the way they were living, but didn't know how to do so on their own. Helping them in that process—and watching them find their way back to lasting health—has been one of the most satisfying, joyful experiences of my life.

None of us gets to choose our genes or our parents or our underlying brain chemistry: Many risk factors for depression are out of our hands. But no matter what life may have handed us, there's abundant evidence that *what we do today* can profoundly lower our vulnerability in the here and now, and in all the days ahead. It's my hope that in the pages that follow you'll encounter just the catalyst you need to reclaim the many powerfully protective lifestyle features from our ancestral past.

---

* As in the case of those who hire a therapist, a personal trainer, or a "life coach."

3
Treating Depression: The State of the Art (and Science)

What's the most effective treatment for depression? When I posed this question to my Abnormal Psychology students, they shot back quizzical stares. They always do. You can see the confusion in their eyes, the wheels spinning: *Is this some kind of trick question? The answer has to be "antidepressant medication," but why would he even ask something so obvious—unless there's a catch?*

I repeated the question, and eventually a thoughtful young man called out from the back of the room, "Dr. Ilardi, I'm pretty sure it's some kind of medication. So are you asking us *which* drug is the most effective?" I shook my head and smiled, and then pointed to a senior in the front row who had her hand raised.

"Okay, even if drugs usually clear up people's depression," she said, "I know this girl who had to quit taking her meds because of all the side effects. So maybe sometimes drugs aren't the best treatment?"

"That's an important point about side effects," I agreed. "And it's something we definitely have to come back to. But right now I'm interested in the first thing you said: 'Drugs usually clear up people's depression.'" Looking out across the room full of three hundred students, I asked, "How many of you believe this? How many of you think antidepressants usually cure depression?" Nearly every hand in the room went up. They always do.

THE EFFECTIVENESS OF DEPRESSION MEDICATIONS: WEIGHING THE EVIDENCE

Virtually everyone now accepts the premise that antidepressants are a potent treatment option for depression. And it's not just because we've all heard the message on a relentless parade of TV ads and public service announcements. Most of us *know* people who've been helped by these meds. Even clinicians who used to treat depression with therapy have jumped on the medication bandwagon. I recently heard a famous psychotherapist claim it would be unethical if he failed to recommend medication for any of his depressed patients.

Besides, with over 300 million antidepressant prescriptions written in the United States each year—a 500% increase since the early 1990s—it seems obvious that these drugs must be providing at least some benefit. Otherwise, people simply would have stopped taking them long ago.

But exactly how much benefit do these medications provide? Of all the depressed patients who take an antidepressant, how many experience a complete and lasting recovery? It turns out to be a surprisingly low percentage—much lower than I would have guessed before I took the time to wade through the hundreds of studies that address this question.

Consider, for example, the landmark 2004 study that followed several hundred patients treated with one of three popular antidepressants: Sertraline, Seroxat, or Prozac. Among those who took the drugs as prescribed, *only 23% were depression-free after six months of treatment.* (As you might expect, patients who failed to take their meds did even worse.) And all three medications yielded roughly the same dismal results.

A fluke result, perhaps? It's actually pretty typical. The recovery rate with antidepressants in similar studies usually falls somewhere between 20% and 35%. Clinical researchers at forty-one treatment sites across the US completed the largest real-world study of antidepressants ever conducted, and the results fit the same overall pattern. This multimillion dollar project, sponsored by the National Institutes of Mental Health, followed about three thousand depressed patients who initially took the drug citalopram (marketed under the trade name Cipramil) for about twelve weeks. By the end of that short-term treatment period, *only 28% of study patients had fully recovered.*

The study's 28% response rate might even be an overestimate of the medication's true effectiveness, because patients received higher drug doses and had more frequent doctor's visits than people do in everyday clinical practice. (In real life, insurance companies sharply restrict the frequency of "med check" follow-up appointments).

Remarkably, the study's authors—a veritable All-Star team of clinical researchers—noted that the observed 28% recovery rate was about what they had expected to see based on comparable studies. That's right: They weren't surprised to find that the majority of study patients failed to recover on an antidepressant. In the study's published write-up, the researchers also raised a provocative question: What percentage of their patients might have recovered if they had received a sugar pill—a *placebo*—instead of the medication? Could it possibly have been as high as 28%?

Better Than a Sugar Pill?

It's hard to believe that anyone with a disabling illness like depression could get better simply by taking a sugar pill—which is medically inert—but the placebo response rate in depression is not trivial. In fact, the U.S. Food and Drug Administration (FDA) won't approve any new depression medication until the drug's manufacturers can provide compelling evidence that the medicine outperforms a placebo.

Although this sounds like a ridiculously easy standard for a new drug to meet, it's not. Irving Kirsch, a clinical researcher at the University of Connecticut, recently showed just how tough it can be. Under the Freedom of Information Act, he petitioned the FDA for the results of every drug-company study submitted over a thirteen-year period (1987–1999) for six commonly used antidepressant medications, including Sertraline, Efexor, Prozac, Cipramil, and Seroxat. Incredibly, he found that *in 56% of these studies, depressed patients taking an antidepressant drug fared no better than those who took a placebo.* Not surprisingly, the drug companies have never published most of these studies.

When Kirsch combined the results of the FDA's antidepressant studies into one huge analysis, he did find some evidence that the drugs worked better than a placebo—but only slightly better. Overall, the placebo effect was 80% as large as that of the medications—equal to a difference of 2 points on the studies' 50-point depression rating scale. This difference was, as Kirsch put it, "very small and of questionable clinical significance." And this shocking result isn't just the handiwork of a single investigator; it's now been replicated by others who have taken an independent look at the FDA database and arrived at the same basic conclusions.

So, what are we to make of all this? Are antidepressants just placebos with nasty side effects? Before we jump to such a radical conclusion, we need to take into consideration an important twist to the story. Among *severely* depressed patients—those whose symptoms are so profoundly disabling that they can no longer function at all—depression drugs have been found to work much better than placebos. Although most severely depressed patients aren't completely cured by antidepressants, at least half of them will experience meaningful improvement within a month or two. By comparison, few such patients ever improve while taking a dummy pill.

But the great majority of people with diagnosable depression don't have such severe disability. They're still able—with some difficulty—to keep working and interacting with family and friends. And among these less severely depressed individuals, antidepressants and placebos work about equally well. This means that most people on antidepressants are receiving no more benefit than they would from a bottle of sugar pills.

And yet if doctors started handing out sham pills—labeled as such—their patients would experience little improvement. Why? Because the placebo effect hinges on an important element of deception: *The person taking the pill has to believe it's an active medication.* They have to believe it's going to help. That's what allows the dummy pills to work their healing magic. Placebo-induced positive expectancies can exert a powerful effect on the brain, increasing activity in circuits of the frontal cortex that are otherwise dormant in depression. Such changes in brain function are sometimes capable of sparking impressive reductions in depressive symptoms.

But it would be unethical for a doctor to deceive patients by giving them sugar pills labeled, say, "Sertraline." That's why no one ever takes a placebo for depression in the real world. It happens only in research studies, where patients can consent to being randomly given either antidepressants or sham pills that look and taste just like medication, but that are medically inert. Surprisingly, most study patients believe they're receiving an active medication, regardless of whether they're taking a real drug or a fake one, and this explains why the placebo can work about as well as an antidepressant under such conditions.

Remember, though, neither placebos nor antidepressants are particularly effective. As we've seen, antidepressants lead to complete short-term recovery for about a quarter of the depressed patients who take them. Another 25% or so will experience significant improvement within a couple months, but will still have some lingering symptoms. And *roughly half of all depressed patients won't improve meaningfully on meds at all.* These numbers appear to be about the same for every major antidepressant medication; there's no conclusive evidence that any particular depression drug works much better, on average, than any other.

Even when antidepressants *are* effective in the short run, their healing effects don't always endure. Over time, the drugs may simply stop working—a phenomenon the experts colorfully refer to as drug "poop out." I've worked with many patients who've experienced it firsthand, and they usually describe it as coming more or less out of the blue. In the typical scenario, they've been taking their meds faithfully for months—sometimes for years—and then simply wake up one day to find their old symptoms returning with full force. Often they can't even point to an obvious stressful event as a trigger. According to the best research, up to 50% of those who respond favorably to antidepressant medications will become depressed again at some point. And because most depressed patients fail to fully recover on their meds in the first place, we know that far fewer than one in four are fortunate enough both to get well and to stay well on antidepressants.

These are sobering numbers. Sometimes when I bring them to people's attention they assume I must be "anti-medication." I'm not. I'm immensely grateful for the relief these medications sometimes provide. I just wish the meds lived up to the immense hype that surrounds them. How wonderful it would be if antidepressants provided a genuine cure for the devastating scourge of depression—if they led to lasting recovery for the vast majority of people who take them. But they don't, and I believe it's important to face the facts head on, especially when other treatment options are available.

Side Effects

There's yet another potential downside to antidepressants: Many people quit taking them because of the unpleasant side effects. According to a recent study, the typical patient goes off his or her prescribed medications after just eight weeks. And of course, when people stop taking their meds, they're much less likely to experience any lasting benefit.

But what are the major antidepressant side effects, and how often do they occur? Although the answers can vary a bit from one medication to another, many adverse effects apply to depression drugs across the board. We'll review the most important of these in this section.

Suicidality. Of all the potential downsides to antidepressant use, none is more troubling than the drugs' reported tendency to cause suicidal thinking and behavior in children and adolescents. It's hard to believe that any drug—let alone one designed to combat depression—could have such a sinister effect. But as the data have accumulated in recent years, it's become clear that these medications pose a genuine risk of increased suicidality in this age group. The evidence on this point is so compelling that the U.S. Food and Drug Administration now requires all antidepressants to carry a "black box" warning label.

This warning, issued in late 2004, came after FDA researchers—under intense public pressure—combed through their database of twenty-four antidepressant studies involving four thousand four hundred adolescents and children. Incredibly, they found that suicidal thoughts and behavior were *twice as likely* among young people on antidepressants compared with those taking a placebo. The risk looks to be particularly high during the first few weeks of treatment, when close monitoring is usually advised.

Although the overall med-related risk of increased suicidality appears to be relatively small—affecting just 4% of the young people in the FDA database—the potential consequences are so disastrous that the finding has to be taken seriously. After all, how many parents would give their child an antibiotic if they knew the drug carried a 4% risk of suicidal thinking or behavior? I believe most people would look hard for other viable treatment options.

And it's not just children and adolescents who face increased suicidality with antidepressant use. A more recent FDA analysis also found a substantially elevated risk among young adults up to the age of twenty-five.*

Emotional numbing. A much more common side effect of medication concerns *emotional numbing,* a decrease in the intensity of emotions—both positive and negative. Although this phenomenon hasn't been widely publicized, there's some evidence that it may afflict the majority of those taking antidepressants. When a person first starts on meds, this emotional blunting can be a welcome experience—providing relief from the wrenching pain of depression. But many people later discover they can no longer feel positive emotions like joy and excitement and romantic love as intensely as they used to.

Interestingly, some patients with this kind of numbness are oblivious to it. It tends to come on so gradually that it just becomes the "new normal." One of my patients said to me last year, after she tapered off Efexor, "It's so amazing just to be able to *feel* again. But how come I never even noticed how numb I was until I came off the meds?" The answer is paradoxical: Emotional numbing blunts a person's ability to notice (and care about) their emotional numbing.

Sexual dysfunction. Some of the most widely prescribed antidepressants belong to a class of drugs known as SSRIs (selective

* Interestingly, no such risk was observed among adults older than twenty-five. The reasons for this discrepancy remain unknown.

serotonin reuptake inhibitors), including Sertraline, Cipramil, Prozac, and Seroxat. These drugs all influence the function of a chemical messenger in the brain called serotonin.

Because serotonin circuits help regulate the brain's pleasure centers, many people taking SSRIs experience sexual side effects—usually in the form of reduced sexual pleasure or desire. Some people completely lose their ability to have an orgasm, and others experience the blunting of *all* romantic feelings, not just their sex drive.

And these problems don't just afflict those on SSRIs. They're common with other drugs that affect the brain's use of serotonin, such as Efexor and Cymbalta.

Weight gain. Although it's rarely reported in the media, weight gain is a possible side effect of most antidepressant medications (especially with long-term use). Since many depressed patients—like the majority of Britons—are already over their ideal weight, the added pounds are almost always unwelcome.

Insomnia. Most SSRIs and similar medications also carry the potential to cause insomnia for a subset of patients. Such drugs sometimes cause people to become physically active while they're asleep—with periodic limb movements and *bruxism* (teeth grinding)—and this can lead to frequent awakenings. The resulting poor sleep may, in turn, cause other depressive symptoms to get worse.

AS GOOD AS IT GETS?

In the signature line from the classic film about obsessive-compulsive disorder, Jack Nicholson (as Melvin Udall) turns to a group of fellow patients—all still suffering the pain of mental illness despite taking their meds—and asks, "What if this is *as good as it gets*?" It's a poignant question, and one of great relevance. For we've seen that antidepressants, by far the most commonly used treatment option for depression, provide a complete and lasting cure for only a small subset of the people who take them. And this sporadic benefit comes at a high cost—an array of potential side effects that range from the merely annoying (weight gain) to the disturbing (loss of sexual function) to the downright terrifying (increased suicidality).

Yet virtually everyone regards these medications as the treatment of choice. Is this because there's truly nothing better? As disappointing as medication outcomes may be, isn't it possible that depression drugs are still as good as it gets? After all, aren't the antidepressants still better than the other options people have at their disposal—things such as traditional psychotherapy or shock therapy?

ON THE COUCH AND BEYOND

Sigmund Freud, the man who put psychotherapy on the map a century ago, was never optimistic about his ability to cure depression. He thought the only possible remedy would require the depressed patient to spend years on the therapy couch delving into the deep, dark, long-forgotten pains of childhood. And, said Freud, they might need to do this painful psychic excavation work at least four times a week.

Why such drastic measures? Freud viewed depression as a break with reality—a form of *psychosis.* Few think of depression this way today, and for good reason: It's just not true. Those suffering from depression are still very much in touch with reality. And most have no deep, dark, painful secrets from their childhood to explore. Even those who do are usually made worse, not better, by dwelling on such painful events while they're still depressed. (After they've recovered, however, it can sometimes be helpful for them to look carefully at past hurts, and to examine how they still influence the present—a topic we'll cover in Chapter 11.)

Simply put, Freudian therapy for depression isn't particularly effective. In the short term, it often makes people feel worse. But because of Freud's towering legacy—and his lasting influence on the public's perception of what psychotherapy is all about—many people just assume that all forms of therapy for depression must be just as ineffective as the Freudian version. They're not.

The Cognitive Revolution

In the early 1960s, a brilliant young psychiatrist named Aaron Beck challenged the Freudian orthodoxy. In the process, he ended up turning the field's view of psychotherapy on its head.

Beck noticed that most of his depressed patients didn't have the deep repressed childhood traumas Freud said they would. Instead, they spent much of their time thinking about things they felt bad about in the present. They tended to dwell—to *ruminate*—on their negative thoughts, which often seemed to reflect a starkly pessimistic interpretation of the world around them.

As Beck observed, even innocuous events could trigger a cascade of negative thoughts. For example, one of my patients last year saw the cashier at the grocery store smiling warmly at the customer in front of him, and he immediately started thinking, "How come people never smile at me like that? That cashier definitely didn't smile at me the last time I was here. She can probably tell there's something wrong with me. I'm sure she doesn't like me. Nobody does."

Beck was convinced that such negative thoughts cause people to feel more depressed. (Makes sense, doesn't it?) So he decided to start urging his patients to do something about it. He had them write down their thoughts and examine them through the objective lens of reason. Patients started disputing their negative interpretations of things, replacing them with less biased perceptions. This new form of treatment, *cognitive- behavior therapy* (CBT), led some patients to start feeling better fairly quickly, often within a matter of weeks. So Beck decided to jettison the Freudian dogma that therapy should last for years or even decades: A full course of CBT takes only three to four months to complete.

And Beck didn't just develop this novel form of treatment; he set out to prove its effectiveness in carefully controlled studies. He also encouraged others to do the same. Over the past three decades, CBT has been evaluated in dozens of carefully controlled research studies. It's now the most thoroughly researched form of psychotherapy in history. And here's the basic gist of the evidence: CBT is every bit as effective as medication in the short term. It leads to complete recovery—that is, the full disappearance of symptoms—for 30% to 40% of patients who start treatment, and it brings about substantial symptom reduction for another 25% or so.

That's not great, but it still compares favorably with antidepressants. And CBT has two big advantages over medications:

There are no noxious side effects, and the benefits of treatment usually last for years after therapy is completed.

Despite this important treatment edge, only a small percentage of depressed patients ever try CBT. Most never even hear of it. How would they? There's no big marketing budget available to inform the public about psychotherapy. Even insurance companies and HMOs—who could conceivably help get the word out—often steer people toward medication, which is cheaper than CBT in the short term (although this cost advantage disappears in the long term).

Do Thoughts Really Matter?

As we've seen, many depressed patients who try CBT—just like many who take antidepressants—find little meaningful improvement. However, clinical researchers in recent years have been searching for ways to make therapy even better. A group of clinicians at the University of Washington appears to have achieved just that. Surprisingly, they did it by taking one small piece of the CBT protocol and expanding it into an entire treatment package.

Although Beck believed it was crucial to help depressed patients stop thinking negatively, he also recognized that *what we do* often determines how we feel. Ever the pragmatist, Beck even outlined a brief set of strategies for changing behavior in order to reduce symptoms of depression. But these behavioral strategies were never the focus of CBT—at least, not until Dr. Neil Jacobson and his research team at the University of Washington decided to see how much therapeutic mileage they could get out of simply changing what people do.

What would happen, Jacobson asked, if depressed patients quit trying to change their thoughts and worked instead on the goal of *doing* things again? How much would patients improve if therapists just helped them become more active and engaged—getting out and socializing and playing and accomplishing things? The answer: They would improve *a lot.* In a landmark study, Jacobson's *behavioral activation* approach was more effective than either antidepressant medication or traditional CBT. An impressive 56% of severely depressed patients recovered with behavioral activation, compared with only 36% in CBT and 23% on medication (Seroxat). No traditional form of psychotherapy has ever performed better in a published head-to-head comparison against antidepressant medication.

Ironically, behavioral activation even helps people stop their negative thinking. It's not that patients are ever asked to change their negative thoughts (that is, to think more positively about things). They aren't. But they *are* taught to interrupt the toxic process of rumination by turning to rewarding activities instead. And this strategy works surprisingly well. According to the latest published evidence, anti-ruminative activity may be the single most effective antidepressant psychotherapy technique ever devised.

Psychotherapy in the Real World

During their medical school training, aspiring doctors are taught to base every treatment decision on an up-to-date knowledge of the relevant research literature, and they generally carry this scientific sensibility with them throughout their careers. So when physicians encounter, say, a patient with a clogged coronary artery, they should automatically begin generating a set of scientifically informed questions: What are the available treatment options? Which option—bypass surgery, angioplasty, medication, and so on—is likely to prove the most effective for *this* patient, given the location and extent of the blockage? What does the research say?

We take it as a given that a doctor's decisions will be guided by the best available scientific evidence, and most of us would be appalled to find a physician who simply ignored or neglected the latest research findings in the field. Surely the same holds true for psychotherapists, doesn't it? After all, just like medical doctors, therapists deal with an array of life-threatening conditions—disorders such as anorexia nervosa and substance abuse and depression. Aren't psychotherapists, like physicians, trained to base their treatment decisions on the best and most relevant research evidence? Sadly, the majority are not.

The problem traces back to the enduring influence of Sigmund Freud, who launched the institution of psychotherapy over a century ago. Despite his superb scientific training as a research neurologist, Freud never felt the need to conduct careful scientific studies on the effectiveness of the psychotherapy techniques he developed. Indeed, Freud was so convinced that his treatment method just *had* to be effective, he asked the world to rely on the "evidence" of mere anecdotes and a smattering of published case studies—some of which were later shown by historians to have been fabricated. Likewise, his followers were encouraged to accept the effectiveness of Freudian therapy as an article of faith, rather than subjecting the therapy to rigorous scientific scrutiny. And for over a century Freud's legacy has persisted: Many practicing psychotherapists still fail to base their clinical practice on sound scientific research.

After decades of tinkering and creative innovation, there are now over four hundred distinct varieties of psychotherapy being practiced by clinicians (with dozens of allegedly new techniques appearing each year), and *the vast majority of these treatments have never been tested scientifically.* Even when it comes to the treatment of depressive illness, many practicing therapists are still using techniques for which there is absolutely no supportive scientific evidence. This is not to say that all of these untested techniques are ineffective. They might work. But then again they might not. The point is that we simply have no way of knowing, and in the absence of solid research evidence we will never know for sure. Freudian therapy was practiced for nearly eighty years before a definitive set of studies showed that it's often ineffective in treating depression.

How many other psychotherapy techniques in widespread use today will prove similarly unhelpful once they're finally subjected to the clear light of scientific scrutiny? Although we have no way of knowing for certain, I believe it is now difficult for any therapist to justify using unproven techniques for treating depression when we have good research evidence that approaches like CBT and behavioral activation—when skillfully implemented—are reasonably effective, with a long-term efficacy at least equivalent to that of antidepressant medication.

THE DESPERATE CURE

Long before the first depression drug was introduced in the 1950s, psychiatrists had a much more radical treatment strategy at their disposal: shock therapy. True to its name, shock therapy entails the conduction of strong electrical currents through the brain. The goal is to induce violent convulsive seizures; if all goes well, they last for about a minute. And for reasons still shrouded in mystery, such seizures can have a profoundly antidepressant effect.

Most people assume shock therapy disappeared from the psychiatric landscape decades ago, a barbaric practice—not unlike the frontal lobotomy—that hasn't been seen since the days of *One Flew Over the Cuckoo's Nest.* But the procedure is still very much with us, albeit under a slightly different name. It's now called *electroconvulsive therapy* (to avoid any lingering negative associations to the word *shock*), and it's been rendered into a somewhat kinder, gentler intervention—with paralyzing muscle relaxants used before each convulsion to make sure the patient doesn't inadvertently break any bones or teeth (as used to happen with some regularity).

In its modern incarnation, electroconvulsive therapy, or ECT, is now used with over one hundred thousand patients every year in the United States and Europe. Most major psychiatric units provide ECT for a subset of their depressed patients—a last resort for those who haven't responded to meds, as well as elderly patients whose bodies can't tolerate the side effects of medication. The typical treatment involves ten to twelve shock sessions in all, scheduled at a pace of three per week.

In the short term, at least, ECT produces much better results than antidepressant medication, with an estimated recovery rate as high as 65%. But there's a big catch: The recovery usually doesn't last long. Most ECT patients, even those who start taking depression meds right after they finish a round of ECT, become depressed again within six months. One important study found that only about 20% of patients treated with ECT got well and stayed well for a full year.

There's another catch: Patients usually have severe memory disturbance for days after each ECT session. Back when I was still an intern at Duke Medical Center, I would be asked every now and then to do psychotherapy with an ECT patient. It was an exercise in futility. Often, I'd walk into the patient's hospital room for a scheduled therapy session, only to have the patient look up at me quizzically and ask, "Who are you again?" This could happen even if we'd already been meeting regularly for days! A patient might tell me the most intimate details of his or her life during a productive session, and then the following day—after undergoing another round of ECT—the patient would stare at me blankly, as if I were a complete stranger.

Some studies suggest that ECT may sometimes cause permanent brain damage. A few investigations, for example, have observed a link between ECT and *cerebral atrophy*—the shrinkage of brain tissue caused by the widespread death of brain cells. ECT can lead to permanent impairment of mental function, as well. Up to 70% of ECT patients complain that they can't remember things like they used to—they fumble over the names of people they've known for years, struggle to pull up the right words in a conversation, and lose everyday objects with startling regularity. There's even evidence that ECT may occasionally induce a permanent drop in IQ.

I have a feeling that future generations will look back on our modern practice of ECT with horror—the psychiatric equivalent of slapping the side of the TV set in a desperate and improbable attempt to render the picture forever clear again.

THE CASE FOR THERAPEUTIC LIFESTYLE CHANGE

As we've seen, the public has been tragically misinformed about treatment options for depression. Sales of antidepressant drugs now exceed $20 billion a year, despite low rates of recovery, high rates of relapse, and an astonishing array of serious side effects. Remarkably, most people still blithely accept the false premise that antidepressants usually offer a lasting cure. They don't.

Traditional psychotherapy isn't much better, at least not as it's currently practiced. Freud-inspired therapy, which involves digging around the patient's psyche for long-repressed childhood traumas, is often of little help when it comes to treating depression. It sometimes even makes matters worse.

Short-term CBT is more promising: It works about as well as medication, but it may yield longer-lasting benefits with no noxious side effects. And there's evidence that CBT can be improved by shifting the focus of treatment to a change in lifestyle—helping the depressed patient become more active, thereby breaking the toxic cycle of rumination. This behavioral activation approach, which builds on one of the key principles of Therapeutic Lifestyle Change, has yielded some of the most promising results of any form of psychotherapy studied to date. In one important head-to-head study, it was found to be considerably superior to antidepressant medication.

But behavioral activation alone doesn't work for everyone. At least 35–40% of depressed patients will not respond favorably to this approach. Why? *When it comes to treating depression, there is no one-size-fits-all cure.* Behavioral activation is a powerful technique—and we will explore in chapter 5 how it can be used to end bouts of rumination—but many people with depression need something more. That's why there are six distinct elements in the Therapeutic Lifestyle Change (TLC) program. It is to those six steps that we now turn.

PART TWO

THERAPEUTIC LIFESTYLE CHANGE

The Six Steps

4
Brain Food

If you can picture a lab rat in your mind's eye, it probably looks a lot like one of these little guys: sleek white fur, long twitchy whiskers, tiny pink ears and feet, and beady black eyes with a reddish cast around the edges. They're called *Wistar rats*, and for many years they've been providing researchers with a useful animal model of depression.

We don't normally think of rats as creatures that get depressed, but they do. Sort of. Actually, when researchers treat them badly, the rats start to shut down in ways that resemble depression in humans. Fortunately for the rats, however, they bounce right back to their former perky selves—usually within a day or two.*

The most widely used technique for depressing a rat these days is the *forced swim test.* It basically involves dropping the animal in a tall cylindrical tub of lukewarm water and watching as it tries to claw its way up the impossibly slippery sides to escape. After about ten minutes of frenetic—and ultimately futile—activity, the rat will just give up and go limp, barely managing to keep even its head above water. When it's plopped back in the tank the next day, the poor creature will be lucky to last two minutes in the water before falling into a depressive stupor.

---

* But they won't bounce back until the researchers stop mistreating them.

But scientists have discovered some techniques that can keep this rodent version of depression at bay. For example, feeding the rats insanely high doses* of drugs like Prozac will do the trick. So will hitting them with the rat version of shock therapy. Recently, however, a group of Harvard researchers discovered a kinder, gentler way to keep the rats from getting depressed: supplementing their diets with *omega-3 fats*.

FAT HEADS

Fat is a fearsome word to most Americans. For several decades, nutritionists and medical professionals have warned us that fats are bad for us: They raise our cholesterol, clog our arteries, and tend to make us . . . fat. But then researchers discovered that this conventional wisdom was, in many respects, just plain wrong.†

We need fats. We'd all be dead without them. They're critical to the well-being of every cell in our bodies, and they're crucial building blocks for the construction of every neuron in our brains. As we saw in Chapter 1, the human brain is mostly made up of fats.

But all fats are not created equal. For example, the body can manufacture most of the fats it needs, but there are some that we can get only from our diets. The essential dietary fats come in

* It sometimes requires doses up to one hundred times higher than those administered to humans (adjusting for body weight).

† It's now known, for example, that most of the fats we eat have no effect on our cholesterol levels. (And some varieties of fat might actually lower cholesterol.) Likewise, the best evidence suggests that reduced-fat diets don't always promote weight loss.

two versions—*omega-3* and *omega-6**—and they play complementary roles in the brain and the rest of the body. When all goes well, omega-3s and omega-6s work in harmony to keep us firing on all cylinders. But when our dietary fats fall out of balance, we become vulnerable to many forms of illness. Depression is one of the most common.

According to recent studies, our hunter-gatherer ancestors maintained a superb balance of omega-6s and omega-3s in their diets, usually not too far from a 1:1 ratio. The typical American, on the other hand, has a radically imbalanced fat intake—heavily slanted in favor of omega-6s. The ratio of omega-6 to omega-3 in the modern American diet now stands at a staggering 16:1. To understand how our diets fell so badly out of balance (and to figure out how to remedy the situation), we need to briefly review where these fats come from.

LEAVES VERSUS SEEDS

Omega-3 fats are made in the leaves of plants, grasses†, and algae. Any animal that eats one of these omega-3 plant sources quickly absorbs the essential fats directly into its own body. So, for example, we find high levels of omega-3 fats in wild game, which feed on grasses and leaves, and in the many species of wild fish that eat algae.

Omega-6 fats, on the other hand, are usually concentrated in plant seeds. These fats are also abundant in nuts and grains,

* The names refer to how far from the end (i.e., *omega*) of each fatty molecule you have to go to find the first carbon double-bond: it's three carbon atoms away for omega-3s and six atoms away for omega-6s.

† Grasses are technically leaves, as well.

which are technically seeds, as well. Few untamed animals feed on seeds, so our hunter-gatherer ancestors got little in the way of omega-6 fats from their meat supply. (After all, who ever heard of grain-fed wild game?) But ancient humans still picked up plenty of omega-6s in their diets from seeds and nuts. Likewise, our foraging ancestors had little trouble getting enough omega-3s: Wild fish and game generally made up a large part of the hunter-gatherer diet, along with some other plant-based omega-3 sources.

The ancestral 1:1 balance of fatty acids started to shift a bit, though, with the invention of farming around twelve thousand years ago. All of a sudden, grains became the biggest part of everyone's diet—wheat, corn, rice, barley, sorghum, oats, rye, and so on. Omega-6 intake soared. And even though people still got some omega-3s from grass-fed livestock and a few plant sources, the ratio of omega-6s to omega-3s skyrocketed to about 5:1.

Remarkably, people all over the globe—in Mesopotamia, east Asia, north Africa, and central America—started suffering ill effects immediately after shifting to the new grain-based diet. According to the fossil record, these more "civilized" early farmers were, on average, considerably shorter and more disease-ridden than their hunter-gatherer forebears. *Their brains even grew smaller.* (We'll see why in just a moment.)

But even as they became less healthy and less brainy than their Pleistocene ancestors, most people stuck with the impressive new technologies of farming and herding livestock. The promise of a steadier food supply was apparently just too good a bargain to pass up.

Fortunately, over the centuries, humans all across the planet slowly adapted to the new farm-based diet. And, over time, cultures in different parts of the world often incorporated a good deal of seafood and other omega-3 food sources into their traditional diets, as if they intuitively realized something crucial was missing. A few agrarian societies—such as the traditional cultures of Crete (Greece) and Japan—even got close to the balanced fatty acid ratio of their hunter-gatherer ancestors, and they benefitted from increased overall health and longevity as a result.

But then in the twentieth century another radical dietary change took place—one without precedent in human history. Throughout most of the industrialized world, consumption of omega-6 fats went through the roof. It's not as if anyone was *trying* to eat more of these fats: It just turned out that way, as traditional farming steadily gave way to the more efficient practice of modern agriculture.

One of the biggest changes involved the shift from leaves to seeds in the diet of livestock. In the nineteenth century, beef cattle would roam on a free range, where they ate grasses and leafy plants and insects. As a result, beef was a rich source of omega-3 fats: hamburgers and steaks were, in effect, health foods. But as the price of corn steadily plummeted in the twentieth century,* grain-feeding livestock became the new norm: Animals grow considerably larger when they're herded onto feed lots and pumped full of corn—a prime source of omega-6 fats. This widespread practice of grain-feeding livestock—especially cattle, chickens, pigs, and fish—is why, in a nutshell, our meat supply today provides us with far too much omega-6 fat.

In a similar vein, the twentieth century saw an explosion in the consumption of seed oils—corn oil, rapeseed/canola oil, soybean oil, sunflower oil, peanut oil, palm oil, safflower oil, and so on—

* This price drop is largely due to innovations like the use of petroleum-based fertilizers, motorized combines, pesticides, and genetic selection of higher-yield seed corn.

and derivative products like margarine and Crisco. Not only do people cook with these oils at home, but they also consume them in nearly every fast food meal (in fries, shakes, nuggets, patties, buns, cheeses, and more) and in most of the processed foods sold at the local supermarket.

So, we're all now swimming in a sea of omega-6 fats. That's why the American diet clocks in at an astonishing 16:1 ratio of omega-6s to omega-3s. This unprecedented dietary shift has taken a dramatic toll on people's brains, which won't work as designed unless the omega fats are reasonably in balance.

CHEMICAL IMBALANCE

The extraordinary rise in depression rates over the last century has closely mirrored the disappearance of omega-3 fats from the Western diet. Similarly, in countries where people still get a better dietary balance of omega-6s and omega-3s, depression tends to be less common. And even in the Western world, people who become depressed have lower omega-3 blood levels than those who don't.

But how, exactly, does an imbalance of the fats we eat make us more vulnerable to depression? Neuroscientists have identified several different mechanisms that play a role. Let's look at three of the most important:

Serotonin. In Chapter 2, we saw that serotonin is a chemical that helps turn off the brain's stress response. When serotonin function shuts down, the stress response system can go ballistic.

Like all neurotransmitters, serotonin is a chemical messenger. It does its job by hopping from one brain cell (neuron) to the next, relaying its signal in an elegant chemical code. Yet when brain cells don't have enough omega-3 fats, they have trouble understanding the message of serotonin, and they start to misfire. This leads to a massive loss of serotonin function throughout the brain, increasing a person's vulnerability to the sort of out-of-control stress response that triggers the onset of depression.

Dopamine. It's much the same story with dopamine, another chemical messenger in the brain. Neurons tend to scramble dopamine signals—just as they do with those of serotonin—when omega-3 levels get too low.

One of dopamine's big jobs is to activate the frontal cortex. People with poor dopamine function may have especially low activity in the *left* frontal cortex—the part of the brain that helps put us in a good mood and pushes us to go after the things we want. And as we've seen, when the left frontal cortex heads offline, this can lead directly to depressive illness.

Inflammation. Throughout the body, omega-6s promote *inflammation*—the blood vessel reactions that make up the body's first line of defense against infection. You can see the body's inflammation response kick into high gear whenever you get a splinter. The surrounding area gets red and swollen as more blood—rich with immune cells poised to attack any offending intruders—is rushed to the site of injury. Without the body's ability to mount a vigorous inflammation response, every cut, scrape, or nick could easily turn into a lethal infection.

Although inflammation is healthy as a local, short-term reaction to a specific injury, the process can also spin dangerously out of control. When inflammation becomes chronic—when it fails to shut down after several days—it starts to affect the entire body. Such runaway inflammation actually causes the body to turn on itself, as if there were treacherous intruders to be attacked in every single one of its cells.

This is not good. In fact, researchers have recently identified chronic inflammation as the common denominator underlying many widespread diseases in the industrialized world: diabetes, atherosclerosis, Alzheimer's disease, heart disease, allergies, asthma, stroke, metabolic syndrome, and even many types of cancer.

Inflammation is also one of the big culprits behind the depression epidemic. Over time, it interferes with the brain's ability to manufacture and use serotonin,* and it can lead to reduced activity in the frontal cortex. It also impairs the function of brain regions such as the *hippocampus*—critical for memory function—that have been implicated in the onset of depression. Finally, chronic inflammation causes the brain to ramp up its stress response in an attempt to put things back in balance, since the stress hormone *cortisol* has powerful anti-inflammatory properties. Unfortunately, chronic cortisol elevation has its own set of depressive effects on the brain.

Tens of millions of people throughout the industrialized world suffer from chronic inflammation, and one major cause is now clear: a radical imbalance in dietary fats. The specialized hormones† that trigger inflammation throughout the body are actually made out of omega-6s. On the other hand, omega-3s can stimulate production of the body's anti-inflammatory hormones. These two essential fats work in tandem to keep the inflammation

* Specifically, inflammation triggers a reduction in blood levels of *tryptophan*, the primary building block of serotonin molecules. The result: less serotonin synthesized in the brain's neural circuits.

† These specialized hormones are known as *eicosanoids*.

response in proper balance—available when you need it for a short-term immune boost at the site of an injury, and yet held in check so it's not able to run roughshod over the entire body for months on end. But with the superabundance of omega-6s and the scarcity of omega-3s in the Western diet, all balance has been lost: inflammatory hormones rule, and chronic inflammation runs rampant.

RESTORING THE BALANCE

In his brilliant book *In Defense of Food*, Michael Pollan tells the story of ten middle-aged Australian Aborigines who abandoned their traditional hunter-gatherer lifestyle in favor of modernity. Perhaps not surprisingly, the adoption of a Western diet took a big toll on their bodies, and they all soon developed adult-onset diabetes and a host of other inflammation-linked disorders like *metabolic syndrome*.* This unhappy turn of events led a clever nutrition researcher to issue the group a provocative invitation: Let's see what would happen to your health if you left civilization and went back to living in the bush. Intrigued, the Aborigines agreed to try the experiment for seven weeks. They returned to their erstwhile hunter-gatherer ways and began roaming the Western Australian coast and inland rivers, subsisting on seafood and kangaroos and insect larvae and wild plants.

When the Aborigines returned to civilization less than two months later, researchers were amazed to discover every one

* Metabolic syndrome is a complex condition that typically involves obesity, high-blood pressure, and disordered carbohydrate and fat metabolism throughout the body.

of them in remarkably better health, with major improvement of their diabetes. Their blood work revealed why: All had undergone a dramatic increase in circulating omega-3 fats (and decreased omega-6s).

Most of us, of course, are not about to make such a trek into the wild, no matter what it might do for our health.* Fortunately, though, we can still reclaim from our collective hunter-gatherer past the many benefits of a balanced fat intake, and we can do so from the comfort of home.

To restore your dietary balance of omega-6 and omega-3 fats, there are really only two major possibilities to consider. You can either:

- Increase your intake of omega-3s
- Decrease your intake of omega-6s

Most of the published research has focused on the first option—consuming more omega-3s. In fact, during the past decade, *lots* of different depression researchers from all over the world—Britain, Australia, Israel, Japan, Brazil, Taiwan, India, and the United States—have studied the effects of omega-3 supplementation. More than two dozen clinical trials have even met the "gold standard" of high-quality drug study design—the inclusion of patients randomly assigned to receive placebo capsules instead of the omega-3 supplement. (The placebo is there for the sake of comparison, to make sure any observed improvement isn't due simply to the positive expectancies that

* And I'm definitely not recommending that you try it. Remember, the Aborigines had already spent years living as hunter-gatherers, learning how to survive under such harsh, challenging conditions.

arise from being in a treatment setting, seeing a doctor, swallowing pills, and so on.)

This impressive body of research now makes one thing clear: *omega-3 fats have a potent antidepressant effect.**

Of the six major elements in the Therapeutic Lifestyle Change (TLC) treatment protocol, the omega-3 supplement is the one my patients most consistently rave about. I've even had several tell me they started feeling better—noticing clear improvement in mood and energy and sleep and appetite and concentration and mental clarity—within a few days of beginning the omega-3 regimen. However, like most depression drugs, the omega-3s usually take at least a week or two—and sometimes up to four weeks—for their antidepressant effect to kick in.

To make sure you get the maximum benefit of adding such a supplement to your diet, we need to dive (briefly) into a few gory details of omega-3 chemistry.

THE LONG AND SHORT OF OMEGA-3

Omega-3 molecules come in three primary versions, and they vary in length: there's DHA (long), EPA (medium), and ALA (short). These three major forms of omega-3 play different roles in the body and brain.

The long one, DHA (*docosahexaenoic acid*), is the only omega-3 molecule that's abundant in the brain. And when brain cells don't have enough DHA, their membranes tend

* The best meta-analyses, which integrate the results of all relevant studies, suggest that proper omega-3 supplementation may have a larger effect (relative to placebo) than antidepressant medication.

to get rigid and inflexible. This makes it hard for them to transmit their signals effectively. Not surprisingly, depressed patients often lack enough DHA in their brains—especially in the critical neurons of the brain's frontal cortex. So it makes sense that a DHA supplement could be helpful.

EPA (*eicosopentaenoic acid*), the medium-length omega-3 molecule, is also crucial for proper brain function. There's little EPA in the brain itself, but the molecule is able to flit in and out of neurons to help them use brain chemicals like serotonin and dopamine more effectively. EPA is also the key building block for many anti-inflammatory hormones, so it can have an additional antidepressant effect by turning off the body's chronic inflammation response.

The short version of omega-3, ALA (*alpha linolenic acid*), doesn't actually affect brain function directly. Instead, it influences cells in other parts of the body. Some studies, for example, suggest that it may help stabilize heart rhythm. But there's no good evidence that it helps with depression.

Since DHA and EPA are the two omega-3 molecules that play an important role in the brain, depression researchers have carefully studied the effects of supplementing with each one. And based on the available evidence, EPA looks like the more potent of the two—by far. Clinicians have also experimented with a wide range of EPA doses, and the best supported daily dosage, used across a number of different studies, is 1000 to 2000 milligrams (mg) of EPA per day.

On the other hand, DHA is not effective as a treatment for depression, at least not when used on its own. But because the brains of depressed individuals are often deficient in DHA, there may still be some benefit in boosting its intake. Fortunately,

DHA always occurs in tandem with EPA in nature, so virtually every commercial EPA supplement will also provide some potentially useful DHA.

THE OMEGA PRESCRIPTION

Based on the available research evidence, I recommend a starting omega-3 dose of *1000 mg of EPA* each day to all of my depressed patients. If you currently have symptoms of depression, or if you want to help prevent the onset of illness in the future, this is the dose I suggest you begin with, as well. Depending on how you respond after a few weeks on this regimen, you might need to tweak the dosage a bit, and we'll discuss that possibility in the next section.

Fish Oil

What's the best way to get your daily dose of omega-3 (EPA)? By far the most convenient approach—and the one used in all the best research studies—is to obtain it in the form of fish oil, the richest natural source of both EPA and DHA. Just a few daily capsules (or teaspoons) of high-quality fish oil will do the job. It's such an easy lifestyle change—requiring less than a minute each day—that most people have no trouble making it part of their daily routine.

I have to admit, though—fish oil can be unappealing. For one thing, it often smells bad. It usually tastes bad, too. The first time I ever took the plunge and tried fish oil capsules (about 18 years ago), I was plagued by a common, nasty side effect: fishy burps. Soon after swallowing the pills, I found myself involuntarily belching up the foul taste of rancid fish every few minutes, and this went on for hours. Not good. It was years before I worked up the courage to try it again.

At that point, I was still ignorant of a crucial fact: All fish oil pills are not created equal. Some are fine, but many are downright awful. The thing is, fish oil rots (oxidizes) quickly in the open air. So if your supplement wasn't processed properly, you'll wind up with rancid oil encased inside a gel cap. Because the capsule is airtight, you won't even know there's anything amiss until your digestive juices release the spoiled oil into your stomach.

Simply put, the fish oil in your supplement should be fresh. You can get a pretty good sense of its quality just by biting into one of the capsules. The taste and odor should be mild and unobjectionable, with only a hint of fishy aroma.

Another rule of thumb for finding a quality fish oil: Make sure the product delivers the omega-3s in their natural triglyceride form. It will typically say on the label if it does. Our ancestors consumed EPA and DHA as triglycerides before the advent of modern chemical processing, which helps explain why our bodies find this molecular form the easiest to use.

Unfortunately, the great majority of fish oil products on the market put their omega-3s in a synthetic state known as ethyl esters. It's easier and cheaper to process omega-3s as ethyl esters, but they're also less bioavailable in this form. This makes them less beneficial to the body. That's why I believe it's worth spending a little more to get a triglyceride-based product. Several options are now available in the UK, including the fish oil supplements produced by Nordic Naturals and Nordic Oil.

Labels. The EPA and DHA content of each fish oil capsule (or teaspoon, in the case of a liquid) should be clearly stated right on the bottle, as depicted on the sample label in Figure 4-1.

Please keep in mind that sometimes—as in the example in Figure 4-1—stated omega-3 amounts are based on a serving size of *two capsules*. So, in this example, each softgel capsule would

FIGURE 4-1.

Nutritional Information from a Typical Bottle of Fish Oil Capsules

Nutrition Info

Serving Size: 2 Softgels

	Amount Per Serving	% Daily Value
Calories	20	
Calories from Fat	20	
Total Fat	2 g	2%*
Saturated Fat	<0.5 g	2%*
Trans Fat	0 g	†
Polyunsaturated Fat	1.0 g	†
Vitamin E (as natural d-alpha Tocopherol with Mixed Tocopherols)	0.5 mg	70%
Natural Fish Oil Concentrate	**2,000 mg**	**†**
Omega-3 Fatty Acids	**1,000 mg**	**†**
Elcosapentaenoic Acid (EPA)**	**500 mg**	**†**
Docosahexaenoic Acid (DHA)**	**250 mg**	**†**
Other Omega-3 Fatty Acids	**250 mg**	**†**

* Percent Daily Values are based on 2,000 calorie diet.

† Daily Value not established.

contain only 250 mg of EPA; it would thus take four such capsules to make up the recommended starting dose of EPA.

Other Important Considerations

To make sure you get the greatest possible benefit from your fish oil supplement, we need to briefly address a few other important points.

Antioxidants. Fish oils and oxygen don't mix: the oxygen spoils it. We all have some harmful forms of oxygen in our bodies, carried around by dangerous molecules called free radicals. These molecules can damage any fish oil you consume just as soon as it hits the bloodstream, making the omega-3s less useful to your brain. Antioxidants—nutrients like vitamin C—can protect omega-3s from such damage.

To ensure that you have enough antioxidants in your system, you could consider adding a low-dose (250 mg) vitamin C supplement to your daily regimen. Or you could resolve to eat at least five servings of vegetables and fruit each day—as nutritional therapists recommend—which will help you reap the full benefits of the omega-3s you consume without the need for another supplement.

GLA. Even though most of us eat far too many omega-6 fats—which are turned into inflammatory hormones that ravage the body—one type of omega-6 is an exception. It's called GLA (*gamma linolenic acid*), and it's a building block for fats that act a lot like omega-3s—they make hormones with a potent anti-inflammatory effect.

When we take a good fish oil supplement, the large amount of EPA can interface with the body's use of GLA. Low levels of

GLA can, in turn, trigger unwanted inflammation. So just to be on the safe side, it's best to make sure you're getting a little GLA in your diet. Luckily, only a small amount is required: 5 to 10 milligrams (mg) per week.

Not many foods have GLA, but oatmeal turns out to be a decent source. It has to be slow-cooked oatmeal, though, not the instant kind. Eating two big bowls a week should give your body the GLA it needs. Another option is to take a supplement of *evening primrose oil,* which you can get at most drug stores or health food stores. However, this oil contains a remarkably high concentration of GLA, so only one capsule each week is necessary. (Some nutritionists explicitly advise against taking it much more frequently than that.)

The freezer trick. Even when using a high-quality fish oil supplement, a few people still experience a bit of burping afterwards. This problem usually can be eliminated, however, by storing the supplement in the freezer and taking it with a meal. The frozen capsule will pass through the stomach and on to the small intestine before it fully dissolves—effectively getting rid of the burping. Taking the fish oil with a meal, or even a handful of nuts, will also help your body make better use of the omega-3s, especially if you're taking them in the cheaper ethyl ester form, rather than the suggested triglyceride form.

Tweaking the Dose

Even though our foraging ancestors kept a nicely balanced 1:1 ratio of omega-6 and omega-3 fats in their diets, our "design specs" as a species also leave some margin for error (thank goodness). Most of us can do just fine with a ratio as high as 3:1.

If you take a high-quality omega-3 supplement at the starting dosage I've recommended—1000 mg EPA each day—there's a good chance you'll shift your omega-6/omega-3 ratio down below 3:1 and into the healthy range. But some people don't. If you eat *lots* of omega-6 fats—fried foods, grain-fed beef and pork (and chicken and fish), vegetable oils, junk food, and so on—you may need a higher dose of omega-3s to balance things out. Likewise, as we've seen, if you don't have enough antioxidants in your system, it may be difficult to keep enough omega-3s available in your body to do the job.

How can you tell if you have a healthy ratio of omega-6 to omega-3? One approach is simply to make an educated guess based on how your body functions. If your ratio of omega-6 to omega-3 is still way too high, there's a good chance you'll have some of the following common symptoms:

Fatigue
Poor concentration
Sluggishness (especially upon awakening)
Sinus congestion
Carbohydrate craving
Dry skin
Dry eyes
Dense stool or constipation
Brittle nails and hair

Most of my patients have reported improvement in several of these symptoms within a few weeks of starting their omega-3 supplement.

Many have also noticed similar symptom relief with other chronic inflammatory conditions. Some, for example, have said their achy knees started to improve within a week or so of starting the omega-3 regimen. A few patients have even told me the fish oil capsules had helped clear up their seasonal allergies. (I have to confess, this last claim sounded far-fetched at first, but I later found research evidence that omega-3s actually help suppress some allergic reactions.)

But for our purposes, the best indicator of your omega-6/omega-3 ratio is your depression itself. If you don't see some improvement in depressive symptoms within four weeks of taking an omega-3 supplement, you may need a higher dose to get into a healthier range. In that case, I'd recommend doubling your initial dose, bumping it up to *2000 mg of EPA each day.* If that doesn't lead to any obvious results within four more weeks, I'd suggest getting a more intensive—and more accurate—reading of your fatty acid profile.

With a simple blood test, it's possible to find your exact omega-6/omega-3 ratio. The test measures both EPA and a key omega-6 fat—called *arachidonic acid* (AA)—and it gives you the precise ratio of AA/EPA (omega-6/omega-3).

The ideal ratio on this blood test is believed to be about 2.0 (not 1.0, as you might have guessed, since the ratio is a little higher in the blood than it is in the brain). But if you're reasonably close to 2.0—anywhere between 1.0 and 3.0—you're probably in a healthy range. And you never want to take so much omega-3 that the ratio gets *too* low, because there's an increased risk of infections when the ratio falls below about 0.7. There's even a small risk for some types of stroke.

You can consult your doctor for options on testing omega-3 and omega-6 fatty acid levels.

FREQUENTLY ASKED QUESTIONS

Now that we've covered the basics of omega-3 supplementation, we'll turn our attention to some related questions that come up from time to time.

1. I'm a vegetarian. Is it possible to get enough EPA (and DHA) from plant-based sources? Every time I give a talk on fatty acids and depression, someone will ask about vegetarian and vegan sources of omega-3s—flaxseed oil, rapeseed/canola oil, walnuts, and so on. It's true that these are all good ways to get ALA (the short molecular version of omega-3), but you may recall that ALA is an omega-3 that doesn't help with depression. Fortunately, our bodies are able to convert a small fraction of dietary ALA to the longer versions of omega-3 that we need (EPA and DHA), and there's evidence that vegans and vegetarians develop a higher ALA-to-EPA conversion rate than meat-eaters*.

According to the best research, some vegetarians convert as much as 20% of their dietary ALA to EPA. But a 10% conversion rate is probably more common (with a lower rate for some men). This would imply a dose of at least 10,000 mg of supplemental ALA to yield our target of 1000 mg of EPA in the body.

One easy and inexpensive supplementation strategy is to take two tablespoons of high-quality flaxseed oil, which provides a whopping 15,000 mg of ALA. Hemp seed oil is another great option. Although two tablespoons contains only about 7,000 mg of ALA, it also contains about 900 mg of a rare form of omega-3,

---

* In addition, women convert up to twice as much ALA to EPA as men. These differences appear to be driven by the effects of estrogen, so they're most notable among women of reproductive age.

stearidonic acid, that is more readily converted to EPA. As an added bonus, hemp seed oil has plenty of GLA, so it eliminates the need to look for other food sources of GLA (as discussed in the preceding section).

2. I'm not sure I want to take fish oil pills every day. Is it possible to get enough omega-3s naturally, by incorporating the right kinds of meat and other foods into my daily diet? Yes, it's possible, but it's fairly difficult. Fatty fish—especially salmon, tuna, mackerel, sardines, anchovies, herring, whitefish, and shad—are by far the richest natural source of EPA and DHA, so the obvious strategy is to start adding plenty of these fish into your daily diet. But it takes a lot of fish to get an antidepressant dose of omega-3s. On average, you'll need two to three servings each day.

The Japanese make up one of the few large populations in the world that eats this much fish. They have an impressive average omega-6 to omega-3 ratio of just under 2:1, and their rates of depression are extremely low. In addition, they're healthier than we are overall, and they enjoy a longer life expectancy.

However, fish are sometimes tainted by toxins such as mercury and pesticides, so you'll want to take some precautions if you choose to add seafood to your diet on a daily basis. In general, ocean-caught fish are safer than farm-raised fish, many of which are imported from countries that don't always make sure they're free of contaminants. Also, large fish at the top of the food chain—tuna and swordfish, for example—normally have higher toxin levels than small fish like sardines and anchovies.

Although it's certainly possible to get adequate EPA and DHA without a supplement—if you're highly motivated and willing to change your diet—such an approach is much harder than taking a few fish oil pills every day. Most of us won't stick with something if it takes too much time, energy, and effort—and that's doubly true for anyone fighting depression, which robs us of initiative. That's why I recommend a high-quality fish oil supplement as the best omega-3 source in treating depression. It's something just about everyone can do.

3. What's the difference between fish oil capsules and liquid supplements? Is one better than the other? They're just different ways of taking the same oil. Few people enjoy the taste of fish oil (even the high-quality stuff), so most prefer taking the oil in capsule form, which prevents us from having to taste the oil itself.

On the other hand, some people don't like swallowing big pills. That's why I'm among the brave souls who take the fish oil "straight-up," right out of the bottle. Luckily, most liquid products now have a lemon flavoring to help mask the fishy taste, and I've found that chasing the oil with a shot of grapefruit juice works wonders to cover up the aftertaste. Still, you'll probably want to have your toothbrush close at hand just to make sure.

4. Is it possible to get my omega-6/omega-3 ratio in balance simply by cutting out the omega-6s from my diet, instead of adding all those omega-3s? It makes perfect sense. We get way too many omega-6s in the Western diet, so why not just cut most of them out? We can and we should.

However, omega-6s stay in the body a long time, so even if you managed to get rid of the omega-6s from your diet, it would take months before your omega-6/omega-3 ratio dropped in a big way. When someone is depressed, they don't have months to wait: They want relief as soon as possible. And omega-3 supplements provide quick relief, because they start improving the omega-6/omega-3 ratio within days.

Certainly, though, as a long-term strategy to prevent future depression, cutting out omega-6s is a great idea. Here are some simple things you can do to get started:

- Switch to grass-fed beef, or simply drop beef from your diet altogether
- Stick mostly with lean meats like chicken breast and fish
- Stay away from fried foods (and most fast food in general)
- Cook with olive oil or coconut oil (fruit-based oils), and avoid seed-based oils like soybean oil, rapeseed/canola oil, canola oil, and sunflower oil; use the same principle when it comes to salad dressing
- Use butter instead of margarine
- Avoid snack chips and baked goods
- Start reading product labels, and stay away from foods that contain lots of seed-based oils (there are thousands of them)

5. I'm not sure I can afford a fish oil supplement in triglyceride form. Can I just take the cheaper kind (in ethyl ester form)? Believe it or not, some triglyceride-based fish oils are available online for only a little more than you'd pay for a lower-grade supplement at your local supermarket.

However, if you can only afford a lower-quality supplement—that is, one that's not in triglyceride form (less bioavailable)—I can pass along some reassuring news. Your body will still be able to use most of its omega-3s, especially if you take the fish oil with a meal or a snack such as nuts. The vast majority of published research on the antidepressant benefit of fish oil was conducted with supplements that carried the omega-3s in the ethyl ester form.

6. I understand how important the fish oil supplement can be, but I just can't remember to take it. What should I do? This is a common problem, but it's usually easy to overcome. It simply requires the use of a memory aid. Over the years, my patients have shared with me several clever remedies they've discovered:

- Store the bottle next to your toothbrush or something else you use every day. (If you need to keep your capsules in the freezer to prevent burping, you can put them in a different container and still keep the empty bottle by your toothbrush as a memory cue.)
- Store the bottle on your pillow or bedside stand.
- Set your mobile phone to ring you every day at a certain time; this will be your "wake-up call" that it's time to take the fish oil.
- Find a friend or family member who's willing to give you a gentle, friendly reminder each day.
- Buy a daily pill box—the kind sold for a pound or so at any chemist—and store the capsules in that.

7. Are there any potential side effects of fish oil supplements? There are some mild, gastro-intestinal side effects of fish oil to bear in mind, such as "fishy burps." Others notice an increase in flatulence (gas), acid reflux, nausea, or abdominal cramps. Fortunately, such problems are usually remedied by switching to a higher-quality supplement or by taking the fish oil with a meal.

If you have an existing allergy to fish or seafood you will likely have an allergic reaction to fish oil. One alternative is algae-derived supplements (see the answer to Question 1, earlier).

Fish oil can have moderate blood thinning (anti-platelet) effects at higher doses, so if you take blood-thinning medication, bleed easily or have trouble with blood clotting, take fish oils only under strict medical supervision. It's advisable to seek immediate medical consultation if you notice that you're bruising more easily or bleeding more readily after beginning a fish oil regimen.

Because omega-3s can modulate the brain's serotonin signaling, they carry the potential to reduce the intensity of our emotions, just as we see with antidepressant medications. A little dampening of negative emotions like anxiety, sadness, and anger can often be a welcome development—especially for those who have battled depression. On rare occasions it appears that fish oil can induce more extreme emotional blunting; I have seen it happen with two people out of the many hundreds whom I've observed on these supplements. Both temporarily lost their ability to care about important things like their work and relationships. In both cases, they returned to normal within a day or two of stopping supplementation. Even though such reactions are extremely unlikely, it's probably a good idea to check in with a friend or loved one to make sure they don't notice any major changes in our emotional expression after we begin taking fish oil.

8. After my depression has lifted, can I then cut back on my omega-3 dosage? Yes, the high daily dose of EPA (1000-2000 mg) used to treat depression may not be necessary or even ideal as a long-term strategy. Most of the published research has patients on this dosage level for about 3 months.

If your depression is markedly improved after supplementing at the suggested EPA dosage for 3 months, it's then reasonable to experiment with a gradual taper over the next few weeks down to a dose of 500 mg (or even 250 mg) per day. If you notice the return of depressive symptoms or inflammation during the taper, you can always return back to the original dose for a few more weeks or months before trying again.

OMEGA-3S: A CLOSING THOUGHT

Change is hard. Yet some new habits are a lot easier to pick up than others. Luckily, the simplest change in the entire Therapeutic Lifestyle Change program—adding a daily fish oil supplement—is also one of the most potent in its ability to fight depression and keep it from coming back. It's a change that takes only a minute of your day, but it can change your life immeasurably for the better.

5
Don't Think, Do

Brenda had been an A student in my Abnormal Psychology class a few years earlier, and had since graduated and begun working in the area. Soon afterward, however, she found herself battling several symptoms of depression, so she decided to drop by my office for some advice.

She told me that right after she'd started feeling depressed, she pulled out her old lecture notes and began reviewing the things I'd mentioned in class about the antidepressant effects of exercise, fish oil, sunlight, and so on. Then, completely on her own, Brenda started putting the Therapeutic Lifestyle Change (TLC) program into practice.

"But I must be doing something wrong," she said, "since I'm not getting better at all. I mean, it's not as bad as it was back in college—when they put me on Sertraline—but I can't let it get to that point again." She sighed. "I was really hoping the TLC stuff would work for me."

"Well," I offered, "why don't we take a look at the things you've been doing, and maybe we'll get some ideas about why they haven't helped."

She quickly ran through an impressive litany of lifestyle changes. In recent weeks, she had started walking about forty-five minutes a day; getting plenty of sunlight exposure; taking a high-quality fish oil supplement at the recommended omega-3 dose; averaging a good eight hours of sleep a night (although she still had occasional trouble falling asleep); and increasing her social connectedness, not only by seeing her boyfriend every day, but also by meeting with a few old friends on a regular basis. She was even taking steps to get closer to her new coworkers.

It was puzzling that none of this had made much of a difference. "Maybe," I thought, "she's the exception that proves the rule." I had never seen someone put the entire TLC protocol into practice and remain clinically depressed, but I certainly couldn't rule out the possibility. On the other hand, one stone still remained unturned. I hadn't asked Brenda yet about rumination.

"Do you remember," I asked, "what we covered in class about rumination?"

She shrugged. "Isn't that just, like, thinking about things?"

"Yes, thinking about them over and over and over. When we're depressed, we tend to dwell on things—especially negative things—replaying them again and again in our minds. And for many depressed patients, that kind of negative thinking can go on for hours."

"Yeah," she offered, "I definitely do that sometimes. A lot, actually. Like when I'm working out or doing the dishes or something, all these thoughts will just be going through my head. 'What if things don't work out with my boyfriend?' or 'Why can't I get closer to people at work?' or 'I can't believe my dad forgot to call me on my birthday' or 'How come I'm getting depressed again?' And then I'll just sit there thinking about things."

"And when you let yourself brood over things like that, does it change the way you feel?"

"Um," she looked down at the floor as she pondered the question for a moment. "It makes me feel worse. Definitely."

"Well, if you're spending a lot of time dwelling on these negative thoughts, it might explain why your depression hasn't cleared up yet."

Brenda shifted in her seat uncomfortably. "But I don't know how to just stop thinking about things. I mean, it's not like you can really control what you think about."

"That's true—we can't always control where our thoughts might lead. But once a thought has popped into our heads, we can decide whether or not we're going to *keep* thinking about it; we can shift our focus onto some other activity instead."

She looked skeptical. "It's not like I haven't tried to get my mind off all this stuff already."

I nodded. "I know. Rumination has become a habit for you—like it is for most people with depression. And habits are tough to break. But I've worked with hundreds of patients who've learned how to stop ruminating, and many of them were more severely depressed than you are right now. Mostly, it just takes a commitment—and some practice."

"Well," Brenda said weakly, "I *want* to stop thinking about all these things all the time . . ." Her voice trailed off. "I'm willing to try, anyway." She smiled wryly, "Even though none of your other TLC stuff has helped."

Brenda worked hard over the next month to break her rumination habit, using each of the major strategies described in the pages ahead. Perhaps because she had already put so many other parts of the treatment protocol into practice, her depressive symptoms lifted in just a few weeks once she brought her rumination under control.

Even though my parents grew up in rural Maine, I was raised in the suburbs. In fact, I was a teenager before I even saw any farm animals up close—on a visit to a relative's cattle ranch in north Georgia. And one of the first things that caught my attention—aside from the pungent smell—was the cows' limited behavioral repertoire: lots of standing around and lots of chewing. I guess there was also a bit of grazing and other activity mixed in there, but after just a short while, the cows would stop eating to regurgitate all the grass (and some unlucky insects) back up in the form of cud—a bolus of semi-digested food. And then they just stood there chomping away for hours, slowly and methodically breaking the cud down into smaller and smaller pieces, until it was ground down enough to fully digest.

The cows' digestive process is known as *rumination.** And it provides a rich metaphor for something similar that we do—not with food, but with our deepest thoughts. It seems that we, too, sometimes need to chew things over for a while before we can actually stomach them.

MULLING THINGS OVER

Rumination appears to be an instinctive human response whenever something goes wrong. It's as if we're hardwired to replay

* Derived from the word *rumen*—the part of the bovine stomach where cud is formed.

our recent trials and tribulations over and over again in the mind's eye—to mull things over for a while before we're ready to move on. And a little such dwelling can be helpful, since it often leads to valuable insights—providing greater clarity about what just went wrong, what can be done to correct things, and what might help us prevent similar negative outcomes in the future.

But after just a brief period of intense pondering, we've usually extracted all the useful bits of meaning from the situation that we're ever likely to find. We soon hit the point of diminishing returns, when any more dwelling is simply a waste of time. But some people stay at it long past the point when enough is enough. And, unfortunately, extended rumination can have several damaging effects.

For one thing, it tends to amplify negative emotions. If you spend some time mulling over very sad events, for example, you'll soon find yourself feeling morose (certainly much more so than when you started). Likewise, when your thoughts become fixated on a potential threat, this process will inevitably start ramping up your feelings of anxiety.

Rumination also makes people less active. It's an inert, inward-focused process that keeps us locked more or less inside our own heads. When we're brooding, we're especially inclined to avoid activity, as it would force us to shift attention away from our internal machinations and out onto the world around us instead.

In a nutshell, when we ruminate, we withdraw. That's especially true on the social front. When someone is locked in a bout of rumination during a social encounter, they're simply not all there mentally. When spoken to, they may nod politely and say "uh huh," but they won't register anything that's being said.

In other words, they'll go through the motions on the outside, while still spinning the ruminative wheels inside their own private little world. When this process becomes a habit, it takes a huge toll on their ability to stay connected with others.

Finally, because it has such a potent ability to turn up the volume on our emotions, rumination sends the brain's stress response circuits into a flurry of sustained activity. And that, in turn, can trigger a full-blown episode of depression.

As it turns out, the link between depression and rumination is a particularly strong one. Through its powerful effects on emotions, behavior, social connection, and brain function, rumination renders us much more vulnerable to depressive illness. It also plays a key role in *maintaining* an episode of depression once it's begun. That's why—as we saw in the case of Brenda at the beginning of the chapter—*when someone continues ruminating on a regular basis, they'll find it extremely difficult to overcome their depression, no matter what else they do in an attempt to get better.*

If you find yourself locked in the vise grip of rumination, however, I can offer some words of reassurance—breaking the habit may sound difficult, but the process is surprisingly straightforward. It only involves two major steps: learning to notice when it's happening (increasing awareness), and learning how to redirect your focus to some other activity.

BREAK THE HABIT: AWARENESS

What is it about depression that causes us to dwell at length on negative thoughts? The answer has a lot to do with human memory.

Although it's miraculous that the brain—a three-pound lump of neural tissue—can store any memories at all, the human memory system has some surprising quirks. Most notably: We forget things. The forgotten information is still there in our brains somewhere; it's just that it's difficult for the brain to put its (metaphorical) hands on any one specific memory when it's needed. There's so much other competing information in there.

To solve this problem, the brain often has to rely on memory *cues*—bits of information related to the thing we're trying to recall—to jog our memories. Pretty much anything can serve as such a cue, as long as it's associated somehow with the information we're looking for. For example, researchers have shown that when people learn a list of words in a particular room, they'll do a better job recalling the words the next day if they're taken back to the same room (as opposed to, say, the one next door). The room setting becomes a cue that helps trigger the words in memory. Likewise, students who study for an exam while drinking coffee will perform better if they consume a similar amount on the day of the test.

As it turns out, *the brain uses our mood state as its single most important memory cue.* The brain actually tags every one of our memories according to the emotional state we're in when the event occurs. And whenever we're in that same mood again later, it can serve as a powerful retrieval cue for that previous event.

When you're sad, for example, the despondent mood starts lighting up all sorts of memories from other moments when you were in similarly low spirits: previous experiences of failure and loneliness and rejection and unhappiness. Like wise, when we're sad, we generally find it difficult to recall any of the specific times in the past when things were going well.

I saw this principle in action years ago when my daughter Abby—a bubbly, upbeat 11-year-old at the time—was upset about a friend who had hurt her feelings. As I tried to console her, Abby assured me—through many heartfelt sobs—"Things *never* work out right. *Everything* is *always* bad. *Always.*" The next day, after she had regained her emotional equilibrium, I asked my daughter about her unusually negative assessment of life the day before. She just shrugged as she smiled blithely and said, "I don't know. It really *seemed* like that yesterday." Exactly—because memory is such a slave to mood.

So, when people are depressed, their intensely sad mood will cause sad memories to percolate—unbidden—up to the surface of their conscious awareness. Such upsetting memories, in turn, cause them to form negative judgments—to infer that horrible outcomes are pretty much the norm. And as all of these upsetting memories and judgments are unleashed, they'll quickly serve to intensify the despondent mood, which in turn primes even more negative thoughts, turning the mood even more negative, and so on. It's a vicious cycle of rumination that can go on more or less indefinitely—until something comes along to interrupt it.

Whenever I bring up the topic of rumination in one of our TLC groups, most patients readily acknowledge that it's something they do. But here's the curious thing: They've often said that until I brought the issue to their attention, they had never even noticed they were doing it.

During an episode of depression, dwelling on negative thoughts is so effortless and automatic—it's possible to spend long stretches of time doing so without any awareness of what's happening.

Think of when you're driving a very familiar route home. If you're like most people, you've probably pulled into your driveway at some point with the jarring realization, "I have no idea how I just got here." You know that somehow you've managed to make a bunch of correct turns and navigate successfully past other cars, but because you've also made the same drive so many times before, you were able to let your attention lapse while doing so.

In similar fashion, people who've battled depression know the well-worn path of rumination by heart; they can navigate it on autopilot. Long stretches of time—sometimes even hours—can pass without their ever once noticing, "Hey, I'm just sitting here ruminating again, and I've been at it for a *long* time already."

That's why the first step in breaking the rumination habit is simply to increase awareness, to *notice* when it's happening. Once you learn to pay attention—moment by moment—to when you're ruminating and when you're not, you'll be well on your way to breaking free. Until then, however, you'll remain at the mercy of a thought process that can hold you in its paralyzing grip more or less indefinitely, with or without your active consent.

Take a Mental Inventory

How do you go about increasing your awareness of rumination? One helpful strategy is to start deliberately monitoring your thought process every hour or so, just to see what you've been paying attention to—and to make a note of any rumination that's occurred since the last time you checked.

Simply remembering to monitor your thoughts on a regular basis can pose a challenge, however, especially at first. If you find this task difficult, try tying it to a specific prompt. For example, phone apps can be set to notify you every hour or so. Likewise, if you happen to own a clock with a chime setting, its hourly clang can provide an effective cue for taking a mental inventory. Or, if you lack any such gadgets, even a periodic, everyday activity like getting a drink or going to the restroom can serve as a memory prompt.

But the single most helpful thing you can do in monitoring your rumination is to keep an hour-by-hour log of your day. Table 5-1 provides an example of what this log might look like.

As you can see, it's just a matter of writing down what you were doing each hour, how much time you spent ruminating, and how intense your negative mood was at the time. This may sound like a lot of work, but it doesn't take more than about five minutes a day to complete. You'll probably find it easiest if you keep such a log with you throughout the day and pull it out briefly every hour or so to fill in your most recent activities. Not only will this provide a useful prompt for periodic self-monitoring, but it will also serve as a superb source of information about which activities tend to make you feel the best (and worst), and which are the most and least effective in preventing rumination.

During the first week or two of monitoring your rumination on a regular basis, you should gradually become more skillful at catching yourself in the act. And the more you practice it, the more the self-monitoring process becomes a habit—something that begins to happen more or less automatically. In other words, with enough repetition, you'll eventually develop your own spontaneous mental alarm to alert you anytime your thoughts

TABLE 5-1. *Sample Rumination Log*

Time	*Activity*	*Rumination (minutes)*	*Negative Mood (0–10)*
6:00	Sleep, then lying in bed awake	25	7
7:00	Breakfast, shower, and so on	20	6
8:00	Drop off kids, commute	15	6
9:00	Work	2	4
10:00	Work—boring staff meeting	30	6
11:00	Work	5	5
12:00	Lunch with coworkers	2	3
1:00	Work	0	4
2:00	Work	0	3
3:00	Work—told about upcoming deadline	30	7
4:00	Work	10	5
5:00	Commute, picked up kids	15	6
6:00	Made dinner, ate with family	0	5
7:00	Helped with homework	0	4
8:00	Watched TV	30	7
9:00	Got kids ready for bed, watched TV	15	7
10:00	Watched TV	40	8
11:00	Bedtime routine, sleep	10	7
12:00	Sleep		
1:00	Sleep		
2:00	Sleep		
3:00	Woke up for 45 minutes	40	8
4:00	Sleep		
5:00	Sleep		

take a ruminative turn. As one patient put it recently, "Before I was in treatment, I was ruminating constantly, but I hardly ever noticed it. Now I'm catching myself all the time. As soon as it starts up, it's like there's this still small voice in my head saying, 'There you go again. You're doing it, and it's time to stop.'"

Watch Out for High-Risk Situations

As you become increasingly tuned in to your mental life, you'll notice that some situations are particularly hazardous to your emotional well-being. The research on this point is clear: *People typically ruminate—and feel the worst—when they have nothing else to occupy their attention.*

And, given the depressed mind's inexorable drift inward upon itself, the single biggest risk factor for rumination is simply spending time alone. This is particularly unfortunate because, as we've seen, depression involves a strong tendency to withdraw from others. In other words, depressed individuals usually seek out alone time, which leads to rumination, which leads to greater withdrawal, and so on—a vicious cycle.

Spending time with others usually helps counteract brooding, unless the person you're with is also depressed. A recent study of depressed teenagers, for example, found that adolescent girls often *ruminate together* in their conversations—a process that brings mood down for both parties. So, if you're spending time with someone who's also prone to dwelling on negative thoughts, it will probably be helpful to discuss the dangers of joint rumination with that person in advance, and for both of you to agree to avoid giving voice to any ruminative thoughts.

Watching television is another high-risk situation. This might seem counterintuitive, since people often look to TV as an escape—something to take their mind off things. But here's the problem: Most programs are simply not interesting or engaging enough to fully occupy the mind, so it's all too easy for our thoughts to wander off when we're sitting in front of the TV. Add to this the fact that depression impairs our ability to concentrate—including the ability to stay focused on a TV program—and it's no surprise that watching television is often a recipe for disaster. It's one of the most effective ways to usher in an extended bout of rumination.

The same basic principle applies to any situation that fails to fully engage your attention. Over the years, my patients have clued me in to numerous potential high-risk scenarios to watch out for, among them: sitting in traffic, binge-watching videos on YouTube or Netflix (or other streaming services), scrolling through social media, listening to sad music, doing routine chores, daydreaming, and lying around the house. (Later in the chapter we'll look at what you can do to minimize the risk when such situations can't be avoided.)

BREAK THE HABIT: REDIRECTING

Once you've learned how to catch yourself ruminating, you're still left with the challenge of stopping it. The solution involves learning to redirect your attention, to turn away from the inner world of thoughts and memories to the outer world of other people and activities. Simply put, it means more doing and less thinking.

In Chapter 2, we saw how depression shuts people down, squelching brain circuits in the left frontal cortex that allow us to translate our thoughts into action. And when that key part of the brain goes dormant, we find it enormously difficult to initiate activity.

So what happens? We start doing less and less. And the less we do, the more we just sit and brood. That only serves to make the depression worse, which then renders the left frontal cortex even less active, which makes it even harder to do things, and so on.

But the vicious cycle can also run in reverse. We can nudge ourselves to do something—or even just to respond to the gentle prompting of someone else—even though we feel like just sitting there instead. This temporary increase in activity helps stimulate the left frontal cortex, which in turn boosts mood and leads to a bit of reduction in depressive symptoms, which then makes it a little easier to initiate more activity, and so on. In other words, by simply engaging in activity—*any* activity—we can change the brain in a way that helps reverse depression.

Find the Motivation to Let Go

Before we examine the redirection process in detail, it's a good idea to address up front a potential obstacle to kicking the rumination habit: lack of motivation. I've discovered over the years that sometimes people don't *want* to let go of the habit. Even though they realize how harmful it can be, they still want to hold on.

One of my patients a few years ago explained a big reason why: Rumination can be seductive. It promises to deliver the goods, but it rarely, if ever, delivers. Here's how she put it, "You know you need to stop, but it's like, 'if only I spend a little more time thinking about this, *then* I'll figure things out, and I'll feel so much better.' Now, deep down you know that's not really true, but it feels true while you're ruminating. So it's easy just to give in and keep at it. And then before you know it, an hour has passed and you're still spinning your wheels—and nothing has changed."

To help combat the seductive quality of rumination—the enticing idea that it will usher in an array of life-altering insights—I usually ask my patients to consider the following question: When you're ruminating, how long does it take to hit the point of diminishing returns, when any more fresh insights are unlikely to emerge? The consensus answer: five to ten minutes.

So, I make a deal with them: When you catch yourself ruminating, give yourself permission to continue thinking about things for a *maximum* of ten minutes. But be sure to set a timer, and then resolve to shut the process down as soon as the timer goes off (if not sooner). This has proven to be a remarkably helpful strategy—making it much easier for them to let go of the toxic thoughts that would otherwise linger indefinitely.

Many patients have even decided to take this last step a bit further. They've begun *writing down* their ruminative thoughts as a prelude to walking away from them. Simply putting our thoughts down on paper actually makes it easier to stop thinking about them. You may have seen this principle at work, say, the last time you found yourself writing out a shopping list or a to-do list: once you've transferred the information to a sheet of paper, you generally feel less need to keep rehashing it over and over in your mind. You can write it down and then promptly turn your thoughts elsewhere.

Find Activities

Whenever you catch yourself ruminating, it's important to have on hand a list of activities engaging enough to capture your attention. As a rule, we can put an end to brooding only when we're caught up in something else—something absorbing. And in most cases, it just takes a few minutes of immersion in a good alternative activity before the spell is broken.

But finding the activities that work for *you*—the ones that do a great job of grabbing your attention—will involve some trial and error. Individual results may vary. Some of the things I find riveting—for example, reading dense academic journals and watching basketball—might seem utterly boring to you.

Fortunately, although there's no one-size-fits-all formula when it comes to finding the right activities, some things turn out to be anti-ruminative for just about everybody:

Engage in conversation. Carrying on a two-way conversation takes a surprising amount of mental focus—so much so that it's virtually impossible to ruminate while also keeping a decent dialogue afloat. (Of course, the verbal exchange has to be reciprocal. If you're unlucky enough to find yourself talking with someone who likes to dominate the conversation, you can easily start brooding as your companion drones on and on.)

In TLC, we ask patients to make a list of all their potential conversation partners, all the people they could conceivably talk with—either by phone or in person—during a bout of rumination. That includes not just members of their immediate and extended family, but also friends, coworkers, neighbors, and anyone else they can think of—even old acquaintances who've moved halfway across the country.

TABLE 5-2. *Conversation Partners*

Contact	*How Comfortable? (1–10)*	*How Available? (1–10)*
Mom	8	10
Dad	4	9
Sally (best friend)	9	5
Jill (sister)	5	3
Danny (brother)	7	5
Bob & Joanie (neighbors)	4	2
Jessie (boss)	3	5
Sandy (friend from high school)	8	?

I invite you take a moment to make such a list (as shown in Table 5-2, above). As you do so, it may be helpful to rate each person according to how comfortable you'd be contacting them (on a 10-point scale), and their availability to talk when needed.

The next time you're in need of a conversation partner, it's best to begin by contacting the people you feel particularly comfortable with, especially if they're also likely to be available when you most need them. The idea is simply to initiate a conversation—or some other form of engaging activity—*the moment you notice yourself dwelling on negative thoughts.*

You may be able to increase your comfort level with some people on your list—and perhaps even their availability—simply by telling them about your plan to use conversation as a tool to interrupt the toxic rumination process. There are no guarantees, of course, but I've observed that friends and loved ones often react with surprising grace and compassion when they're confided in like that. Probably the most frequent response my patients have received is, "Thank you for trusting me enough to tell me about this, and feel free to call anytime you need me."

Pursue shared activities. Many of the most effective anti-ruminative activities are the ones we can share with others. There's something about the mere presence of another person that helps keep our thoughts from drifting inward.

For example, a few years ago I treated a lonely, depressed housewife who began volunteering with Habitat for Humanity after her youngest child went off to college. The first time she told me about how much better this activity made her feel, I assumed it was because she had made new friends while volunteering. But I was wrong. She was still very socially withdrawn, and she hadn't really connected with anyone there. Instead, what had helped her was simply having specific tasks to do—pounding nails, moving boards, sanding sheetrock—things she could focus on with others. "If I had done any of those things by myself, at home," she said, "I wouldn't have enjoyed it, and I probably would have ruminated the entire time. But just having someone else there with me made all the difference. I'm not sure *how*, exactly, but it kept me from getting lost in my own thoughts—even though we never really did much talking while we worked."

I've certainly found this principle to be true in my own life. (And it's been observed that men are often more comfortable connecting around shared activities than around intimate conversations.) For example, back when I was in graduate school, I sometimes struggled with ruminative, stress-filled thoughts about my yet-to-be-completed dissertation (which ran into some serious snags along the way). The most effective remedy, by far, involved simply leaving my books and jumping into a game of full-court basketball down at the local playground. Within a few minutes of running up and down the court (often with a group of complete strangers), I became swept up in the challenge of the game as it unfolded in front of me, and my mind soon became a worry-free zone.

Play. Interactive games represent a particularly effective way to end rumination. This is especially true if you can take part in a game that involves physical activity—tennis, golf, softball, racquetball, volleyball, basketball, bowling, and so on—because the mere act of coordinating your body's movement requires a great deal of focus from one moment to the next. (Such active games also provide the antidepressant benefit of physical exercise and—often—enhanced social connection.)

An interesting new option on this front has emerged with the advent of gaming systems that use that a wireless controller to simulate active sports and games. Surprisingly, they have become a huge hit even among people who normally avoid vigorous activity—nursing home residents, for example—because it allows them to savor the taste of otherwise inaccessible experiences (like tennis, golf and baseball) through the magic of a wireless remote linked to on-screen simulations.

But even card games and sedentary board games can serve a similar anti-ruminative purpose, especially when they bring us into contact with other people. And, again, technology can make such gaming experiences available in a way that would have been unimaginable a few decades ago. Specifically, there are websites that can connect you in an instant to thousands of potential online gaming partners eager to join you in play anytime, anywhere in the world. In literally less than a minute, you can find yourself caught up with others in a game of online Scrabble, Monopoly, checkers, bridge, chess, backgammon, spades, or any number of other engaging distractions from your rumination.

Listen to music. Although sad music can serve as a trigger for rumination—as can any music that we merely *associate* with upsetting events—most people find at least some types of music absorbing enough to interrupt a bout of brooding. If this is the case for you, it will open up a wide range of anti-ruminative possibilities. Most importantly, you'll be able to listen to music to prevent dwelling on negative thoughts during otherwise high-risk activities: driving, resting, performing mundane chores around the house, doing gardening and yard work, and so on. (As we'll see in Chapter 6, many forms of exercise also lend themselves to rumination especially when you work out alone but engaging music can serve as a wonderful antidote.)

Listen to audiobooks or podcasts. Depression can temporarily rob us of our ability to concentrate, which makes reading very difficult. Many patients have told me, however, that listening to an audiobook or podcast is a much more realistic possibility. It can even serve a function similar to that of listening to music—especially useful during those times when you're alone and engaged in a mindless activity that would otherwise lend itself to rumination.

Watch films and TV programs. Spending time passively in front of a screen—watching TV or movies—is usually something depressed patients should avoid, since it can so easily lead to rumination. (It can also decrease activity in the left frontal cortex, making depressive symptoms even worse.) However, in a pinch—when no other effective alternatives are available—you'll likely find that some movies and TV programs are absorbing enough to help break an episode of rumination. For this reason, it's probably not a bad idea to have a few ideas for films to stream or favourite DVDs around for when you're alone and in need of a quick, easy distraction.

Brainstorm. We've barely scratched the surface of activities you can use to help end a bout of rumination. Over the years, my patients have mentioned dozens of other options, including playing an instrument, cooking, shopping, listening to talk radio, playing with a dog or cat, visiting an animal shelter, going to a karaoke bar, volunteering at a museum, watching children play in the park, writing a letter, needlepoint, and hiking.

With a little brainstorming, you'll doubtless be able to come up with additional activities to add to your own list. I encourage you to take a moment now to compile a list of at least ten things you can turn to when you next find yourself ruminating. It can include options we've already covered, as well as some others that you've come up with on your own. Please note: If you've been depressed for some time, it may help to think back to things you used to enjoy before the illness struck. You can still reclaim many of them as anti-ruminative activities in the present.

Take charge. Earlier we discussed the importance of identifying the high-risk situations in your life—times when you're most likely to get stuck in an extended bout of brooding. The most effective way to address such situations is by taking an active approach: map out each day's schedule in advance and fill in any times of potential inactivity or social isolation with engaging activities.

For example, if you look at my patient's sample rumination log, shown in Table 5-1, you'll see that much of her brooding took place during two high-risk activities: commuting and watching TV. How might she improve things? First, the big block of time devoted to TV viewing after work could be targeted directly—circled on her calendar as a vulnerable period each day, and then filled in with alternative activities (any of the dozens described in this chapter). Likewise, the time spent commuting—while probably not avoidable—could still be rendered less toxic through such simple strategies as listening to engaging music or audiobooks (or, alternatively, through finding someone to carpool with—which would provide a conversation partner).

If you haven't done so already, I encourage you again to begin keeping an hour-by-hour log to track your own rumination (and the activities that promote it and prevent it, respectively). This exercise will not only help you identify and address the troublesome spots in your calendar (when rumination is the most likely), but will also serve as a catalyst to increase your overall activity level.

ACHIEVE BALANCE

Some of the effective anti-rumination strategies we've looked at—socializing and exercising, for example, are intrinsically antidepressant in nature, and most people would benefit from devoting more time to them. On the other hand, some of the activities we've covered—like playing games and watching films—are valuable mostly because they happen to provide a momentary distraction from upsetting thoughts.

As we've seen, a bit of distraction can be enormously helpful. But when the strategy is used too often, it can turn into full-blown avoidance—serving as an escape, not just from negative thoughts, but from the rest of life, as well.

That was the case for Julie, a patient in one of our TLC groups last year. She discovered that she could effectively divert attention from her rumination by spending time on her computer—playing video games, surfing websites, and so on—but before long she was spending most of her day glued to the screen. And that led her to avoid many other important—but less enjoyable—activities: paying bills, doing laundry, grocery shopping and cleaning her apartment. The nagging sense of guilt over such neglect, in turn, began to overtake her whenever she took a break from the computer. Paradoxically, her chronic avoidance led to an *increase* in ruminative thoughts (e.g., *I really need to pay that bill before it's overdue*) during every unguarded moment of downtime, which in turn led her to spend even more time on the computer as an escape.

When she brought up her dilemma in our group, there were knowing, sympathetic nods all around the table. Depression can so completely rob a person of their energy that even simple tasks start to feel overwhelming; it becomes all too tempting to avoid them. And that avoidance eventually becomes a habit, one that can linger long after depressive symptoms begin receding. Fortunately for Julie, however, her fellow patients gently pushed her on the point, helping her recognize the dangerous trap she'd fallen into and her need to bring the pattern of avoidance to an end.

When the use of distraction morphs into a habitual avoidance of things that need our attention, the process can still be turned around fairly quickly. But there are a few important principles worth bearing in mind.

First, when an avoided task feels overwhelming, it can usually be broken down into smaller, less daunting steps. If, say, cleaning the entire kitchen feels like it's too much to handle right now, you can divide the project into simpler tasks: unloading the dishwasher, putting a new load in, wiping down the counters, washing the pots and pans, sweeping the floor, and so on. These subtasks can then be taken on one by one, for as long as your energy holds out.

It's also helpful to make a list of all tasks that you've been avoiding, and to start with the easiest ones first. Simply completing any task—even a short, straightforward one like paying a bill—often brings a nice feeling of accomplishment. And for most of us, merely crossing something off a to-do list is an innately rewarding experience. It helps create a sense of momentum we can build on.

However, in taking up long-neglected tasks, it's important to *set realistic goals for how much you can accomplish at any one time.* As a general rule, it's good to start with modest goals, especially if you've been using avoidance a great deal, or if your depressive symptoms are still severe. A realistic starting goal for some of my patients has been to spend just ten minutes a day on previously avoided tasks like paying bills or doing housework. But they've usually been able to increase that time by a few minutes a day as their stamina grew.

Finally, keep in mind the timeless principle: *everything in moderation.* In overcoming rumination, and in healing from depression itself, maintaining a sense of balance is crucial. Spending some time on long-neglected tasks is beneficial (and it can be anti-ruminative), but devoting too much time to chores can itself be overwhelming—and can make things worse.

Likewise, a moderate use of distraction—playing video games and watching movies and surfing the Internet—is just fine, especially when it serves to end a bout of rumination, but excessive distraction can easily turn into a perilous avoidance of responsibility.

Similarly, as we've seen, even a moderate amount of rumination can serve a constructive purpose when it leads to important insights into an upsetting situation. But a little bit of dwelling on our problems goes a long way. For most people with depression, the balance between thinking and doing is easily lost, and rumination becomes a persistent habit that borders on addiction—amplifying depressive symptoms and standing as a formidable roadblock on the path to recovery.

But by putting into practice the strategies and principles covered in this chapter, you'll find the rumination habit is one that can, indeed, be broken. In so doing, you'll make the all-important journey from the inner prison of your own depressive thoughts to the vastly more rewarding world you were designed for—that of other people and activities.

6
Antidepressant Exercise

Like most of the patients who enter our treatment program, Alice had been clinically depressed for a long time—in her case, about twelve years. And nothing had ever helped. Not meds. Not therapy. Not even the passage of time. At sixty-one, she had pretty much given up hope of ever making a full recovery. But then she saw a story about our Therapeutic Lifestyle Change approach in the local paper and decided it might be worth a try.

Even before contacting us, Alice had noticed that going for a stroll often made her feel a little better. So, when we told her about the antidepressant benefit of regular exercise, it struck a resonant chord. She asked if walking was an intense enough activity to make a difference, and we assured her that it could be, if she were willing to start walking faster, longer, and more regularly. To help her with this, we asked one of our personal trainers to begin meeting with Alice each week for brisk hikes together. Not only did Alice enjoy the invigoration of these outings, but she also valued the companionship, which made the time pass by much more quickly. She also timed her outings to take full advantage of the mood-elevating effect of sunlight exposure. Before long she was taking brisk walks several times a week, often in the company of her husband or a friend. To her surprise, she started noticing a gradual improvement in her sleep, energy level, mood, and ability to think clearly.

Within three months, Alice was, as she put it, "99% depression free." She felt better than she had in years. And while she credited each part of our treatment program with helping her recover, she was convinced that exercise made by far the biggest difference.

THE EXERCISE DILEMMA

According to recent fitness research, over 20 million Brits are classed as "physically inactive." It's not a surprising finding, but it does raise an interesting question: Since just about everyone *wants* to be physically fit—wants to be exercising on a regular basis—why are so few of us doing it? Well, for one thing, we all have a litany of excuses. We're too busy, too tired, too overworked, too sore, too unmotivated, too strapped for cash, too burdened with responsibilities, too discouraged by bad weather—maybe even too embarrassed to be seen exercising in public. But such excuses often serve to mask a deeper truth: Working out is just plain *hard*.

If you're like most people, you've probably even vowed at some point to start an ambitious new exercise routine, only to find your resolve crumbling in a matter of days. Unless you're one of the lucky ones—someone who actually enjoys working out for its own sake—you may even approach the topic of exercise with a vague feeling of dread.

I'm with you. In fact, I believe there's something about trying to exercise that's downright *unnatural*. To understand why, we need to return to the fact that our bodies and brains are still largely designed for life in the Stone Age, for the hunter-gatherer conditions that existed for most of human history. And here's the thing: hunter-gatherers never work out. They don't need to. They get so much physical activity in the flow of daily life—several hours each day—that they actually avoid extra exertion whenever possible.

Why? Imagine if one of your hunter-gatherer ancestors had decided to start working out. On top of the ten miles he already traveled each day while hunting, hauling water, and scouting out campsites, perhaps he went off and decided to run a few extra miles a day just for fun. Not a very wise choice, I'm afraid, since all that extra running would have burned off thousands of precious calories—calories that could have been stored as body fat, reserve fuel during the next inevitable food shortage. Frankly, given the ever-present risk of starvation in the ancestral environment, it's a safe bet that few Stone Age runners ever survived long enough to pass on their "working-out genes" to future generations.

So our wisest ancestors were the ones who followed a simple rule: *spend your energy only on activities that have a clear purpose*. This rule was so important to people's survival that it ultimately became part of our genetic legacy, part of the brain's built-in programming. It's a rule that's still with us. Many people discover this the hard way when they try to work up the willpower to work out. As they approach the dreaded treadmill or stationary bike, it's as if a part of their brain is screaming out, "Don't do it! You're not actually *going* anywhere on that thing. You need to conserve the calories!"

We can even observe this same principle—the same built-in programming to avoid needless activity—in laboratory rats. Exercise researchers have a devil of a time trying to get the little guys to run on a treadmill. The rats will go to incredible lengths to avoid running, even to the point of just squatting down on their haunches until the machine starts to wear the fur and skin off their backsides. When it comes to forced exercise, they feel our pain. But unlike the rats, we have a nagging feeling that we *should* be working out more.

THE BENEFITS OF EXERCISE

Doctors have been telling us for years that we need to get more exercise. Most of us can even recite a long list of health benefits that accompany physical activity: lower blood pressure, boosted immune function, greater bone density, and a reduced risk of diabetes, obesity, and heart disease. Regular exercise even helps our bodies remain youthful. According to aging researchers, it can slow down the pace of biological aging by a decade or more by the time we reach our 50s.

But even though everyone knows that exercise is a key to maintaining physical health, few realize that it's equally important for preserving *mental* health. The latest research shows that exercise can even stop depression in its tracks.

When I was a graduate student at Duke University in the early 1990s, one of my professors, Dr. Jim Blumenthal, was beginning to study exercise as a treatment for depression. It's embarrassing to admit now, but when I first heard about Blumenthal's research I thought the idea was kind of nutty. I can still remember talking with one of my classmates about it. "Sure," I said, "you might feel better for a few minutes after working out, but how in the world is that supposed to help you if you're seriously depressed? I just don't see it."

But Blumenthal knew the powerful antidepressant effect of exercise from firsthand clinical experience. At the time, he was carrying out the most ambitious study of exercise and depression the world had ever seen. The study involved 156 depressed patients—mostly middle-aged and pitifully out of shape—who were randomly assigned to treatment with either Sertraline (a commonly prescribed antidepressant medicine) or exercise.

You might imagine that an exercise regimen would have to be pretty grueling to be effective against depression. Maybe hours of running every day? Or some kind of strenuous weight lifting—the kind that makes people's neck veins bulge? Incredibly, however, Blumenthal simply had his patients take *a brisk half-hour walk three times a week*. That's it. And yet this remarkably low "dose" of exercise proved to be more effective than the Sertraline. The two treatments worked about equally well for the first few months, but by ten months into the study, the exercisers were much more likely than those taking Sertraline to remain depression-free.

And this study wasn't just a fluke: Over two dozen clinical trials now show that exercise can effectively treat depression. How does it work? As we saw in Chapter 1, *exercise actually changes the brain*. Like an antidepressant medication, it increases the activity of important brain chemicals like serotonin and dopamine. It also stimulates the brain's release of a key growth hormone (BDNF), which in turn helps reverse the toxic, brain-damaging effects of depression. It even sharpens memory and concentration, and helps us think more clearly. Simply put, *exercise is medicine*—one that affects the brain more powerfully than any depression drug.

THERE HAS TO BE A BETTER WAY

Yet, at this point it's fair to ask: What good is it to know about all the benefits of exercise if we still can't bring ourselves to do it? After all, we've seen that we're designed to *avoid* extra physical activity. So how can we possibly find a way to make regular exercise a reality?

Fortunately, there's a way out of the dilemma. Yes, we're wired to avoid extra physical activity—but what about *necessary* activity? Have you ever noticed how much easier it is to be physically active when you're caught up in something that has a clear goal or purpose?

This point hit home for me recently when my wife, Maria, told me about her Grandma Peterson. Well into her eighties and hampered by arthritic knees, Grandma had taken to spending the better part of each day with her pet Chihuahua on a recliner in the living room. She was almost completely inert. Her doctors got on her about it, of course. They told her if she would just get a little exercise, she'd probably notice an improvement in her arthritis. But it didn't matter; she couldn't get motivated. Family members would beg and plead for Grandma to join them for a walk around the neighborhood, but she wasn't having any of it. "It's too *hard* for me now," she'd say. "You go on ahead while I finish watching my show."

Then one day the family hit on a different tactic. They invited Grandma to join them on a trip to the local shopping mall. After all, she used to love shopping, but she hadn't been to the mall in years. Fortunately, she found their offer too tempting to pass up, so off they went. Maria estimated—charitably—that her grandmother might last about ten minutes before pooping out. But to everyone's surprise, Grandma was still going strong after three solid hours. She got caught up in the fun of a day out with the girls, and simply forgot all about her sore knees. Somehow she was able to keep on "hunting and gathering" right there with the best of them.

As it turns out, *whenever we're caught up in enjoyable, meaningful activity, our tolerance for exercise goes up dramatically.* Tim McCord is a man who puts this principle to better use than anyone I know. An unassuming junior high teacher from Titusville, Pennsylvania, Tim has been in the national spotlight for chasing an outrageous goal: to get every student in his school district involved in an intensive daily exercise program. Through years of heroic effort, he's managed to get Titusville's students working out—vigorously—more than forty minutes a day. Many kids even make their way to school voluntarily over the summer vacation to get a workout in.

In one of life's wonderful coincidences, I found myself seated next to Tim on a flight sevaral years ago. The more we talked, the more I was blown away by what he's accomplished with his students. I don't know about you, but I used to dread going to gym class, and I certainly don't remember anyone getting in great shape there (rope burns, yes; great physical conditioning, not so much). How in the world, then, did Tim get so many kids on board with his fitness program?

"The most important thing," he said, "is to make the workouts as engaging as possible. When the kids are really into it, they don't notice how hard they're working. Take the exercise bike. It's a boring piece of equipment, right? Put most kids on that bike, and they'll give it a little half-hearted effort and then hop off after a few minutes. But a couple of years ago we hooked some of our bikes up to a video game interface—it's called *Game Riders*—where the kids have to pedal to play. Now they're so caught up in it, they sit there and pedal like crazy. You can't get 'em off the darn things!" He laughed and went on to give one example after another of students getting absorbed in their workouts: The kids were able to get caught up in activities ranging from dance contests to virtual reality games to team sports to old-school playground games like tag and keep-away.

It makes perfect sense, doesn't it? Time really does fly when we're caught up in something enjoyable, even when there's physical exercise involved. It's a principle that worked beautifully for Tim McCord's students—and for Maria's grandmother. It's the same principle we're going to keep clearly in view as we begin to outline an antidepressant workout routine you'll actually be able to stick with.

FIRST: MAKE IT AEROBIC

How hard do you have to work out to see an antidepressant effect? Researchers have looked at the question extensively, and they've consistently observed a powerful therapeutic benefit from *aerobic* exercise—the kind of workout that causes your heart rate to stay elevated for several minutes at a time. Common aerobic activities include jogging, brisk walking, swimming, cycling, racquetball, team sports, hiking, dancing, and climbing stairs.

Technically speaking, a workout is aerobic whenever it gets your pulse between 60%–90% of your maximum heart rate. You can estimate this maximum—the greatest number of times your heart can possibly beat in a minute—with a simple formula: It's just 220 minus your age. But you won't have to do any math on this one. Instead, Table 6-1 displays your estimated maximum heart rate, along with the aerobic values that range from 60%–90% of this maximum number. (These values are listed for every adult age group.) We'll return to these numbers shortly.

TABLE 6-1. *Maximum Heart Rate by Age*

	Aerobic Range			
Age	*60% Maximum Heart Rate*	*75% Maximum Heart Rate*	*90% Maximum Heart Rate*	*100% Maximum Heart Rate*
20–24	120	150	180	200
25–29	117	147	176	195
30–34	114	143	171	190
35–39	111	139	166	185
40–44	108	135	162	180
45–49	104	131	156	174
50–54	102	127	153	170
55–59	99	123	149	165
60–64	96	120	144	160
65–69	93	116	140	155
70+	90	113	135	150

Before you can exercise aerobically, you'll also need to have a reliable way of measuring your heart rate, or pulse. Chances are, you've had your pulse taken at the doctor's office many times, so you probably remember the basics: They hold your wrist, look at a watch, do a little counting and some quick math, and that's about it. Not much to it, right? But it turns out to be a little trickier than it looks (especially in the middle of a workout).

Although taking your pulse seems easy enough, most people need a little coaching and some practice to get it right. If you feel up to the challenge, many nurses and doctors are happy to walk you through the basic steps during a routine office visit.

You may want to invert in a simple, portable heart rate monitor. This is a little watch-like device (used with a chest strap) that gives an accurate, continuous readout of your pulse. It's an investment that will pay big dividends, helping you stay within your target aerobic range during every workout. You might have a basic heart monitor on your smart phone or smart watch that will do the job.

However, even if you never buy a heart rate monitor or learn how to take your pulse, you can still use some low-tech rules of thumb to get a rough idea of whether or not your heart rate is in the optimal range. For example, if you're able to effortlessly carry on a conversation during your workout, it's probably not aerobic. Making conversation is always a bit tougher when you're in the aerobic range; your sentences become choppier because you're breathing so hard. Likewise, if you're able to *sing* while working out, you're definitely not in the aerobic range! On the other hand, if you ever find yourself gasping for breath, you've likely gone *above* your aerobic range, and need to slow down.

Having covered these important basics, we're now ready to move on to the process of choosing an aerobic activity.

SECOND: CHOOSE AN ACTIVITY

Engineers who study the human body—its structure, joints, musculature, and so on—marvel at how exquisitely well-designed it is for walking. It's an activity that comes to people so naturally, so effortlessly, that even babies who receive no prompting will eventually just start to walk on their own, as if propelled by instinct. Walking is something we're truly born to do.

And for the vast majority of human history—until the advent of the automobile a few generations ago—people walked a lot. Our remote ancestors walked an estimated ten miles a day. For them, "a day at the office" often meant a day spent tracking down dinner. Even as recently as the nineteenth century, when most Americans still made their living on the farm, people spent the better part of each day working and traveling on foot. Before car ownership became the norm in the 1940s, most people continued to walk several miles every day. But things are different now. Each day, the average American travels over forty miles in a car, and less than one mile on foot.

Because our bodies are designed for it—and because it's something just about everyone can do—walking is an ideal antidepressant exercise. Sometimes when I tell this to my patients, however, they ask, "Is walking really intense enough to make a difference?" It really doesn't seem like it should be, does it? And yet walking had a surprisingly potent effect in Jim Blumenthal's famous exercise study (the one in which exercise beat Sertraline). The key: Blumenthal's patients walked briskly enough to get their heart rates up into the aerobic range, and long enough to allow that aerobic activity to work its healing magic on the brain.

In light of its many advantages, I suggest that you consider walking as the place to begin your antidepressant workout routine. But this is not a one-size-fits-all recommendation. For example, some people can't walk due to injury or illness. If that's the case for you, you'll need to consult with your doctor to find an aerobic alternative your body can tolerate. (I have a paraplegic friend, for example, whose workouts include kayaking and wheelchair racing.) Likewise, some people already have another favorite aerobic activity, something they know they'll want to do on a regular basis. If that's true for you, then by all means, go with it.

The most important thing is to find an activity you'll be able to stick with. Although my clinical experience suggests that brisk walking usually fits the bill, individual results may vary. Because finding the right workout routine sometimes involves a little trial-and-error, it actually will be useful for you to identify *three* aerobic activities you might enjoy. This will give you plenty of options to work with as we outline an exercise program in the remainder of the chapter. And to help get your creative juices flowing, I've listed several aerobic possibilities in Table 6-2. You may notice that even weight lifting (at home or the gym) is on the list, since it can be aerobic when rest breaks between sets are very brief.

THIRD: DETERMINE HOW MUCH, HOW LONG, AND HOW OFTEN

How much time will you need to invest in all this? The best research suggests that it takes only *ninety minutes of aerobic activity each week* to provide an antidepressant effect. That's the weekly target I'm asking you to aim for. (It's much less time than

TABLE 6-2. *Some Aerobic Possibilities*

Outdoor Activities	*Competitive Sports*	*Activities in a Gym*
Brisk walking	Basketball	Treadmill (jog/walk)
Jogging	Soccer/football	Aerobics class
Swimming	Tennis	Weight lifting (circuit)
Cycling	Racquetball	Dance class
Cross-country skiing	Handball	Jumping rope
Inline skating/ice skating	Netball	Row machine
Hiking	Volleyball	Water aerobics
Rock climbing	Squash	Elliptical trainer
Physical work	Badminton	Spinning (cycling) class

the average Brit spends watching TV in a single *day*.) Here are some related points you'll also need to keep in mind:

It takes about five minutes of working out before most people get their pulse into the aerobic range. So, it's best if you consider the first five minutes of each workout as warm-up time. This brief warm-up period will not count toward your weekly ninety-minute target.

Plan on splitting your ninety minutes of exercise each week into at least three shorter workouts. If you're in reasonably good physical health and at least somewhat active already, it's ideal to plan for three workouts of thirty minutes each. (If you add five minutes of warm-up time, the workouts will each take thirty-five minutes). Why split things up like that? Because unless you're already in exceptional shape, your body just won't have the stamina to last more than about thirty minutes in the aerobic range. It's truly best not to overdo it.

In fact, if you've been completely sedentary over the past several months, I suggest starting with an even briefer workout time, and gradually building up to that thirty-five-minute target. You might, for example, begin by walking only five or ten minutes a day for the first week, and then add five minutes to your daily walk time every few days—until you've increased your stamina enough to last for thirty-five minutes without becoming physically exhausted.

Although you're technically in the aerobic range at 60% of your maximum pulse rate, the best research studies have asked people to work out somewhat harder—usually in the middle-to-high end of their aerobic range. Therefore, I suggest that you set your target pulse at 75% of your maximum. (You can refer to the corresponding heart rate value for your age group in Table 6-1.) During each workout, try to keep your pulse reasonably close to this 75% target.

FOURTH: MAKE IT ENJOYABLE

We've already talked about how important it is for each workout to be as enjoyable as possible. But how can you make this ideal a reality? Following are some discoveries we've made along the way with the Therapeutic Lifestyle Change program:

Make it social. Whenever possible, it's best to work out with someone else—especially someone whose company you enjoy. Because spending time with others tends to be highly absorbing, it makes the workout pass more quickly; it also gives you the mood-elevating benefit of social support. The latest research suggests that exercising with others may be even more effective in fighting depression than working out alone.

So, the next time you're planning a brisk walk, consider inviting a friend or loved one to join you. Or, if you own a dog, you might try having a regular canine workout companion. (Dogs, like us, are built for much more physical activity than they usually get.)

Another option—one that many of my patients highly recommend—is to meet regularly with a personal trainer. Not only can they provide important companionship during your workouts, but most trainers will also give expert coaching and timely pointers along the way. Any local gym or health club should have a list of personal trainers in your area.

Of course, some aerobic activities already have a built-in social component. Sports such as basketball, racquetball, and tennis are fantastic in this respect (Table 6-2 lists several others), and many communities now offer year-round recreational sports leagues for men and women of all ages and skill levels.

Make it absorbing. Sometimes it's just not possible to exercise with someone else. But there are other ways to make your workout absorbing.

Most of us, for example, find it easy to get caught up in our favorite music. This is true for many of the patients I've worked with. Swept up in the rhythm of a great song, they find themselves carried along by the music—with a level of stamina and vigor they'd never achieve when working out in silence. So the next time you're exercising by yourself, you might consider listening to a playlist of up-tempo songs on your phone with earbuds or headphones. You can also mix things up by downloading same engaging podcasts.

Listening to audiobooks is another great possibility. Melanie, a friend of mine who overcame her depression using the TLC approach, struggled for months to work up the willpower to use her home treadmill. It mostly just sat in her basement gathering dust. And no matter how hard she tried, she couldn't make herself stay on the thing for more than a few minutes before the sheer drudgery wore her out. But then she took a long road trip, and happened to bring along some books on CD. Remarkably, the hours on the road simply *flew* by. And that's when it hit her—maybe the books would help her on the treadmill, too. So she got a few audiobooks and made a deal with herself: She was allowed to listen to the books *only* while she was on the treadmill. It worked beautifully. Melanie soon found herself putting in more workout time than she had imagined possible (over two hours a week). Remarkably, she even started looking forward to the time on the treadmill as one of the highlights of her day.

Games also tend to be good at capturing our attention, so any workout that has a game-like quality to it will be especially engaging. Stan, one of the patients in a recent TLC group, told us that when he's out on the racquetball court, an hour will go by in what seems like the blink of an eye. I've heard the same thing from others about sports as varied as basketball, squash, tennis, football, ultimate Frisbee, and volleyball. Several active video games on the market can also provide a surprisingly good aerobic workout; these are especially popular with kids and teens, of course, but many grown-ups find them great fun as well. One of our patients, for example, loved to work up a sweat playing *Dance Dance Revolution* (a fast-paced dance contest) on the PlayStation with her teenage daughter.

One more thing about absorbing activity: *Nature itself has an uncanny ability to capture our attention.* We're all hardwired to enjoy the beauty of natural settings, and there's something almost transcendent about being immersed in the sights and sounds and smells of the great outdoors. Most of us will find hiking in nature to be among the more absorbing (and peaceful) workout activities in our repertoire.

Make it purposeful. As we saw earlier, exercise is easier and more enjoyable when it incorporates a goal or purpose. For example, the average visitor to Walt Disney World walks about seven miles—nearly on par with the daily workout of hunter-gatherers. But how many of these visitors will ever work out like that again after leaving the park? Without all the built-in purposeful activity—checking out the next cool ride or exhibit around the bend—they just won't have the motivation.

As a rule, people are usually willing to walk much farther when they're doing it for a specific reason; it can even be an indirect reason—enjoying the beauty of nature, the companionship of a friend, or the satisfaction of giving a dog some badly needed exercise. But the most obvious reason for walking is simply to *get* somewhere.

So the next time you go for an aerobic walk, you may want to choose a destination that matters to you. It could be a friend's house, a coffee shop, a book store, a scenic waterfall, a restaurant—

anyplace at all, as long as it's someplace you want to be, and someplace you can walk to safely and comfortably.

You can also put the principle of purposeful activity to work for you right in your own backyard: mowing, raking, shoveling, mulching, hauling, or gardening. Because yard work is so goal-oriented, many people find it highly energizing—which allows them to stay at it for long stretches of time. And believe it or not, this sort of activity is usually aerobic. (You can test this by taking your pulse the next time you're out working in the yard.)

One more thing about purpose before we move on: Over the years, many of my patients have reminded me that exercise already carries an intrinsic sense of meaning for them—the goal of fighting depression. In other words, the quest to overcome depression can itself become the purpose sufficient to motivate and energize each workout. When viewed in this light, each stride you take can literally be seen as another step on the path to recovery.

FIFTH: CREATE A SCHEDULE

One of the most important things I've learned about antidepressant exercise is how helpful it is to write out a workout schedule. When we set aside space in our calendars for working out in the week ahead, we're much more likely to reach our exercise goals. Following are some key principles to keep in mind.

Set aside an hour. Even though you only need about thirty-five minutes to get in an antidepressant workout, you'll want to set aside at least a full hour to give yourself enough time to change into comfortable clothes and shoes beforehand and to shower afterwards. You'll also want to build in ample additional time if you need to travel to your workout destination.

Create a routine. Whenever possible, set aside the same blocks of time every week. Habits are hard to break—even a seemingly arbitrary habit like working out the same time every Tuesday. See if you can identify at least three openings in your schedule that are guaranteed to be free from week to week.

Space things out. It's best to space out the exercise evenly over the week (as opposed to working out three days in a row and then taking the next four days off). That usually means taking a day off in between each workout, a practice that has the added benefit of giving your body plenty of time to recover each time.

Avoid ending late. When we work out aerobically, our bodies experience a powerful adrenaline rush. Although this can be invigorating, it can also lead to insomnia if we don't allow enough time to cool down before bedtime. As a rule of thumb, you'll want to finish your workout at least two hours before you turn in for the night.

Bearing all this in mind, please take a moment now to schedule three blocks of time—each one at least an hour long—for working out in the week ahead.

SIXTH: MAKE YOUR WORKOUT SPECIFIC BUT FLEXIBLE

After you've completed your first three workouts, take a few minutes to reflect on how things went. Remember, your goal is for each exercise period to be at least somewhat enjoyable. So even though the pleasure of exercising tends to increase for most people over time (especially during the first several weeks), you should find at least *some* enjoyment in your workouts from the outset. If you don't, it's important to incorporate one (or more) of the strategies we covered earlier, such as exercising to music or audiobooks, or including a workout partner. You can also shift to one of the other workout activities on your list.

SEVENTH: BE ACCOUNTABLE

The biggest single obstacle to working out—especially for those battling depression—is simply to overcome the profound sense of inertia that sets in when we're inactive. Virtually every patient I've ever worked with has told me they enjoy exercising once they're doing it, but they often lack the motivation and energy to get started.

Reduced initiative is a hallmark of depression. The depressed brain actually has an impaired ability to initiate activities, so those battling depression usually have a difficult time starting anything new. But they typically do just fine with a new activity if someone else can help them get going.

That's why it's so important to have someone who can give you the nudge you may need to get off the couch and into your exercise routine. One obvious possibility is a workout partner—someone committed to joining you at a specific time and place. The sense of accountability that comes with this arrangement—the fact that you won't want to disappoint your workout companion—is usually enough to get you started, and your partner's presence and encouragement can help you stay with it. As a bonus, you'll feel good about providing the same incentive and encouragement for your companion.

But if you don't have someone in your life right now to work out with, a personal trainer can play this role. Or, if need be, your accountability could come from someone who doesn't even work out with you. It just has to be someone who's willing to check in with you (even if only by phone) at the beginning of each workout to hold you accountable for getting started, and to provide gentle encouragement to stick with it.

A good friend or trusted family member can often play this role. But so can a therapist, a nurse, or a coworker. And even though it may be a little scary to think about asking for help, it can be well worth it. In fact, our TLC patients have been consistently and pleasantly surprised at how willing other people usually are to provide such accountability. In most cases, others will be profoundly impressed with your commitment to the recovery process and honored to support you. They may even be inspired to start working out themselves.

As we've seen, our bodies are designed for a high level of physical activity. And exercise is extraordinarily important for maintaining both physical and mental health. Aerobic exercise is the most potent antidepressant activity ever discovered, with the ability to reverse the toxic effects of depression on the brain. Physical activity even has mood-elevating effects that can usually be felt in a matter of minutes. As one personal trainer told me recently, "I don't think I've ever seen someone leave the gym in a worse mood than when they arrived."

And, despite the fact that most vigorous physical activity has been engineered right out of our twenty-first-century lives, it's still possible to recapture the benefits of regular exercise. The key steps laid out in this chapter provide a clear sense of what this process looks like, and I've watched patient after patient make it happen. They always do so by simply taking it one step at a time. *Anything more can be overwhelming; anything less can lead to inertia.*

I invite you to take that first step. Remember, you were designed to be physically active, free of depression, and surrounded by people who can support and encourage you along the way.

7
Let There Be Light

This was unexpected. Callie had been symptom-free for nearly a month, and yet there she was in my office, a complete wreck. I could tell she was starting to get depressed again the minute she walked in. It was as if the light had gone out of her eyes.

Plopping down in the chair next to my desk, Callie—a tall, athletic preschool teacher in her mid-twenties—stared absently out the window, as if trying to gather her thoughts. "I don't know what went wrong," she said softly. "I thought I was better, but I guess I'm not. The depression is back." Her voice rose in desperation. "It's like I'm right back to square one."

I tried to reassure her that we'd get to the bottom of things—figure out what had caused her setback—and turn things back around. But I have to confess: I was a little rattled.

Callie had first come to see me three months earlier for help with her depression. Hearing about my research in the local newspaper, she said she'd felt some rekindling of hope. And her motivation in treatment was exceptional. Week after week, she pushed herself to add exercise, fish oil, engaging activity, and social interaction to her daily routine. Within eight weeks, she said she was feeling "pretty much back to normal."

But that was before the setback.

"So," I asked, "did anything happen? Anything unusual or upsetting you can think of?"

"No. It's not like anything happened. I just started feeling run-down all the time. And it's taking me forever to fall asleep; then once I finally do, I can't wake up. It's like I could sleep in until noon, but even that's not enough. And it affects everything else, you know? I feel like crap, dragging around all day. I'm eating all the time, my mood's awful, I can't focus at work . . . it's just like it was before."

This was puzzling. And there were dozens of possibilities we might have to explore in sorting it all out. But I had a hunch about where to begin. "Remind me again: You first started getting depressed back in December, right?"

"Uh, it was right after Thanksgiving last year. Yeah, I think it was maybe early December."

"And you told me you'd been depressed three times before that—once in high school and twice in college?" She nodded. "Can you remember when those episodes started? What month of the year?"

She glanced up at the ceiling. "Uh, well, back in high school I was depressed for two years. It started sophomore year. I guess it got bad after Christmas break, maybe January. And then in college . . . my freshman year it was at the end of fall semester, so probably December. And then junior year—I think it was pretty much the same thing."

Bingo. Four episodes of depression, and each one started in December or January. It was the classic seasonal onset pattern: depression triggered by a lack of sunlight during the short, cold, dreary days of winter. I floated the idea past Callie.

"But it's only October," she said. "Isn't that too early?"

"Maybe. But think about what it's been like out lately." It had rained for several straight days, and had been unseasonably cold and cloudy, to boot. "You usually spend a lot of time outside with your job, right? What about this week?"

She shook her head. "I normally have the kids outside for a few hours every day, so sunlight is never really an issue for me. But it's been so gross out lately; it was indoor play every day. I haven't been out in a week." She leaned forward. There was a little more life in her eyes. "Do you really think that's the problem?"

"I don't know. It could be, but there's only one way to find out for sure." I asked Callie to sit tight while I ran down the hall and grabbed a light box from my lab. We set it up right next to her, and she spent the final thirty minutes of our session basking in light as bright as the morning sun. There was no immediate effect, though she said her mood was maybe a little better by the session's end.

Since it was Friday afternoon, I sent her home with the box to try over the weekend, a half hour after getting up each day. And then on Monday morning I got a call at the office. "Dr. Ilardi? It's Callie. You're not going to believe this, but my sleep's getting better, and I'm kind of starting to feel like myself again. Thank you so much for the light box! Oh, and I just ordered one for myself online; FedEx should have it here by tomorrow."

For my ninth birthday, my parents got me a Polaroid camera. It was one of my favorite gifts of all time. I can still remember the thrill of hitting the shutter and watching as it spit out one of those humble little blank prints, promissory notes that could morph magically into true-to-life images in a matter of minutes. It was like instant gratification in slow motion.

One of the things I always wondered about that camera, though, was why I always had to use a flashbulb inside, but never outside, even on the dreariest, cloudiest day. Sure, it might be a *little* brighter out there, but it didn't seem like that much of a difference. After all, I could see just fine indoors, so why couldn't the camera? I even tried taking pictures inside without a flash, but they always came out a dark, muddled mess.

What I didn't realize at the time was just how *much* brighter it is in broad daylight. As shown in Figure 7-1, *the natural light of a sunny day is over one hundred times brighter than typical indoor lighting*. That's a huge contrast. We don't notice it only because our eyes and brains are so cleverly designed—adjusting effortlessly to nearly any change in lighting conditions, and hardly ever missing a beat.

FIGURE 7-1. *Brightness in Lux*

10	100	1,000	10,000	100,000
	Indoor Lighting	Overcast Day	← Sunny Day →	

But here's the thing: Even though our eyes *can* work okay inside, they're designed for the great outdoors. Our hunter-gatherer ancestors were outside all day, every day. Even as recently as a century ago, most people spent the majority of their waking time in natural daylight.

So it makes sense that our eyes are engineered for the lighting conditions outside. They even have special light receptors, hard-wired straight to the middle of the brain, that respond only to the brightness of outdoor lighting. Why don't they work inside? Because they're looking for light at least as luminous as a gray, overcast day outside—which is over three times brighter than your living room with all the lights on.

If you spend most of your time inside—as people generally do these days—your eyes' light receptors simply aren't getting the stimulation they need. And that, in turn, can have a major effect on both your brain chemistry and your body clock.

THE SEROTONIN CONNECTION

Bright light stimulates the brain's production of serotonin, that crucial chemical emissary. And making sure we have adequate serotonin function is a big deal: It's a neurotransmitter with widespread effects on mood and behavior.

Stress and depression. As we saw in Chapter 2, serotonin circuits help calm the brain's depressive stress response. Thus, bright light, by ramping up the brain's serotonin activity, exerts an antidepressant effect. And unlike traditional medications, the therapeutic effects of bright light can kick in quickly, often in less than a week. (In contrast, the typical lag time with drugs like Prozac and Efexor is two to four weeks.)

Well-being. Bright light doesn't just suppress stress-related emotions; it also boosts feelings of well-being. That's another nice benefit of increased serotonin activity. According to the latest research, people usually feel some elevation of mood within an hour of two of exposure to bright light. I've even had patients tell me they could sense their mood beginning to lift within *minutes* of basking in the sun.

Social activity. When your mood is upbeat, you're also more inclined to socialize. According to the latest research, bright light propels us to seek out more social contact, and to find it more appealing. A recent study also showed that people under the influence of bright light are less likely to argue or fight with others. These effects, too, are due in part to a light-based serotonin boost, which can even stimulate positive social interactions in rodents and monkeys.

ON THE CLOCK

The brain works hard to keep the body running like clockwork. And buried deep inside the cranium is a nifty little chronometer—the so-called *body-clock**—that stays remarkably accurate, *as long as we get enough light each day.*

When we're deprived of ample light, however, the body clock falters, our one hundred trillion cells quickly fall out of step with each other, and all hell breaks loose: Hormone levels get out of whack, sleep grows erratic, and energy ebbs and flows at all the wrong times. For some individuals, these effects actually can usher in a full-blown episode of depression.†

---

* The body clock is a cluster of neurons in a region of the brain called the *suprachiasmic nucleus*

† Among those who are less genetically vulnerable, the effects of prolonged light deprivation usually aren't as catastrophic: They may range from mere sluggishness to feeling blah (or, on occasion, agitated).

Here's the thing: The body's built-in timepiece is *pretty* accurate, but it's not exactly a Rolex. (It's more like the wind-up job you'd buy from some guy in a trench coat.) If it doesn't get reset regularly, the body clock starts to drift—losing or gaining up to an hour a day. And a week or two of drifting is all it takes to send the body into a tailspin.

So resetting the clock each day is an important priority, and it all hinges on those specialized light sensors at the back of the eyes, which are exquisitely sensitive to minute-by-minute changes in brightness. They send continuous input back to the brain, which uses all that lighting information to lock in on the timing of sunrise and sunset each day. (Since these events take place at the same time every day, they can be used like beacons to keep our internal clocks in sync.)*

How much bright light exposure is required? Luckily, it's not that much. For most people, fifteen to thirty minutes each morning† is enough to keep the body clock reasonably on track.

Despite our penchant for staying indoors, most North Americans and Europeans still get enough light in the summertime, when the days are sunny and warm and it's bright outside from early morning until late in the evening.

It's a different story in the winter, though, when the days are dark, dreary, cold, and short. Across much of the industrialized

---

* Although the timing of both sunrise and sunset always varies by a minute or two each day, such small, *gradual* changes are easy for the body clock to account for.

† The body clock is especially tuned in to the timing of sunrise each day. To figure out when sunrise has occurred, it looks for a telltale lighting pattern that goes from very dark (nighttime) to semibright (at sunrise) to very bright (about a half-hour after sunrise). Even inside our modern houses, the first two steps of the sunrise pattern hold: It goes from dark at night to semibright inside when we turn the lights on after waking up. But the brain also needs to see that third step of the pattern—the much greater brightness that quickly follows sunrise. When we're missing that part, the body clock doesn't get reset accurately.

world, people spend virtually all day, every day cooped up inside. Not surprisingly, the typical American is dangerously light-deficient from November through March. (And in more northern locales, the light deficit can last from October through April.)

SEASONAL AFFECTIVE DISORDER (SAD)

According to researchers, Americans and Europeans tend to be less happy (and more sluggish) during the winter. The rate of clinical depression goes up, as well—and the more northern the latitude, the greater the increase. An estimated 20% of the population battles the "winter blues," with at least some clinically significant depressive symptoms between November and March.

And, as we've seen, this pattern can be explained by a lack of light exposure, which disrupts the body clock and depletes the brain's serotonin circuits—leading to social withdrawal, depressed mood, and an elevated stress response.

Clinicians refer to the winter-onset pattern of depression as *seasonal affective disorder*,* or SAD. Diagnostically, it's simply a subtype of depressive illness. But SAD does have a few distinctive clinical features.

For example, while most people with depression struggle with insomnia, those with SAD tend to sleep too much—often up to twelve hours or more each day. And even after they finally wake up, they usually feel extremely groggy and sluggish.

---

* The DSM doesn't actually use this term, however. Instead, it notes some major depressive episodes follow a "seasonal onset pattern."

SAD sufferers also frequently find themselves gaining weight—with a voracious appetite for sweets and other simple carbohydrates* that the body can convert directly to sugar. Many researchers now believe this sugar craving represents an attempt to "self-medicate," since surging blood glucose can trigger more serotonin activity in the brain, temporarily lifting mood. But there's a big downside: eating sugar (and other simple carbs) promotes inflammation—and as we saw in Chapter 2, chronic inflammation is a major culprit in promoting depression. So, the sugar-based self-medication strategy ultimately fails—in a big way.

Those with SAD also tend to be extremely sensitive to light deprivation year-round. This means they can develop depressive symptoms any time of year—whenever there's a long stretch of gloomy weather that keeps them from getting enough bright light.

BRIGHT LIGHT THERAPY

The clear treatment of choice for SAD is bright light therapy. It's now been evaluated in over seventy research studies, and often yields even better results for SAD patients than medication (with far fewer side effects).

But bright light therapy turns out to be useful in treating *all* forms of depression. It's not just for those whose symptoms follow the winter onset pattern, or for those who have the distinctive symptoms we usually see in SAD (things like sleeping too much, weight gain, and sugar craving).

---

* Simple carbohydrates are starchy foods like snack chips, white bread, noodles, pasta, and fries.

Remember, we were all designed to get bright light on a regular basis. That's why it has such widespread beneficial effects: boosting mood, turning down the brain's stress response, keeping the body clock in sync, and even making us more likely to socialize.

Nature versus the Light Box

For most people suffering from depression, thirty minutes of light exposure each day is all it takes to provide an antidepressant effect. However, as we've seen, the light needs to match the brightness of a sunny day—an intensity of at least 10,000 lux—in order for that thirty minutes' worth of exposure to do the trick. (On an overcast day, it's much less bright out—often only about 1000 lux—so you'd need at least a few hours of exposure to such dim lighting to achieve the same clinical effect.)

Getting your bright light exposure the natural way (that is, by spending time outside) has some clear advantages. For example, we're all hardwired to find outdoor settings appealing, since our bodies and brains are still adapted to the Stone Age—a time when people were immersed in nature 24/7. Researchers have discovered that people all over the world generally prefer the beauty of nature to any man-made creations. And mere exposure to a natural setting—especially the sights and sounds of the great outdoors—can lower stress hormone levels and reduce feelings of anxiety. This holds true even when we're only enjoying the "natural setting" of an urban park or a suburban backyard.

An additional advantage of light exposure outside: We can easily combine it with other antidepressant lifestyle elements like exercise and social interaction. Some of my patients, for example, have scheduled weekly meetings with their friends at restaurants that offer outdoor seating. Likewise, others now combine their bright light exposure and aerobic exercise by taking a brisk thirty-minute walk each morning.

The light box, on the other hand, has two clear advantages of its own: It's reliable and it's convenient. As long as you have access to a power supply, it will give you all the bright light you need at the flick of a switch.

Of course, if you're lucky enough to live in a sun-drenched locale—someplace where you can count on access to sunlight year round—you can probably do without a light box. Simply going outside each day will be the best way to get your bright light fix.

Many of us, though, don't have that luxury: We live in places where sunny days are sometimes few and far between. Here in Kansas,* for example, my wife and daughter and I endure long stretches of overcast weather each winter. There are some weeks when we might not see the sun at all!

If you live in such a less-than-hospitable clime, you have three options for making sure you can always get an antidepressant dose of light, especially during the harshest months of the year. You can move someplace sunnier; you can spend at least two hours outside on every dim, overcast day (no matter how cold or rainy it might be out); or you can buy a light box. Since most people will find the first two options undesirable or impractical (or both), a light box can be essential to have on hand for those days when we lack access to natural sunlight.

* We live in the college town of Lawrence, just outside Kansas City.

Thinking Inside the Box

A few different light box technologies are now available. In this section we review the two most promising.

10,000 lux box. By far the most widely researched type of light box for depression—and the one I've employed in my studies—involves the use of *fluorescent* bulbs to provide 10,000 lux of white light.* In essence, this simulates the brightness of a sunny morning. Because we know this technology works—numerous studies back it up—it's the one I recommend.

Even if you go this route, you'll still have an important choice to make because there are dozens of different fluorescent light boxes on the market. They vary quite a bit by size, weight, design quality, and price.

As you might imagine, these boxes can be expensive—ranging from £40 to well over £300, so cost can be a big consideration. Unfortunately, the less expensive devices, especially those costing less than £100, tend to produce dimmer light, which usually means you would have to sit very close (25 cm or less) in order to receive the necessary 10,000 lux. I recommend using a box that delivers 10,000 at a distance of at least 40 cm.

One of the most important features to look for in a light box is an adjustable stand, which allows you to position the box slightly overhead, with the light shining down on your eyes from above—just as the sun does when you're outside. This positioning provides the best possible angle for stimulating the eyes' specialized light sensors.

---

* It's also known as *broad-spectrum* light, since white light includes all the colors of the visible light spectrum.

It's also helpful to keep in mind that some fluorescent lights flicker, causing potential eyestrain and headache. I recommend looking for a box that uses flicker-free technology.

Blue-spectrum box. A newer entry onto the light therapy scene is the *blue-spectrum* box. Because the eyes' light sensors respond best to light on the blue end of the spectrum, it doesn't take a lot of blue light to reset the body clock: About 400 lux seems to be enough to get the job done. That's twenty-five times less light than you need with a fluorescent (white light) box, which allows manufacturers to put out a much smaller, lighter box.

But researchers have only recently begun to test the effectiveness of blue light boxes in treating depression. Although the evidence so far is promising, at this point the jury's still out. And there's also a potential health concern to keep in mind. Blue light turns out to be hard on the retina,* and there's evidence that it might not be good for that part of the eye. (Since pure blue light doesn't occur in nature, it's not far-fetched to think the eyes might have trouble with it.) So, until this safety concern is adequately addressed—and until there's more solid evidence that blue light boxes truly work in treating depression—I suggest you stick with the tried-and-true fluorescent light box technology for the time being.

Light box tips. Here are a few additional points to keep in mind for getting the most out of your light box:

- It's best if you can set the box up about 15 cm or so *above eye level.*
- If possible, position the box so it's centered in front of you, not off to one side.

* The retina contains the light-sensitive cells lining the back of the eye.

- Light boxes usually work best when they're positioned about 45 to 60 cm from your eyes. But there's an interesting tradeoff when it comes to distance. The farther away the box is, the more it will reach every part of your eyes (a good thing) but the lower the number of lux it will deliver (not so good). Most high-quality boxes can deliver 10,000 lux at a distance of at least 35 cm, but some boxes need to be a bit closer. (The product insert will tell you just how close you need to be to receive 10,000 lux.) However, positioning the box any closer than 25 cm can cause uncomfortable eyestrain.
- Never stare directly at the box itself. It will be far too bright, and very hard on the eyes. Instead, fix your gaze on something in front of you—a computer screen, a book, a newspaper, a conversation partner—with the light shining down into your eyes from above.
- If you can't position the box above you for some reason, it will still work okay if you locate it slightly off to your side—as long as it's still facing you from the front. But make sure to keep things balanced by switching sides (from your left to right or vice versa) halfway through the exposure period.

BRIGHT LIGHT EXPOSURE: TIMING

The single most important thing to keep in mind with bright light exposure is that *it has to happen at the right time of day.* Although that "right time" will be in the morning for most people, some will benefit more from light exposure in the afternoon or evening. More than anything, finding the ideal time depends on your current sleep habits. Please take a moment to see which one of the following four sleep patterns most closely matches your own:

- *Late shift:* You experience morning sluggishness, with difficulty waking up on time; you usually have trouble falling asleep at night as well. People with this pattern often find their bedtime drifting later and later, as they stay up to the point of exhaustion so they can fall asleep. They're sometimes able to sleep ten or more hours and still feel tired.
- *Early shift:* You have little trouble falling asleep, but have a tendency to wake up way too early in the morning. Often, people with this pattern are awake at least two hours before their desired wake-up time, but are unable to go back to sleep.
- *Fragmented sleep:* You wake up frequently throughout the night, with no obvious time pattern to the awakenings.
- *Healthy sleep:* You have little trouble falling asleep, staying asleep, or getting up in the morning.

In this section we describe light exposure guidelines for each of these basic sleep patterns.

Late Shift

About 80% of people with the winter blues experience a *late shift* sleep pattern: Their body clock has slowed down and needs to be reset to an earlier time. All it usually takes is thirty minutes of bright light exposure soon after waking up each morning—ideally, within the first hour upon waking. But it's important for the light exposure to occur at about the same time every day, which means you'll need to keep roughly the same wake-up time each morning, even on the weekends.

Let's say, for example, that you normally stumble out of bed at 7:30 on weekdays (after hitting the snooze button on your alarm clock several times). On the weekends, however, you sleep in past noon. In this scenario, you'd have to begin your light exposure each morning by no later than 8:30—even on Saturday and Sunday—because that's one hour after your usual wake-up time.

Most of my patients with this late shift pattern have opted to sit in front of a light box at home for a half hour soon after getting up, usually while eating breakfast or reading the newspaper. Others have enjoyed sitting outside on a patio or deck in the morning when it's nice and sunny out.

Of course, you may have to start waking up a little earlier to make room for a thirty-minute block of light exposure in your morning routine. Then again, you might have a work setting that allows you to sit in front of a light box at your desk. (Many people like to set up the light box right next to their computer monitor.) In that case, you could keep your normal wake-up time, as long as you're able to begin the light exposure at work within an hour or so of getting up.

Within a week, most people start noticing at least some benefit from the light exposure. They often experience less trouble falling asleep at night, an easier time waking up in the morning, and an improvement in mood and energy throughout the day. Some people, however, need more than thirty minutes of light exposure to get good results. If you don't notice any improvement within the first week, I recommend extending the exposure time to one hour.

You may also find it helpful to get another half-hour of bright light exposure in the late afternoon, especially if you're usually dragging later in the day. However, please note that this afternoon light exposure *can't be as bright as the light you get in the morning*, or you could throw your body clock off even more. The safest approach is simply to sit twice as far away from the light box for your second exposure. Or, if you want to get that afternoon light exposure outside, you can wait until about thirty minutes before sunset to make sure it's not too bright out.

Most people with the late shift pattern gradually find their sleep returning to a regular schedule—and other depressive symptoms improving—within two to six weeks of the bright light therapy we've outlined. If you have this sort of favorable response, you can eventually cut back on the amount of bright light exposure you need each day. I'd suggest dropping the exposure time by five minutes every day until you're down to fifteen minutes—an ideal maintenance dose. (However, you may still want to get additional natural light exposure throughout the day to take advantage of its mood-boosting effect.)

Early Shift

Early shift is the most common pattern in clinical depression. If you have this problem, you probably have no trouble falling asleep at night, but you wake up far too early in the morning and find it difficult to get back to sleep. This pattern is a sign that your internal clock thinks it's much later than it really is: It needs to be reset to an earlier time.

The most effective approach is to get thirty minutes of bright light exposure in the early evening. For the first week, it's best to start the exposure five hours before your usual bedtime. So, for example, if you normally go to bed at 11:00 pm, you would begin getting bright light at 6:00 pm. Also, while you're resetting your internal clock like this, you'll need to avoid getting any bright light exposure in the morning, because such exposure can actually shift the clock in the wrong direction. This means you'll have to wear sunglasses whenever you're outside in the morning, at least until your sleep is back to normal.

After a week on this exposure schedule, some people find their sleep greatly improved. But if you're still not able to sleep through the night by then, it's best to shift your light exposure a half hour later. (In the preceding example, you'd slide the starting time from 6:00 to 6:30 pm.) Keep the new exposure time for three days, and then keep pushing the time back another half-hour later every three days until you're no longer waking up too early.

There's an important limit to bear in mind, however: Bright light exposure can't occur within two hours of bedtime, or you'll likely have trouble falling asleep at night. But what if you've pushed your light exposure time all the way back to that two-hour threshold and you're still not sleeping through the night (or seeing improvement in other depressive symptoms)? If that's the case, you can try extending your exposure time from thirty minutes to sixty minutes for a few additional weeks. There's a good chance that will help.

After you've reestablished a healthy pattern of sleep and maintained it for a month, you can start slowly cutting back the late light exposure. But it's best not to quit cold turkey, or you could end up with a rebound effect that can make your symptoms return. Instead, taper off gradually, reducing the exposure amount by five minutes each day until you're down to a duration of fifteen minutes. You can then shift to a maintenance schedule of fifteen minutes of exposure in the morning.

Fragmented Sleep

Some people have fragmented sleep—waking up frequently throughout the night—but they have no obvious pattern to the wakenings that could indicate a major shift in their body clock.* If you're in this category, you may still benefit from bright light exposure. It can actually strengthen activity in the brain circuits that signal a need for sleep, which can in turn make your sleep deeper and more restful throughout the night. In addition, the bright light can have an antidepressant effect by boosting serotonin function in the brain.

With a fragmented sleep pattern, it's best to get your bright light exposure in the morning. But you don't want to start too early or you could wind up accidentally shifting your body clock ahead—causing you to start getting drowsy too early at night and waking up too early in the morning. Accordingly, I recommend waiting a half-hour to an hour after your normal wake-up time.

Start with thirty minutes of exposure for two weeks, and then take stock of your sleep quality. If you're still experiencing fragmented sleep, try increasing the duration of morning light

* In other words, they're neither waking up way too early nor finding it impossible to fall asleep at a regular time each night.

exposure to sixty minutes. (After your sleep quality improves, you can then reduce the duration of light exposure by five minutes a day, until you reach a maintenance dose of fifteen minutes.)

Healthy Sleep

If you have a pattern of healthy sleep, fifteen minutes of bright light exposure in the morning can help make sure that it stays that way. It's best to wait at least a half hour after your normal wake-up time, but to get the exposure within two hours of awakening.

There's one exception to this guideline, however. If you have symptoms of depression—which is rare (but not unheard of) among people with healthy sleep—you'll benefit from a full thirty minutes of bright light in the morning for its antidepressant effect. After two weeks, if you're still not seeing any improvement in your depressive symptoms, you can extend the exposure time to sixty minutes. (Some people need a full hour of bright light exposure to trigger an antidepressant increase in serotonin function.)

FREQUENTLY ASKED QUESTIONS

Now that we've covered the basics of bright light exposure, we can address some of the questions people commonly have about it.

1. Should I check with my doctor before using a light box? Researchers have found light boxes to be safe for the vast majority of people who use them.* Nevertheless, it's always a good idea to check with your doctor before starting any new treatment that can affect your body.

A few medical conditions, especially eye problems, can be made worse by a light box. It's definitely *not* recommended for use by anyone with a serious eye disorder such as macular degeneration, retinopathy, or retinitis pigmentosa. Likewise, you should avoid using a light box if you have extreme light sensitivity, even the temporary kind caused by a medication.

In addition, if you have bipolar disorder (formerly known as *manic depression*), you should never start light therapy except under a clinicians direct supervision, because bright light can occasionally trigger symptoms of mania† in vulnerable individuals. Similarly, if you have a seizure disorder, there's a very small risk that a light box could cause an epileptic reaction, so you should consult with your doctor before using one.

Finally, many people with diabetes experience eye complications along with the disease itself. So if you're diabetic, it's recommended that you talk with a physician about whether or not a light box would be safe for you.

2. Are there any other possible side effects of using a light box? Most people experience no side effects. Of the many patients we've treated in our TLC research, no one has ever reported any. However, it's possible that you could have some eye irritation (especially burning or itching sensations), headache, or mild

* These devices have been evaluated with thousands of patients across many different studies.

† Mania is a condition marked by elevated mood, impulsiveness, reckless behavior, racing thoughts (and feeling "sped up"), distractibility, irritability, and a decreased need for sleep.

nausea the first few times you try a light box. All of these annoyances usually clear up within several days as your eyes adjust to the device, so it's important to stick with it if you can. You can also move the box farther away—double your original distance—to see if that helps, and then gradually move it back toward its original location. If that doesn't work, try reducing your daily exposure to five minutes, and then increase it by a few minutes each day until you get back to the full (original) exposure time.

3. Is there ever a risk of getting too much bright light? As you'll recall, bright light stimulates serotonin activity in the brain. While that's usually a good thing, some people produce too much serotonin after extended light exposure. That can lead to nervousness, jitteriness, or nausea. If this happens to you, it's a good idea to stop the light exposure until you talk with a clinician about how to slowly build back up to a level you can tolerate.

Another possible effect is a shift in your body clock. With excessive morning light, you may find yourself waking up too early and getting drowsy too early at night. If that happens, it's a good idea to cut your light exposure time in half, and to shift it to an hour later, as well.

The same type of problem can be seen in reverse with too much light exposure in the early evening, which can make it harder to fall asleep at night. In that case, you would want to cut your light exposure time and schedule your exposure at least an hour earlier.

4. Can I get enough morning light exposure when I'm driving to work? It's possible, but conditions outside have to be just right. For example, it's not very bright out at sunrise—only 400 lux—and it doesn't usually reach 10,000 lux until about forty minutes later. Even then, it still won't be bright enough inside your vehicle, because the tinted glass cuts your light exposure by about 50%. This means you'd need to wait until the brightness reaches 20,000 lux, and it doesn't get that bright until about an hour after sunrise on a crisp, sunny day.

Similar considerations apply if you're trying to get late afternoon or evening sunlight during your drive home from work: Within an hour or so of sunset, the brightness will dip below 10,000 lux inside your car.

Also, please remember: If you have the late shift sleep pattern, you need to avoid bright light exposure in the late afternoon and early evening, so you should wear sunglasses for your evening commute if it's still very bright out. Likewise, if you have the early shift pattern, you'll need to avoid bright light in the early morning; you may need to wear sunglasses for your drive in to work.

5. I've seen ads for full-spectrum light bulbs that are supposed to mimic sunlight. Will they work just as well as a regular light box? Full-spectrum simply means the light includes all the colors of the visible spectrum, along with invisible forms of light such as infrared and ultraviolet. But most full-spectrum bulbs fall far below the target brightness level—10,000 lux—that's been shown to have an antidepressant effect in carefully controlled research. And even if you could find a full-spectrum light box that puts out 10,000 lux, there's still no evidence that full-spectrum light is any better than regular white light* (the kind used in most light boxes) when it comes to treating depression.

---

* Regular white light is sometimes called *broad spectrum light*. (Not surprisingly, people often confuse it with *full-spectrum light*.)

6. I'm supposed to get light exposure in the morning, but I missed out on it today because I was running late. Is it better to try to make up for it later in the day or just wait until tomorrow? When you miss your scheduled light exposure, it's usually better to make up for it later in the day, as this will still allow you to get the mood-elevating benefit of increased serotonin activity in the brain. However, if you're supposed to get your light exposure in the morning, it's important not to wait too late in the day before you begin. (Evening light exposure can throw off your internal clock and cause you to have trouble falling asleep when you turn in for the night.) If possible, try to complete your light exposure within five hours of your bedtime; if you can't, it's generally better to wait until the next morning instead.

7. I've heard that some people are particularly sensitive to the effects of bright light. Is there any truth to that? Yes. People with fair skin and blue eyes sometimes require less light exposure than others to achieve the same effects. If you have very fair features, you may be able to adjust downward by about 30% all the recommended exposure times in this chapter. For example, where I've suggested thirty minutes of light exposure, you can try it with only twenty minutes. Likewise, instead of a recommended fifteen minutes, try ten. If you don't see adequate results with those briefer exposures, you can always go back to the original suggested times.

8. I like to use a tanning bed in the winter, and I know it makes me feel better. Am I getting enough light exposure just by tanning? No, you can get enough light exposure only when you keep your eyes *open*, and it's definitely advisable to have one's eyes closed inside a tanning bed.

Still, there is something to the claim that tanning boosts mood, despite the fact that dermatologists commonly warn against the practice (and for good reason, because it can age your skin and increase the risk of some forms of cancer). Of course, much of the mood-elevating effect of tanning rests on basic psychology: If you feel better about yourself with a tan, seeing your skin newly aglow might put a bounce in your step. But some people also get a rush of endorphins—the body's natural feel-good chemicals—while tanning, and that can induce a pleasant, relaxed sense of well-being. Finally, tanning increases exposure to ultraviolet light, which causes the skin to start making vitamin D. As we'll review in the chapter's final section, vitamin D can also have a potent antidepressant effect.

THE D PRESCRIPTION

Vitamin D is absolutely essential for life. We'd all be dead without it. It isn't even a proper vitamin at all: Vitamin D is a *hormone*, one of the most important ones ever discovered. A chemical key, it unlocks hundreds of genes that control the day-to-day functioning of your brain, heart, immune cells, bones, skin, nerves, and blood vessels. In fact, a vitamin D deficiency can induce an extraordinary range of health problems. Rickets—a disorder that causes children's bones to grow weak, brittle, and misshapen—is the one most people know about. But scientists have more recently linked vitamin D deficits to an array of much more common diseases* ranging from multiple sclerosis to colon cancer to atherosclerosis to Crohn's disease—to depression.

On average, depressed patients have perilously low blood levels of vitamin D. Supplementation, however, has been shown to lift mood among those with deficiencies. In one intriguing clinical trial, giving SAD patients just a single vitamin D megadose—two hundred and fifty times higher than the amount in your multivitamin—was found to have a large antidepressant effect.

How does vitamin D fight depression? In part, the effect follows from the nutrient's role in regulating gene function in the brain and other vital organ systems. But vitamin D also has a powerful anti-inflammatory effect throughout the body. This is important because—as you'll recall from Chapter 5—chronic inflammation is a major culprit in depression; it interferes with serotonin function and shuts down activity in key brain regions. Accordingly, vitamin D's anti-inflammatory properties turn out to be antidepressant, as well.

Because Vitamin D is such a crucial hormone, our bodies are endowed with the ability to make all we need. But it takes a little sunshine to get the process going. Basically, when the sun's ultraviolet (UV) rays† penetrate the skin, they kick off a chain reaction that converts cholesterol (of all things) into vitamin D. It's an efficient procedure, and most of us can get an entire day's supply with a bit of midday sun exposure, except in the winter.

Our hunter-gatherer ancestors never had to worry about getting enough vitamin D, because they spent hours in direct sunlight each day. And those who lived in more northerly climes—where the sun wasn't strong enough to make vitamin D in the winter—

* Vitamin D deficiency is not the only cause of these diseases, but it contributes to the risk of contracting them.

† These are the same UV rays that stimulate melanin production and cause us to tan.

simply stored in their bodies all the excess they made during the summer and fall, so they had enough to last all year.

But vitamin D deficiency is a big problem today throughout the industrialized world. Over half of the British population is now deficient at the end of each winter, and many people have perilously low levels all year long. Interestingly, the well-intentioned, widespread practice of fortifying milk and dairy products with vitamin D hasn't protected us the way it was supposed to. For one thing, people aren't drinking nearly as much milk as they did in the past; and there isn't a great deal of vitamin D in milk to begin with. More importantly, the molecular version that's widely used in milk—vitamin D_2 (*ergocalciferol*)—isn't the same as the version made by our bodies. We need vitamin D_3 (*cholecalciferol*), and much of the D_2 we get from milk (and from some other supplements) is simply unusable.

How, then, can you make sure you're getting enough vitamin D to keep your brain and body in good working order? There are two main possibilities worth exploring: taking a high-dose supplement of vitamin D_3, or spending a little time in the sun on a regular basis. We'll briefly address each option.

Vitamin D Supplement

If you take a multivitamin, the chances are it will contain 10 mcg of vitamin D—the EU RDA (recommended daily allowance). But, as we now know, vitamin D has dozens of other critical roles in the body (beyond ensuring healthy bone development), and it takes a lot more than 10 mcg each day to get the job done on these other fronts.

A group of Canadian medical researchers tried to find out just how much more. They recruited volunteers from their own hospital, and measured everyone's blood levels of vitamin D during the dead of winter. Most people, of course, were deficient. So the human guinea pigs were randomly assigned to start taking either 25 mcg or 100 mcg of vitamin D_3 each day. Surprisingly, even after a few months, many people taking 25 mcg a day—two and a half times the recommended amount—still didn't get their blood levels up high enough. It took 100 mcg a day—for a period of up to three months—to bring everyone up into the ideal range.

Doctors can get skittish, though, when you starting talking about such a large daily dose of vitamin D. The biggest worry is that it might throw off your calcium balance, since vitamin D helps regulate the body's ability to use this key mineral. However, no one in the Canadian study had any calcium-related problems (or any other adverse health effects) at the 100 mcg dose. Even more reassuring, a study last year looked at a group of multiple sclerosis patients taking *1000 mcg of vitamin D_3 every day* (one hundred times the recommended daily allowance), and none of them had any adverse medical effects, either.

Still, the official medical *tolerable upper intake level* for vitamin D, published by the European Food Safety Authority in 2012, is listed at only 100 mcg per day. Anything above this level is considered potentially unsafe. Although numerous researchers in the area say this recommendation may be outdated doctors are understandably reluctant to practice outside the field's official guidelines.

So what should you do if you want to go the supplement route to make sure you have enough vitamin D? I'm afraid there's no perfect solution, but you at least have some decent options.

The simplest approach is to start by taking 100 mcg of vitamin D_3 in supplement form each day. (You can pick up a couple months' supply at a local health food store for a few pounds.) This dose is high enough to push most people up into the ideal range for vitamin D blood levels. However, because the dose is also right at the tolerable upper intake level, it's important to check with your doctor before starting on such a high-dose regimen. In addition, after a few months of supplementing at this dose, it would be a good idea to have your doctor do a blood test to make sure you're actually getting *enough*. According to the best published evidence, your blood level of vitamin D* should be at least as high as 30 ng/mL (or 75 nmol/L) for optimal health.

A more aggressive approach—but one you should definitely consider if you're currently depressed, or if you have a history of seasonal affective disorder—is to see your doctor right away to have your blood level of vitamin D evaluated. If it's very low (below 15 ng/mL or 37 nmol/L), you can talk with your doctor about taking a high dose of vitamin D_3—up to 250 mcg per day—for several weeks under his or her supervision, with regular monitoring to make sure there are no side effects, and to ensure that your blood levels make it quickly into a healthier range.

Sun Exposure

The other option is to let your body make enough vitamin D on its own, with an assist from the sun. It's an approach that many

* It's measured in a molecular form called 25(OH)D.

will still find attractive, and there's even some research evidence that the body can use its own natural vitamin D more effectively than the kind we get from a supplement.

How much sun exposure does your body need each day to make enough vitamin D? The answer depends on several factors: the time of day, the time of year, local weather conditions (how cloudy it is), where you live (how far north or south), and your complexion (how fair or dark-skinned). As a rule of thumb, adequate vitamin D synthesis takes about the same amount of sun exposure that's required to develop the faintest hint of a tan (or to turn your skin ever-so-slightly darker).

Let's start with an optimal exposure scenario, the one that would take the least amount of time. A person with fair skin in a swimsuit would get a full day's supply of vitamin D in about two minutes on a sunny midday in the summertime in Miami. But as we start tweaking parameters (time of day, season, complexion, clothing, and location), the required exposure time changes. Finding the exact time needed on any given day can get complicated, but there are three easy guidelines you can follow:

- In the continental United States and Europe, your body should make enough vitamin D from May through August if you average ten to twenty minutes a day of sun exposure between 11:00 in the morning and 3:00 in the afternoon. (That's assuming you aren't wearing any sunscreen and that your arms and face are exposed.)
- In March, April, September, and October, it will probably take at least twenty to thirty minutes per day.
- If you have a dark complexion, you may need to double all recommended times.

Even at this low level of recommended sun exposure, you'll likely build up some vitamin D reserves for your body to draw on in the winter. But just to be on the safe side, it's still a good idea to supplement from November through February, as described in the previous section.

Direct sun exposure has obvious benefits, but it also comes with its inherent downsides. Not only can it age skin prematurely, but it can also elevate the risk of skin cancer (a condition that will afflict up to one in five Americans). However, while the link between sun exposure and skin cancer is strong for the experience of sunburn, there's not as much evidence of a link at the relatively low levels of exposure needed for vitamin D synthesis. In fact, the website of the National Institutes of Health has recently added a recommendation of ten to fifteen minutes of sun exposure (periodically) as a way most people can avoid vitamin D deficiency. Still, before scheduling any time in the sun, you should weigh the pros and cons of the issue with your doctor. Depending on your skin type, your medical history, and your family history of skin cancer, you may conclude that sun exposure isn't worth the risks—especially since viable alternatives are available. Whichever way you decide, the critical thing is to ensure that you benefit year-round from the healing, antidepressant effects of vitamin D.

8
Get Connected

Some animals are natural-born loners. Parasitic wasps, for example, can live out their entire lives without any meaningful social contact—nothing, at least, beyond a few brief bouts of mating. But we humans find isolation an unnatural state of affairs. Extended seclusion is so uncomfortable that it constitutes a form of criminal punishment.

We are literally born to connect. The drive is etched deeply into our DNA: From the first moments of life, we crave the company of others. And it's not just for the food and protection they provide. Babies even need social contact to help regulate their breathing and heart rate. They're exquisitely attuned to the biological rhythms of those around them—the ebbs and flows of respiration, heart rate, alertness, and so on—and they mimic these natural cadences to keep their own bodies in sync. That's one reason babies howl in protest when they're left alone: They instinctively know it's a recipe for biological disaster.

You might suppose that such abject dependence is something we all eventually outgrow. But we never do—at least, not completely. Even as adults, we still rely on the presence of others. When we're deprived of it for just a few days, our stress hormones escalate, mood and energy plummet, and key biological processes quickly fall out of balance. On the other hand, our bodily rhythms readily synchronize with those of others—even pets—in our immediate vicinity. (The process happens even while we're sleeping.)

Our innate dependence on others is an ancient legacy. For hundreds of thousands of years, our ancestors lived in small, intimate social bands, facing together the relentless threat of predators, the forces of nature, and hostile neighboring clans—a context in which survival was impossible apart from the support and protection of the group. Even brief periods of isolation carried overwhelming risks, to be avoided at all costs.

Such a clannish sensibility is still keenly present among modern-day foraging bands (and other traditional, pre-agrarian societies). According to anthropologists, "alone time" is virtually unknown among such groups. They spend nearly twenty-four hours a day in the company of friends and loved ones: hunting together, walking together, gathering food and water together, eating together, playing together, and sleeping together. Often, they even wander off to relieve themselves together (a smart policy in a world where predators and unfriendly neighbors might be lurking nearby).

Within such traditional societies, isolation is regarded as an obvious hardship, and those who are able to endure a few days of solitude—shamans, for example—are revered for their heroism. In the industrialized West, on the other hand, we've strayed far from this ancient sensibility. Many now find solitude to be the default mode of existence: They work alone, eat alone, recreate alone, and sleep alone. According to the latest research, nearly 25% of Americans have no intimate social connections at all, and countless others spend the bulk of their time by themselves. Because the obvious physical risks of social isolation have receded—most predators now reside on endangered species lists, after all—we've become increasingly oblivious to solitude's equally real *psychological* dangers.

As we saw in Chapter 1, isolation is a major risk factor for depression: Those who lack the benefit of meaningful social connection are highly prone to becoming depressed, especially in the face of severe life stress. And, unfortunately, once a person starts experiencing depressive symptoms, they tend to withdraw even further from the world around them. This, in turn, exacerbates the depression, sparking a vicious downward cycle of illness and seclusion that often proves difficult to break.

But why, exactly, should depression prompt social withdrawal in the first place? In large part, it's because the brain responds to depression as it does to any other serious illness, directing us to avoid activity—especially *social* activity—so the body can focus on simply getting well. This withdrawal response is triggered by a decrease of serotonin activity in the brain, which, as we addressed in Chapter 2, is one of the major features of depression. (Because the brain's serotonin levels plummet when we're fighting a serious infection, some scientists even speculate that the ensuing withdrawal response evolved to help fend off the spread of disease.)

Think about the last time you had the flu. How much did you feel like socializing? When I had a bad case of the illness a few years ago—complete with a 103-degree fever, shakes, chills, and assorted body aches—I just wanted to crawl into a hole and wait for it all to go away. That's a typical reaction. And, interestingly enough, it's similar to the way people react when they're fighting a severe episode of depression.

But there's one crucial difference: With the flu, such withdrawal helps to promote recovery—with depression it only makes things worse. So, even though depressed patients feel—right down to the core of their being—that pulling away from others is going to help, that's only because their brain has been misled. In effect, depression tricks the brain into thinking something akin to an infectious illness needs to be fought.

Tragically, the ensuing social withdrawal amplifies depression. It stands as a major obstacle on the path to recovery. Conversely, anything that enhances social connectedness—increasing either the quantity or the quality of our bonds with others—proves immensely valuable in fighting (and preventing) the disorder.

FINDING CONNECTION

Of course, increasing social connection is easier said than done. And the process raises a host of practical questions. Who's available to connect with? What should I be doing with them? Should I focus more on family or friends? What about coworkers? And what if certain people make me feel worse every time I'm around them? Am I supposed to spend more time with them, as well?

In navigating this tangled maze of questions, it helps at the outset to keep in view one critical fact: There are many varieties of social connection, and all of them are potentially helpful. For example, members of traditional societies like the Kaluli of Papua New Guinea—among whom social support is abundant, and depression virtually unknown—benefit from social ties that span multiple levels of closeness: from the deep intimacy of immediate family and friends to the comforting familiarity of extended family to the profound sense of belonging provided by membership in the clan itself (a hundred or so people linked by a shared identity and a common destiny).

Anyone lucky enough to draw upon such deep, multilayered sources of social support will be unlikely to get depressed. But these fortunate individuals are now the exception, not the rule, throughout the modern industrialized world. Sadly, the past few decades have seen the steady erosion of social bonds across every domain of British life.

Compared with our counterparts from even a generation ago, we're much less likely to know our neighbors, to invite friends over for dinner, to join social clubs, to participate in a local church or synagogue or mosque, or to take part in community sports leagues (football, netball, tennis, and so on). We're less likely to get married, and less likely to stay married when we do take the plunge. We also spend less time developing and maintaining friendships. According to a recent landmark study of American social life, half of all adults lack even a single close friend they can rely on. The picture in Britain is similar.

What's happened? I believe many of us now live as if we value things more than people. In both the US and UK, we spend more time than ever at work, and we earn more money than any generation in history, but we spend less and less time with our loved ones as a result. Likewise, many of us barely think twice about severing close ties with friends and family to move halfway across the country in pursuit of career advancement. We buy exorbitant houses—the square footage of the average American home has more than doubled in the past generation—but increasingly we use them only to retreat from the world. And even within the home-as-refuge, sealed off from the broader community "out there," each member of the household can often be found sitting alone in front of his or her own private screen—exchanging time with loved ones for time with a bright, shiny object instead.

Now, I'm not saying that any of us—if asked—would claim to value things more than people. Nor would we say that our loved ones aren't important to us. Of course they are. But many people now live *as if* achievement, career advancement, money, material possessions, entertainment, and status matter more. Unfortunately, such things don't confer lasting happiness, nor do they protect us from depression. Loved ones do.

For most of us in this culture of isolation, there's considerable room for improvement when it comes to enhancing social connectedness. This is especially true for those who've battled depression, because the disorder—with its characteristic pattern of withdrawal and negativity—has a corrosive effect on relationships.

In the pages that follow, we'll outline strategies for improving connections with friends, family members, coworkers, and other members of the community. The ideal, as we saw earlier in the case of the Kaluli people, is to benefit from abundant support across each of these important domains.

Achieving this ideal takes some time, and it may not be a realistic goal for everyone in the short-term, especially for those currently in the midst of a depressive episode. Fortunately, however, any improvement in social connection can be of some immediate benefit in the fight against depression, so the focus of each section ahead will be on those changes that can make a difference right away. (We'll also point out some potential longer-term goals for those who are not depressed, but still want to reduce their risk of illness in the future.)

FRIENDS

Over time, depression can take an enormous toll on friendships. When someone first becomes depressed, there's a natural tendency for friends to rally to their side—to provide increased support, and to try whatever else they can think of to help. But as the weeks pass and the symptoms persist, the illness starts to weave its toxic spell of social isolation, straining even the strongest of bonds.

For those friends who don't understand the seriousness of depression, the disorder's characteristic withdrawal can become a source of great pain and frustration. Simply put: It's hard to watch someone pulling away from you and shutting down, especially when you can't figure out why in the world it's happening.

Even friends who know that social withdrawal is a core symptom of depression may find themselves feeling rejected. After all, it's only human to feel hurt when a friend starts shutting you out—failing to return phone calls, refusing offers to get together, and sending signals about their complete lack of interest in connecting.

Ironically, those suffering from the disorder commonly feel as if they're doing their friends a favor by pulling away. My patients tell me this all the time. Under the influence of depression's starkly negative thinking, they say things like: "My friends are better off without me." "I'm such a downer to be around, no one could possibly want to spend time with me." "They're only calling me out of pity." Even though such thoughts may be wildly distorted and off-the-mark (as they are in the vast majority of cases), such perceptions still feel true to the person in the grip of depressive illness.

It's little wonder, then, that most patients withdraw from even their dearest, closest friends—with predictably tragic results. Fortunately, however, it's almost always possible to turn things around, to renew the bonds of friendship, no matter how much depression may have strained a relationship. In my clinical experience, the following steps usually prove helpful in that respect.

Disclose. Because of the lingering stigma associated with depression, many people are reluctant to let even their closest friends know about their struggle with the illness. It's understandable: No one wants to risk being viewed as "crazy" (or weak, or lazy, or any number of other qualities mistakenly attributed to those suffering from depression). But I believe our friends have a right to know what we're going through, especially when we're facing a treacherous enemy like depression. Honest disclosure about our struggles is essential to maintaining (or reestablishing) the health of any friendship.

Educate. Often, however, mere disclosure is not enough. Many friends need to be educated about depression as well. In particular, they have to understand three things: Depression is an illness—one that robs people of their ability to function; like many other forms of illness, depression typically leads its victims to withdraw from friends and loved ones; nevertheless, social support can play an important role in the recovery process. It's also often useful to ask friends to read a good overview* of the disorder that covers these points in some detail.

---

* Peter Kramer's *Against Depression* provides a superb comprehensive summary. Chapter 2 of this book also includes a brief overview of the disorder.

Ask. Many of us find it difficult to ask for help, even from our closest friends. But depression is such a serious affliction that most people are eager to do whatever they can for a friend who's been laid low. When I speak about depression in the community, the most common question I get is, "What can I do to help someone who's fighting this illness?"

The most useful thing, by far, is to spend regular time together in shared activities: walking, working out, grabbing a meal, playing games, going to a concert, attending a play, watching a film, and so on. As we saw in Chapter 5, such activities are especially effective in combating depressive rumination. They also help to reactivate the brain's left frontal cortex, which itself provides a direct antidepressant effect. Accordingly, in our Therapeutic Lifestyle Change (TLC) groups, each patient is asked to adopt the goal of scheduling at least three such activities each week with friends or other close acquaintances.

Jamie, a fortyish real estate agent in one of our TLC groups, was intimidated by this goal, but she told us she was willing—despite her fear of rejection—to start by calling her best friend Deb (whom she hadn't seen in weeks) to see if she might want to get together sometime. With trepidation, she began the conversation by telling Deb some of the things she'd learned in treatment: that depression had caused her to withdraw, that her isolation was making the depression worse, and that she needed help from friends and loved ones to break the destructive pattern of withdrawal. To Jamie's immense relief, her friend told her, "Look, I'm here for you—for anything you need, and I'm so glad there's something I can do that might help." Before hanging up, they penciled a weekly lunch date into their calendars, and even made plans to hit a karaoke bar together that weekend.

Jamie also asked Deb for help *initiating* their future get-togethers. As we've seen, depression shuts down activity in those areas of the brain that allow us to initiate things. So, good intentions, including the plan to spend more time with friends, don't always get translated into action. Acknowledging this point openly with her friend, Jamie told her, "I really want us to get together more often, but because of the depression, I might have trouble taking the initiative sometimes. Would you be willing to stay on me about it—to call me anytime you haven't heard from me in a while, and to insist that we set something up?" Predictably, her friend was more than willing to help on this front, as well.

Avoid negativity. Under the bleak spell of depression, people's thoughts often turn starkly negative, even when they're in the company of friends. Although sharing such dark thoughts might seem like a natural thing to do, excessive disclosure on this front can quickly turn counterproductive. Remember, spending time with others is helpful in part because it's a powerful way to interrupt rumination—the depressive habit of dwelling on upsetting thoughts—but it can do so only if the social interaction centers on something other than the depressing thoughts themselves. Unfortunately, the process of sharing negative reflections with friends can easily lead to a full-blown episode of rumination.

Consider the following dialogue, based on a conversation one of my patients, Becky, had while meeting with her friend Joan (after several weeks of self-imposed isolation):

Joan: It's so good to see you. I've really missed you, you know?

Becky: Yeah, I've missed you, too. (*Awkward pause.*) God, I'm such a mess right now—I can't even make small talk. I'm just not much fun to be around.

Joan: Hey, come on. You know that's not true. [illegible] we all go through rough patches sometimes. T[illegible] need our friends the most, right?

Becky: I guess so. But I just hate being such a burden [illegible] all the time . . .

Joan: What are you talking about? Becky, you're not a burden.

Becky: I'd probably say the same thing if I were you. But no one wants to be around someone who's like this. I mean, look at me. I feel like crap, I'm cranky as hell, and my mind doesn't even work right half the time. (*She starts crying softly*.)

Joan: (*Holds her hand reassuringly*.) Look, I'm sorry you're going through such a hard time right now, but I want you to know I'm here for you.

Becky: Even though I'm ruining your whole day?

Joan: Becky, that's crazy! You're not ruining my day.

Becky: (*Sighs*) Well, you sound kind of irritated . . . I guess I don't blame you.

Joan: No, I'm not irritated, I'm just—it's just hard to see you being so tough on yourself.

Becky: I'm sorry. I don't mean to be so hard to be around. That's the only thing I'm really good at right now—making people upset. I knew it was a bad idea for me to come over . . .

Notice that the more Becky gave voice to her negative thoughts, the more she was unable to turn her attention away from them, despite her friend's reassuring attempts to help her see things in a more positive light. Sadly, once a conversation takes this sort of ruminative turn, it can be difficult to prevent the ensuing downward spiral. That's why it's usually a good idea to

more engaging social activities that have the power to lift mood and shift the brain into a less negative mode of thinking.

FRIENDS AT A DISTANCE

During one of our very first Therapeutic Lifestyle Change groups, I asked each patient to write down a list of all the people they felt the closest to, no matter how far away (geographically) they happened to be. Not surprisingly, given our highly transient society, every single patient said some of their dearest friends lived hundreds (or thousands) of miles away.

I also learned that most of them were rarely in touch with their faraway friends, despite the deep feelings of affection that remained. It was as if the imposing physical distance had somehow ruled out the possibility of keeping such relationships alive in the present. But as my patients and I thought this through, we realized that it didn't have to be that way, especially in the age of cheap long-distance phone rates and high-speed Internet connections.

So I asked them to identify at least three people they still felt close to in spite of geographic separation—childhood friends, college buddies, long-lost cousins, old roommates, former coworkers, erstwhile neighbors, and so on—and to schedule time in their calendars to contact them within the following week. There was a surprising amount of enthusiasm for the idea. It did, however, raise some important questions:

- *Should I tell them about my depression?* ("Yes," I said, "by all means.")

- *How much can I talk about my problems before it turns into rumination?* ("It's probably helpful to briefly describe what you've been going through, but then try shifting the focus to the things you're doing to get better. That should serve as a safeguard against excessively dwelling on the negative.")
- *What else should I talk with them about?* (My response was, "Pretty much anything that doesn't lead to rumination. You can reminisce about good times you shared together in the past; ask to hear in detail what they've been up to; talk about common interests; get updates on mutual friends and acquaintances; and so on.")

In most cases, my patients have found it enormously helpful to reconnect with their old friends like this. They've usually been pleased to discover how easily they're able to pick things back up where they'd left off, and how much they enjoyed the process. And many have had old friends open up to them about their own battles with depression and other painful experiences life had thrown their way. As a result, my patients have often been able to provide as much support and encouragement as they've received, and they've experienced the deep satisfaction that comes from helping a loved one in need.

Video chats. With the advent of free computer software like Skype,* the Internet now makes it possible to have virtual face-to-face chats with old friends (and just about anyone else on the planet).

Because we humans are such a highly visual species—with much of the brain's cortex devoted to vision—we're designed to get much more out of a conversation when we can see the person

---

* You can download Skype at www.skype.com.

we're talking with. Not surprisingly, then, it's even easier to feel close to a friend during a video chat or a FaceTime conversation than it is during a regular phone call.

Internet friends. It's also now possible—through Internet chat rooms and forums—to forge meaningful friendships with strangers online. For example, my friend Linda recently endured a painful battle with anorexia, and in her search for friends who could truly understand what she was going through, she stumbled onto several virtual communities on the Internet—forums where hundreds of other people gathered to share their struggles with eating disorders, and to offer one another words of support and encouragement. Linda credits her online friends with playing a major role in her eventual recovery, even though she's never met a single one of them in person.

Dozens of such virtual communities are now available to those suffering from depression—places where fellow-travelers on the path to recovery gather to chat and encourage one another on a 24/7 basis. Some of the more popular sites at the time of this writing are depressionforums.org, healingwell.com, and beatingthe beast.com.

TOXIC RELATIONSHIPS

In my clinical experience, most friends and loved ones are eager to help facilitate healing from depression in any way they can. But there are some important exceptions: toxic relationships that stand as major obstacles on the path to recovery.

In some cases, the harmful influence of others is unintentional. For example, psychologists have documented a powerful effect of emotional contagion: the spreading of our emotional states to others, just as we might transmit a cold or flu bug. When two friends or loved ones are fighting depression at the same time, they can inadvertently ramp up the intensity of each other's sadness just by spending time together. This process is especially common in marriage, and it helps to explain why the risk of getting depressed goes up for anyone whose spouse is fighting the illness.

Please bear in mind, however, that such emotional contagion isn't inevitable. It can be prevented, even when you're spending lots of time with someone who's severely depressed. But both parties have to avoid the temptation of dwelling on their negative thoughts together, since joint rumination is a particularly damaging process in depression. So, you'll probably need to set firm limits in advance when you're talking about one another's problems, sharing disappointments, airing complaints, and so on. I'd suggest a time limit of five minutes of verbal negativity per interaction.

Interestingly, after they learn about the process of emotional contagion, my depressed patients often start to worry about *me*—fearing they'll somehow "infect" me with despair, and cause me to lose my emotional balance. It's a touching concern, but it turns out to be unnecessary. You see, emotional contagion works in both directions: It can spread *positive* moods just as readily as negative ones. So, believe it or not, I always look forward to spending time with my patients, including those still in the depths of despair, because it provides an opportunity to help infect them with an authentic sense of hope about their eventual recovery.

If you're currently struggling with depression, I encourage you to put the power of positive emotional contagion to work for you. You might, for example, write out a list of the people you know—even casual acquaintances—who are consistently upbeat and sunny, and make a deliberate effort to start spending more time in their company. If no one in your life fits the bill right now, a good psychotherapist could even play that role for you on a weekly basis.

Conversely, you may need to limit the amount of time you spend with those whose negativity consistently rubs off on you. Again, it's not that you should avoid interacting with others just because they happen to be depressed. But it *will* be important, if you do spend time with someone who's blue, to steer most of your time with them toward upbeat activities and conversations.

Toxic Beyond Repair

Although many unhealthy relationships can be improved with some effort, others are so destructive they make recovery impossible. For example, I have a friend, Karen, who found herself in a horrifically abusive relationship while she was struggling to heal from severe depression some years ago. Although she had already put many of the principles of Therapeutic Lifestyle Change into practice, the toxic impact of her boyfriend's relentless emotional and physical abuse kept her brain locked in a depressive runaway stress response. Yet, because she loved him, she found it impossible to simply let go and walk away. She hung on for months—telling herself that he would change, that she couldn't live without him, that things weren't really that bad—until her growing desperation finally brought about an epiphany: The relationship, by perpetuating her depression, was slowly killing her. In a genuine act of courage, with the support and encouragement of her therapist, pastor, and loved ones, she cut off all contact with him and—despite the searing pain of separation—gradually found her way back to health. (She's now happily raising boisterous twin boys, and working to help others combat the depressive illness that almost took her own life.)

Likewise, I worked years ago with a twenty-one-year-old college student, Annie, who hung out with a clique in her sorority that could have come straight out of the movie *Mean Girls*—a group of snobbish, hypercritical elitists who tortured one another with impossibly high standards of physical beauty, status, wealth, and style. Although Annie was a sweet young woman, her deep insecurity caused her to find these girls irresistible, as she desperately wanted to win their acceptance and approval—which, of course, never came. Week after week, she told me how everyone in the clique made her "feel like crap," and yet she continued spending all her free time with them. She also wondered why her depressive symptoms—while greatly improved since she began treatment—never completely cleared up.

So I asked her a simple question. "Annie, are there any other girls in your sorority who make you feel good about yourself when you're around them—people who accept you for who you are?"

"I guess so," she said. Then she rattled off a list of a half-dozen names.

"And how much time do you spend with these girls, the ones who make you feel good about yourself?"

Annie started laughing. "Pretty much none."

"Does that make sense to you?" I asked. "I mean, does it make sense that you'd spend all your time with girls who criticize you, who don't even seem to care about you, and then ignore these other girls who actually like you? Can you help me understand that?"

"It sounds crazy when you put it like that. But it's like I just don't care as much what people think about me when they're really nice to everyone. It's like it doesn't count then, or something."

"Okay, that makes sense," I reassured her. "But I wonder what would happen to your mood if you started limiting your time with these 'toxic friends' of yours, and started spending time instead with girls who accept you for who you are. Do you think it would make a difference with your depression?"

She shrugged, and then did her best to change the subject. Clearly, she didn't want to go there. I wasn't at all surprised, since toxic relationships are usually hard to let go of, no matter how destructive they might be. They hold out the tantalizing promise of something desirable—love, acceptance, approval, protection—even though they never really deliver. In Annie's case, it took her two full months to finally admit to herself that the "mean girls" were the main source of depressive stress in her life, and to recognize that she would never gain their approval, no matter how hard she tried. Following this tearful revelation, she was finally ready to start limiting her contact with these girls. And that, in turn, freed her to begin connecting with others who genuinely appreciated her, to start forming a new set of healthy, authentic friendships that laid the groundwork for a full and lasting recovery.

When to Let Go

But how can you tell if a relationship is so harmful to your psychological well being that it needs to be limited or cut off altogether? Unfortunately, there is no simple set of rules that applies to every case. I can, however, offer a few time-tested principles that may prove useful as you evaluate the troublesome relationships in your life.

First, it's important to ask yourself: "Do I usually feel worse when I spend time with this person?" If so, you'll need to identify: (a) what it is about the interaction that's the source of distress, and (b) whether or not it's something that can be improved. For example, as we've seen in the case of relationships that drift toward joint rumination and negative emotional contagion, it's often possible to redirect the focus of interaction toward something less toxic (e.g., shared activity or non-ruminative conversation). But, if you have a friend or loved one who is unwilling or unable to make such a shift, it might be helpful to limit the time you spend with them—at least until you've made a full recovery.

Sometimes, of course, people find themselves in relationships that are clearly toxic beyond the point of repair. That was the case with Karen and her abusive boyfriend, just as it was with Annie and her malicious sorority "sisters." Such harmful relationships are pretty easy to spot, since the offending party is typically abusive: harshly critical, demeaning, demanding, hostile, and controlling. And because depression causes its victims to "beat themselves up" anyway, such abusive partners only serve to strengthen the depressive sense of self-loathing—a process that makes full recovery impossible.

SPOUSES

Although the principles we've covered so far can be applied to virtually any relationship, in this section we'll address some specific ways they're relevant in marriage and other romantic partnerships. (Much of the content can also be applied to any emotionally intimate relationship, romantic or otherwise.)

Whenever a person is caught in the grip of depressive illness, the situation is agonizing for their spouse, as well: It's horrible to see someone you love in pain. Almost invariably, the spouse winds up feeling powerless. After all, they know they can't just encourage their partner to "snap out of it." (Or else they learn the hard way that this only makes the situation worse.) And in many cases they're even told by clinicians there's nothing much they can do to help—that they simply need to stand by and wait for the effects of treatment (usually medication) to kick in.

But in most cases, this is utterly wrong. Spouses can be an invaluable resource in the recovery process. They can do so in two ways: by helping their depressed partner put into practice the six core elements of Therapeutic Lifestyle Change (TLC), and by serving as an unwavering source of social support.

Helping with TLC

Again, because of the reduced activity in the depressed patient's frontal cortex—the part of the brain that helps translate intentions into actions—most depressed individuals have great difficulty initiating activity. Even things they desperately want to do may go undone. And that includes putting into practice the various elements of the TLC protocol. One of my patients recently put it like this: "I just sit there thinking 'I need to get up and go for a walk while it's still sunny out' or 'I should really call my friend right now,' but then I just keep sitting there on the couch, and nothing happens."

That's where a spouse can come in: they can, in effect, serve as a proxy for their partner's frontal cortex, providing—when necessary—a nudge of initiative that the depressed brain often fails to give. I mentioned this idea a few months ago at a presentation for fellow clinicians, and one of them told me afterward that a little lightbulb went off in her head. As it turned out, her husband had been struggling with depression for some time, and he found it difficult to make himself do many of the things (exercise and light exposure and omega-3 supplementation and social activity) that he knew could help. So she went home that night and talked with him about the whole "frontal cortex angle," asking how he would feel if she were to provide gentle nudges to help him initiate the lifestyle changes he'd been unable to put into practice. To her considerable surprise, he thought it was a fantastic idea.

Of course, it takes great care to make sure this brain-inspired nudging doesn't start to feel like outright nagging—which could lead to resentment and ill will. The best safeguard is simply for the couple to have an open, honest conversation about the issue, and to decide together up front on some basic ground rules: when it's okay to nudge and when it's not, which activities (if any) are off-limits for nudging and which ones need to stay on the front burner. With such clear lines of communication in place, it's possible for a spouse to serve as a superb catalyst for antidepressant lifestyle changes.

Providing Social Support

As we've seen, extended social isolation is unhealthy for anyone, especially for those fighting depression. And yet virtually every depressed patient I've treated has spent far too little time in the company of others, and missed out on the benefits of positive emotional contagion.

Spouses are in a unique position to help on this front, but it doesn't always work out that way. All too often, depressed patients pull away from their marital partners just as they withdraw from everyone else, becoming isolated—physically and emotionally—even within the confines of their homes. Although it can be tempting for spouses in this situation to allow the distance in the marriage to grow (after all, it's hard to maintain closeness with a partner who keeps pulling away), it's a temptation to be avoided.

Simply having a spouse provide their physical presence—even if it's just a matter of spending time together in silence—is of some benefit to depressed individuals, since the mere company of another person can help put the brakes on the brain's depressive stress response. A more potent benefit is provided by caring physical contact—hugging, holding hands, sitting next to each other on the sofa, and so on—which sends a strong anti-stress signal to the depressed brain. It's also helpful for spouses to plan engaging activities together, and to steer conversations away from negative topics that might lead to rumination. (Again, this is not to say that upsetting events shouldn't be discussed, but simply that such conversations should be limited and infrequent.)

Finally, it's important to note that no spouse can serve as an effective resource for their depressed partner unless they're also taking exceptionally good care of their own emotional well-being. Remember, emotional contagion runs in both directions. So, the more the spouse attends to their own needs (making time for friends, regular exercise, restorative sleep, and so forth), the more "immunity" they'll have from their depressed partner's gloom, and the more they'll be able to serve as a source of support and inspiration.

THE IMPORTANCE OF GIVING

It's more blessed to give than to receive. This proverb may sound paradoxical, but psychologists now have the data to back it up. For example, when research subjects were given large sums of money and told either to keep the cash or to spend it on someone else, they consistently reported greater happiness when they gave their bounty away. (This experiment has been replicated in several different variations.) Todd Kashdan, a psychologist at George Mason University, saw a similar result with the students in his Science of Well-Being course, who were assigned to compare the psychological effects of two activities: 1) something they found innately pleasurable (scuba diving was one option), and 2) a selfless act of kindness for someone else (for example, collecting clothes for a battered women's shelter). Remarkably, students discovered that the latter activity consistently brought them a greater sense of happiness and well-being.

The same general principle holds true for those fighting depression: One of the surest paths to boosting mood is giving to someone else in need. Such giving can take many forms.

In our TLC groups, I've had the joy of watching patients put the principle into practice each week by providing one another with heartfelt support and encouragement—listening to each other's stories, cheering each success, and offering words of comfort with every setback (along with a shoulder to cry on). Many patients have told me this opportunity to give back to others was the single most meaningful thing they experienced during the entire course of treatment.

Likewise, many have grown deeply connected to others through volunteer activities: building houses with Habitat for Humanity, "adopting" a lonely child though Big Brothers Big Sisters, serving as a tour guide with a local museum, knocking on doors for a political campaign, serving meals at a soup kitchen, and working with abandoned animals at the local shelter. The number of volunteer possibilities is nearly infinite, and there now exist some extraordinary online resources to help match people with placements that fit their interests. One of my favorites is www.volunteermatch.org, which has over fifty thousand volunteer organizations in its vast nationwide database.

CARING FOR ANIMALS

We touched briefly in the last section on the possibility of caring for animals, but the topic is so important it deserves a bit more elaboration. As many pet owners know from experience, the bonds we form with animals can be just as emotionally powerful as those we share with other human beings. And caring for animals can be a profoundly therapeutic experience. I've seen patients with symptoms so debilitating they could barely find the energy to eat or get dressed miraculously spring back to life when faced with a helpless puppy or kitten in need of care.

Pets have an almost magical ability to increase our sense of well-being through their affectionate physical contact, which lowers stress hormones and boosts the activity of feel-good brain chemicals like dopamine and serotonin. Pets also provide us with a faithful source of social companionship, and a deep feeling that we truly *matter*: They literally depend on us for their very lives. As we'll see in the next section, this sense of mattering to others is something we're all designed to have, and something we all need.

FINDING COMMUNITY

Twelve thousand years ago, before the invention of agriculture, everyone belonged to a community. Within each intimate hunter-gatherer band, people lived and worked together with a common purpose and a powerful sense of belonging. In a world filled with predators and hostile neighbors, the members of each band were profoundly linked together by their shared fate: Without the group, each individual would die. And, because every person contributed to the well-being of the entire clan (through hunting, foraging, collecting water, child-rearing, scouting, and so on), no one ever had to worry about whether they were valued by others. Simply by being a member of the community, each person was intrinsically important.

For hundreds of thousands of years, this deep sense of belonging was simply part of what it meant to be a human being. It's an experience we all still crave; the longing seems to be embedded in our very souls. Those lucky enough to find authentic community today are much happier (on average) than those who live in its absence.

But it's become increasingly difficult to experience community in the modern world. The small, intimate societies of our ancestors all have long since been replaced by towns and cities with populations that number well into the millions. And lifelong bonds of commitment—forged between people who rely on one another, moment to moment, for their survival—have been usurped by fleeting ties that often signal nothing more than a desire to pursue leisure activities together (when it's convenient). So, where can we moderns still find authentic community, and the profound sense of belonging it confers?

Church. One likely place, according to sociologists, is the local church or place of worship.* That's not to say that every place of worship is a gateway to such intimate, meaningful connections. But at least *some* are, and they tend to share a common set of features:

- Size: According to an interesting line of research, people are most likely to flourish in a church that's about the size of a typical hunter-gatherer band. Once the congregation gets much bigger, exceeding two hundred or so members, people often start to feel more anonymous and unimportant. However, some larger churches (even so-called *megachurches*) have effectively addressed this problem by involving members in smaller groups—often known as *home groups*—where they can still find intimate community.
- Purpose: Nothing binds people together more effectively than a shared purpose and a set of common goals.

* For the remainder of this section, I'll use the term *church* in the generic sense to refer to any place of worship, of any faith—Christian, Jewish, Muslim, Hindu, Buddhist, and so on.

Churches that provide their members with a clear sense of mission—whether it be caring for the poor and disenfranchised, reaching out to the "unchurched," or trying to change society for the better—tend to foster a greater sense of community than those that don't.

- Investment: Not surprisingly, people who invest heavily of themselves in a church—their time, energy, and resources—are those most likely to find a genuine experience of community there. It's only by spending time with a group of other people on a regular basis—sharing our lives together as we work toward common goals—that any of us can hope to form the deep, intimate connections that make community possible.

Church is not for everyone, of course. Fortunately, other options are available for those who find involvement in a religious community an unattractive prospect. But the same factors that foster community in churches still apply to nonreligious groups: small group size, a strong sense of shared purpose, and a high level of investment among group members.

Volunteer organizations. Many volunteer groups excel at bringing together people who share a specific passion: saving the environment, ending homelessness, protecting battered women, feeding the hungry, promoting a political party, sheltering abandoned animals, and so on. If this prospect sounds appealing, you might reflect on the one or two causes or goals that matter to you the most, and try identifying a group of like-minded souls joined in pursuit of that purpose.

Social organizations. Most towns and cities are host to numerous social organizations and clubs that provide their members with a sense of community. These range from civic societies and Rotary Clubs to special interest organizations like Veterans UK and political campaign groups.

Self-help groups. Organizations such as AA (Alcoholics Anonymous), Bipolar UK, and NAMI (National Alliance on Mental Illness) bring together individuals dedicated to overcoming various forms of mental illness. In speaking to such groups, I've observed firsthand the tight social bonds that often form among their members.

Interest groups. Myriad groups help bring together people with shared recreational interests: reading, hiking, crafting, cycling, running, writing, rafting, photography, film, visual arts, drama, history, and so on.

Sports leagues. I've also witnessed genuine community spring up among team members in any number of different sports leagues, including football, basketball, cricket, golf, volleyball, ultimate Frisbee, bowling, and tennis.

The workplace. Increasingly, we invest so much of our time and energy at the workplace that it actually becomes our primary vehicle for the experience of community. This is a development I view with some ambivalence, since it would be healthier for most people to invest less of themselves at work—to spend more time cultivating relationships elsewhere. But given the ongoing reality of American and British workaholism, it's certainly much better for people to experience community at work than never to find it at all.

Developing close bonds with coworkers usually involves carving out ample time to spend with them in a nonwork setting. It also takes a commitment to sharing life's triumphs and failures. But some employment cultures discourage this level of coworker intimacy, so it won't always be attainable, even for those who seek it. In fact, given the loss of balance that easily comes from wrapping up the bulk of one's time and energy in the workplace, I generally advise people to look for their primary experience of community elsewhere.

CONCLUDING THOUGHT

All of us are born to connect, hardwired to live in the company of those who know and love us. When we draw from deep wells of social support—the care and concern of close friends, family, and community—we're more resilient to the slings and arrows of fortune, and we're considerably less vulnerable to depression. Social connection helps push the brain in an antidepressant direction, turning down activity in stress circuitry, and boosting the activity of feel-good brain chemicals like dopamine and serotonin. That's why it makes sense to swim hard against the tide of our "culture of isolation" and to place our relationships at the very top of the priority list. Truly, nothing in life matters more.

9
Habits of Healthy Sleep

Sleep that knits up the ravell'd sleeve of care,
The death of each day's life, sore labor's bath,
Balm of hurt minds, great nature's second course,
Chief nourisher in life's feast.

—William Shakespeare, *Macbeth*

Why do we sleep? What is sleep *for*? For centuries, scientists had no satisfying answers. As recently as fifty years ago, many thought sleep was useless—a mere period of biological downtime.

That view has now changed. Recent advances in the neurosciences have brought the discovery that adequate sleep is indispensable for both physical and mental well-being—just as Shakespeare intuited four hundred years ago. In fact, it is only during sleep that the body and brain have a chance to do their major repair work—to undo the subtle damage suffered by millions of cells over the course of each day—and to perform a daily tune-up so things continue running smoothly. Sleep is what keeps us firing on all cylinders.

Because sleep is so essential to our well-being, it takes only a few nights of deprivation before adverse effects start piling up: memory and concentration wane; mood turns irritable; judgment grows poor; reaction times slow; coordination deteriorates; energy dims; and immune function declines.

Even more dire consequences follow prolonged sleep loss. The body starts shutting down, and we begin to experience the sleep deficit as physically painful. That's why intentionally depriving someone of sleep is now regarded as a form of torture,* and rightfully so.

Sadly, sleep disturbance and depression go hand in hand. Not only is disordered sleep one of the telltale symptoms of depression, but it also plays a major role in triggering the illness. As we saw in Chapter 2, the loss of slow-wave sleep—the most restorative phase of slumber—can directly account for many of depression's most debilitating features. Not surprisingly, before the onset of depression, four out of five people suffer from some form of sleep disturbance.

The implications are clear: Anything we can do to improve our sleep can help combat depression and render the disorder less likely to occur in the future.

Fortunately, several elements of the Therapeutic Lifestyle Change (TLC) program carry the potential to enhance sleep. For example, physical exercise profoundly improves sleep quality. It leads to more restorative slow-wave sleep throughout the night, and also helps cut down on the number of

---

* It's viewed that way by, for example, the *U.S. Army Field Manual.*

nighttime awakenings. Similarly, bright light exposure strengthens the brain's internal body clock, which in turn makes it easier both to fall asleep and to stay asleep throughout the night; it also spurs a desirable increase in slow-wave sleep. And strategies like omega-3 supplementation and anti-ruminative activity and enhanced social connection—by helping slam the brakes on the brain's stress response circuits—can improve both the quality and quantity of sleep.

For some, putting such lifestyle changes into practice is all it takes to restore healthy sleep each night. But that's not always the case. Many people need additional help on the sleep front. That's why the TLC program has a sixth (and final) element: an array of sleep-enhancement strategies drawn from an effective treatment program for insomnia* that's proven superior to popular sleep medications in long-term clinical trials.

DETERMINING HOW MUCH SLEEP YOU NEED

According to the best research, most adults need about eight hours of sleep each night for optimal physical and emotional well-being. Unfortunately, the average Brit gets only 6.3 hours. Most of us, therefore, are chronically sleep-deprived. That's why over 90% of US ingest caffeine or other stimulants on a daily basis: It helps mask a staggering national sleep deficit,

* This treatment approach integrates an array of effective behavioral and cognitive insomnia interventions. One of the best summaries is found in *Cognitive Behavioral Treatment of Insomnia: A Session-by-Session Guide* by Perlis, Jungquist, Smith, and Posner (2005).

easing drowsiness so we can make it through the day. But caffeine does nothing to reduce the heightened risk of depression brought on by our collective lack of slumber.

Interestingly, people do vary somewhat in their sleep needs. A few lucky souls get by perfectly well on six or seven hours a night, while others require as much as nine and a half hours. Although it's possible that you need much less sleep than average, it's not likely. (Most people greatly underestimate how much sleep they require.)

In my clinical work, I've found it best to have each patient start with a goal of eight hours of sleep each night. And, unless you're certain you need less sleep than that, based on careful attention to your experience over a long period of time, I'm going to ask you to adopt an initial target of eight hours per night, as well. (After a few weeks you can always adjust your nightly sleep goal up or down based on how you respond—a point we'll address later in the chapter.)

Of course, when asked to carve that much time out of their lives for sleep, many people object, at least at first. The most common protest: *I can't afford to spend so much time in bed.* Stacy, a successful executive with a local nonprofit organization, was typical in that respect.

"I'm just not sure eight hours is a realistic goal for me," she said during an early treatment session. "I've got *way* too much to get done. And it seems like things take me longer than they used to. If I let myself sleep more than six hours, I don't think I'll ever be able to keep my head above water."

I reminded Stacy that her depression was going to be hard to clear up until she started getting more sleep, but she still insisted it simply wasn't possible. We were at an impasse, so I came at it from a different angle.

"What happens to your ability to get things done," I asked, "when you get a really good night's sleep? Does it make any difference if, say, you let yourself get a full eight hours?"

She shot back grudgingly, "I suppose I can get more done when I've had a good night's sleep, but I doubt if it's enough to make up for all that time wasted in bed. I don't know, I guess it's possible."

Encouraged by her concession, I asked Stacy if she would be willing to try an experiment—to adopt a goal of eight hours of sleep each night for a full two weeks, after which we could evaluate whether or not it was a good investment of her time. If she concluded that the added sleep truly wasn't worth it, I told her I would drop the subject. To my surprise, she agreed to give it a try.

Since Stacy had already done a good job of implementing some of the other lifestyle changes in the TLC program—and was also willing to put into practice some of the habits of healthy sleep outlined later in this chapter—she encountered little difficulty sleeping for a full eight hours once she set aside the time in her schedule. When I asked her at our next session about the preliminary results of the experiment—only a week into her trial run—she rolled her eyes.

"Okay, fine, you were right—the extra sleep is helping. It's hard to explain it—it's like my head is just clearer. And I've definitely had more energy this week. My husband even said I haven't been as cranky. It's funny: I'm not really any better at getting things done, but that part doesn't even seem to matter. Somehow, I've been finding a way to fit everything in anyway, because the sleep is a priority now."

When it comes right down to it, we usually find the time for things that truly matter to us. As Stacy discovered, when sleep is a priority, we'll make room for it in our busy lives. And, as the research shows quite clearly: In the battle against depression, sleep belongs high up on the priority list.

THE HABITS OF HEALTHY SLEEP

Unlike Stacy, many people set aside adequate time for sleep, only to discover that their bodies still won't cooperate after they've crawled into bed. They're among the millions who suffer from insomnia.

This ubiquitous sleep disturbance comes in three varieties. The most common form in depression is known as *terminal insomnia**: waking up too early—usually an hour or two before intended—and being unable to fall back to sleep. *Middle insomnia*, marked by frequent awakenings throughout the night, is also fairly widespread. The final variety—*onset insomnia*—is a hallmark of seasonal affective disorder and many forms of anxiety; it refers to an initial inability to fall asleep at night.

Believe it or not, much of the problem of insomnia stems from unhealthy sleep habits people develop. In this section, we'll

* Technically, terminal insomnia simply means that the awakening comes at the *end* (or termination) of the sleep period.

identify the most common culprits and outline ten healthy habits of sleep that can help remedy the problem.

Conditioning Your Body to Sleep

One of my friends has perfectly normal blood pressure at home, only to find that it shoots through the roof when he has it measured at the doctor's office. This phenomenon—*white coat hypertension* (that is, blood pressure that spikes only in the presence of white-clad medical specialists)—is a common problem, and it nicely illustrates how the body can be influenced by our surroundings.

Just like Pavlov's iconic dog—trained to salivate merely upon hearing a nightly dinner bell—each of us can be conditioned to respond reflexively to the sights and sounds and tastes and smells of our environment. For example, having endured some unpleasant visits to the dentist's office as a child, I still find my pulse racing every time I hear the shrill hiss of a dental drill—even if the sound is just coming from a nearby TV set. Likewise, when I smell fresh-baked apple pie, fond memories of my grandmother's cozy kitchen percolate, unbidden, to the surface of my mind, where they induce an involuntary wave of relaxation.

Our ability to sleep can also be influenced by our surroundings, although most of us are oblivious to the process. Specifically, our brains can be programmed to fall asleep—trained to enter a state of slumber reflexively and automatically—in the presence of certain cues from the world around us. (Conversely, we can also be conditioned to stay awake under certain circumstances.)

When someone consistently enjoys healthy sleep, the sights and sounds and sensations of the bedroom—and the bed, in particular—become strongly associated with the act of sleeping. Night after night, the brain is conditioned to follow a pretty ironclad rule: When you're in bed, you sleep; when you're not, you don't. And scientists have proven that people benefit from this conditioning, reflexively growing drowsier from the mere act of entering the bedroom, turning out the lights, and crawling into bed.

When a person battles insomnia, a different sort of conditioning takes place. Instead of associating the bed with sleep, they link it with the experience of lying wide awake, tossing and turning in frustration. They often inadvertently weaken their sleep programming even further by pairing the bed with all sorts of non-sleep activities like watching TV, reading, eating, and chatting on the phone.

Unfortunately, the more they lose the benefit of a conditioned sleep-bed association, the more their struggle with insomnia grows. But it's possible at any point to reprogram the body on this front. It simply requires adhering to a basic principle, the first of our habits of healthy sleep.

Habit #1: Use the Bed Only for Sleeping

You can condition your body to fall asleep in bed—and to stay asleep—only if the overwhelming majority of your time in bed is actually spent sleeping. The following guidelines will help make sure this is the case:

- *Anytime you've been lying awake for fifteen minutes, get up, leave the bedroom, and do something relaxing until you feel drowsy enough to return to bed.* This rule is essential because it prevents the bed (and the bedroom) from becoming associated with a state of wakefulness—which would undermine the sleep-bed conditioning process. Although getting out of bed when you've had trouble sleeping may feel like a hassle, it can be made more enjoyable by, say, setting aside a good book or magazine to be brought out only on such sleepless occasions.*

- *Avoid getting into bed anytime you aren't already drowsy.* If you're only allowing yourself a fifteen-minute window for falling asleep, you need to make sure you're already sleepy before climbing into bed; otherwise you'll quickly find yourself hopping right back out again. So, you'll want to avoid any arousing activities—for example, exercising, watching a scary movie, working, or surfing the Internet—right before bedtime.
- *Anything you do to increase your drowsiness should be done somewhere other than the bedroom.* This may seem a little counterintuitive. After all, if you're in another room reading or watching a movie to become groggy, won't the walk back to the bedroom unweave the somnolent spell? Wouldn't it make more sense just to read in bed, where you could simply reach over to turn off the light and fall asleep the instant you're ready? Actually, when you're truly drowsy, there's little chance of getting too stimulated merely by walking to your bedroom (assuming you don't decide to do some exercise along the way). And, because our goal is to

* Obviously, reading a book to get drowsy—instead of simply staying in bed and resting—might lead to a decrease in your total sleep time, but it's a key part of a process, and it yields greatly improved sleep in the long run. As sleep researchers have discovered, the trade-off is well worth it.

strengthen the association between sleep and bed, anything you do in bed other than sleep—even something relaxing like reading or watching TV—will interfere with the conditioning process.

- *You can make an exception in the case of sex.* For reasons that are still mysterious scientifically, sleep specialists have found that pairing the bed with sex does nothing to weaken the sleep-bed conditioning process. (One theory: Sex helps train the body to associate the bed with positive feelings, which counters the strong feelings of dread many insomniacs have upon getting into bed.) This is the only exception, though.
- *Avoid sleeping anywhere other than your own bed.* Pairing sleep with any other setting—the sofa, the recliner, or a guest room—interferes with the process of programming the sleep reflex to occur in your bed.

Habit #2: Get Up at the Same Time Every Day

Did you know your brain comes with a built-in sleep meter? A cluster of neurons deep in the brain tracks how much shut-eye you've been getting, and it estimates how much more you need at any given time. Based on its calculations, it sets your *sleep drive*, which you can usually feel on a moment-to-moment basis as a sense of drowsiness (or, if sleep drive is low, a sense of wakefulness). When sleep drive is appropriately high at bedtime, problems with insomnia tend to be minimal. And there are some pivotal things you can do to enhance this drive.

When your body clock is working properly, it provides a huge boost to your sleep drive at bedtime each night and sustains it until the next morning. This makes it much easier to get a good night's sleep. But if your internal timepiece starts to malfunction—thinking it's time to wake up when it's only, say, 3:00 in the morning—insomnia is one of the many unfortunate consequences.

One of the best ways to keep the body clock running on time—and, thus, to ensure healthy sleep—is to get up at the same time every morning. I know from my own experience that this isn't always convenient, but it's an essential weapon in the battle against disordered sleep.

Many people are tempted to sleep in on weekends—and pretty much any other time they get the chance (especially if they've been sleep-deprived). But this natural impulse to catch up on sleep turns out to be counterproductive in the long run: It ultimately serves to weaken sleep drive. So, I encourage you to resist the urge to sleep in, even if it means missing out on a golden opportunity for some extra rest. The temporary sacrifice will prove well worth it in the long run, as you find both the quality and quantity of your sleep improving.*

Habit #3: Avoid Napping

Simply put, anytime you nap, it strongly reduces the brain's sleep drive, which then sets you up for potential insomnia later that night. There's also evidence that napping can cause a reduction in restorative slow-wave sleep. So taking a nap is a bad idea

* We can also make an important exception to the "no-sleeping-in rule": After you've established a consistent pattern of healthy sleep, sleeping in for an extra hour or two on occasion will likely do little to throw off your body clock, provided you don't make it a habit.

for anyone with sleep difficulties (and anyone who's depressed), even though it might feel like the most natural way in the world to spend a sleepy afternoon.

But for those who have no sleep problems, the occasional nap is unlikely to pose any risk. Some people find they can nap every day and still maintain healthy sleep. (The key point is that if you have disordered sleep, napping will almost always make things worse; but taking a siesta won't pose a problem if your sleep is already healthy.)

Habit #4: Avoid Bright Light at Night

Even though indoor lighting is dim in comparison with direct sunlight, a well-lit room is still about as bright as the clear sky at sunset. As we saw in Chapter 7, indoor light can trick the brain into thinking it's still not nighttime yet, even if it's been pitch dark outside for hours. Such trickery can interfere with sleep, because the brain won't allow your sleep drive to kick into high gear until it thinks the sun has been down for at least an hour or so.

Many people who have onset insomnia—trouble falling asleep at night—are unwitting victims of this phenomenon. They keep all the lights on until the moment just before their head hits the pillow, and then they wind up having to lie awake in the dark for an hour before their brain finally gets the message that it's time for sleep.

Fortunately, there's a simple solution: Turn off all the lights about an hour before bedtime, and use only candlelight or very dim lamp light from that point on. You'll need to turn off your computer late at night as well, because its monitor (at close range) is bright enough to simulate twilight. So is your smartphone. (A TV screen is usually okay, provided you sit across the room with all the other lights out).

Light exposure in bed. Once you're in bed, it's best to keep your bedroom pitch dark. One of my patients discovered this the hard way last year. After having a few nightmares, her five-year-old son begged her to start leaving the hallway light on overnight so he could spot any monsters trying to sneak into his room. She agreed, and since her bedroom was on the same hallway (and she kept her door ajar so the cat could come and go), a fair amount light came streaming into her room each night. Although she didn't mind—she said she hardly even noticed the increased light—her sleep quickly started to deteriorate, with frequent awakenings throughout the night.

It takes very little light—even when it's filtered through our eyelids—to convince the brain that it's daytime and (therefore) time to be fully awake. So I advise you to turn out all nightlights, bathroom lights, and any other light sources (TVs, for example) before you climb into bed. Likewise, if there are certain times of year when the sun rises before your usual wakeup time, you'll likely benefit from installing blackout curtains in your bedroom. (A much cheaper alternative is to start wearing a sleep mask; they do a great job of blocking out ambient light.)

Late sunlight exposure. Sunlight exposure in the early evening can suppress sleep drive for hours. And when such exposure occurs several nights in a row, it can even throw off the body clock, making you want to go to bed and wake up much later than usual. Therefore, unless you actually need to recalibrate your body clock like this*—a process described in detail in Chapter

* If you tend to wake up far too early, such recalibration could be helpful.

7—it's wise to avoid getting regular sunlight after about 7:00 in the evening. (You can always wear sunglasses, however, if you still want to enjoy being outside past that hour in the summer.)

Habit #5: Avoid Caffeine and Other Stimulants

As you might expect, stimulants like caffeine and nicotine strongly suppress sleep drive. Caffeine has a typical half-life in the body of about four hours. (This means that every four hours, your blood level drops by 50%.) So, let's say you have a strong cup of coffee—with 200 milligrams (mg) of caffeine—at noon. By 4:00 in the afternoon, you still have 100 mg of caffeine in your body, and at 8:00 pm, there's still 50 mg in your system. Even at midnight, you're left with 25 mg of caffeine coursing through your veins; that's about the equivalent of a cup of green tea, and it's enough to disrupt your sleep.

You probably won't have any problem with a single cup of coffee or tea (or a caffeinated soda) first thing in the morning, because your body still has a full sixteen hours or so to clear it from your system before bedtime. But it's a good idea to avoid caffeine after you've been awake for more than a few hours. (Also, please note: Oral contraceptives can extend the half-life of caffeine by several hours, so even greater caution with caffeine intake is required.)

Habit #6: Avoid Alcohol at Night

Many people with onset insomnia use alcohol in an effort to increase drowsiness before heading off to bed. This strategy sometimes works, but it also causes a horrible rebound effect—with frequent awakenings and poor-quality sleep throughout the night. For this reason, it's a good idea to avoid any alcohol within a few hours of bedtime.

Habit #7: If Possible, Keep the Same Bedtime Every Night

By going to bed at the same time each night, you program your body to give a massive boost to sleep drive—usually starting about thirty to forty-five minutes before bedtime. The ensuing drowsiness makes it much easier to fall asleep. Remarkably, the brain also learns to optimize its sleep algorithms whenever it faces a predictable bedime schedule, making our sleep more efficient and restorative.

However, you may still face the occasional night when you're simply too wound up at bedtime to drift off to sleep. On such nights, it's best to delay going to bed for a while, and to engage instead in some form of relaxing activity until you're drowsy enough to climb into bed and fall asleep fairly quickly.

Habit #8: Turn Down Your Thermostat at Night

There's evidence that a mild drop in temperature at night helps increase sleep drive. This may seem a little puzzling until you consider that our remote ancestors always slept outside (or in open huts), where it got noticeably colder right around bedtime. And, since our bodies are still largely designed for life in the

Pleistocene, a nighttime dip in temperature actually sends us a primal signal that it's time to sleep. Accordingly, you may want to try lowering your thermostat by about five degrees an hour before bedtime.

Habit #9: Avoid Taking Your Problems to Bed with You

Nancy Hamilton, a noted sleep researcher, recently passed along a memorable formula for falling asleep: "All it takes is a tired body and a quiet mind." We've now addressed the *tired body* part of the formula in our review of the many ways to enhance sleep drive, so we'll turn our attention to strategies for cultivating a quiet mind.

For many people, the prime time for dwelling on negative thoughts is when they're lying in bed, trying to fall asleep. Such rumination revs up the brain's stress response circuits, and this, in turn, makes it virtually impossible to fall asleep. So it's crucial to make sure you don't succumb to any bouts of bedtime brooding.

As we saw in Chapter 5, the best way to put an end to rumination is by redirecting your attention to some type of engaging activity. But this particular strategy seems tricky to put into practice while you're lying in bed, waiting to fall asleep. What sort of activity could you possibly engage in, anyway?

There's really only one option: *mental activity*. The challenge is to find some sort of mental task that's engrossing, and yet simultaneously relaxing enough to allow you to fall asleep. Apparently, some people find counting imaginary sheep helpful—if the old cliché is to be believed. I have to admit, though,

I've never met a person for whom this worked. But I have had patients tell me they've successfully directed their thoughts away from rumination with one or more of the following mental exercises:

- *Replay scenes from a favorite movie in your head.* On nights when the tendency to ruminate is particularly acute, you can even try watching a relaxing film right before you turn in for bed: This will keep all the movie's details fresh in your mind as you attempt to replay them.
- *Visualize a relaxing scene.* Many people find it easiest to choose a favorite vacation spot or some other pleasant venue. Some, for example, like to imagine themselves walking along a scenic beach or a majestic mountain pass; for others, it's sitting in a childhood tree house or strolling through a verdant forest. It simply has to be some place you know well and can bring to mind with great clarity.
- *Play a round of golf (or any other outdoor game) in your mind's eye.* Visualize in detail the look of every fairway and bunker and green, the smell of the cut grass, the feel of the wind, the sound of birds and crickets, and so forth. (I also find it helpful to imagine myself playing at the skill level of a Tiger Woods; otherwise the mounting frustration over my erratic swing can quickly undo any relaxation I might otherwise achieve.)
- *Use progressive muscle relaxation.* This highly effective relaxation technique simply involves momentarily tightening and then relaxing each major muscle group in the body. It's easy to learn, and apps and CDs are available to guide you through the process. Because this technique takes a bit

of concentration, it's an effective antidote to rumination, and a particularly useful activity on nights when you need to get your thoughts off something that's troubling you.

- *Use another proven relaxation technique. Diaphragmatic breathing* involves learning how to inhale and exhale slowly and deeply from the diaphragm (the large muscle that sits right below the lungs). *Autogenic training* makes use of guided imagery to create a pleasant feeling of warmth in each part of the body. Both are highly effective in focusing attention and preparing you for sleep.

Although each of these strategies can redirect your attention away from upsetting thoughts, in some cases the problem of nighttime rumination can best be addressed by doing something before you turn in for the night. Specifically, if you have troubling thoughts on your mind in the evening, you can try one of these strategies to make rumination in bed less likely:

- *Talk things through with a trusted confidant.* This allows you to get any distressing thoughts off your chest, which usually weakens the desire to keep mulling them over later.
- *Write down your ruminative thoughts.* This process often makes it easier to leave them behind for the night.
- *Fill your mind, right before you go to bed, with explicitly positive thoughts and images.* Because of the contextual nature of human memory, loading your mind with such positive information will temporarily make it more difficult to recall any upsetting memories, and much harder to get stuck in a ruminative thought process.

Habit #10: Don't Try to Fall Asleep

Sleep is an inherently paradoxical state: The harder you try to attain it, the more elusive it becomes. Sleep can never be stalked and caught—like some sort of wild animal—when you hunt it with intense, focused effort. Instead, it will appear unbidden, sneaking up on you gently after you've fully let go of the struggle.

This means it's always counterproductive to worry about how long it's taking you to fall asleep—a process that quickly turns into outright rumination. That's why sleep specialists generally advise you to turn your clock away from the bed, so you can't see at a glance what time it is.*

Likewise, whenever you lie in bed worrying about the negative consequences of sleep deprivation the next day, it will make it much harder to fall asleep. If you find such worrisome thoughts springing up on occasion, you may find it helpful to remind yourself that a single night of poor sleep is never catastrophic (though it can certainly be frustrating). Also keep in mind that temporary sleep deprivation actually serves to increase sleep drive on the following night. In other words, tonight's sleep loss means tomorrow night's sleep will likely prove much better. And, ironically, once you let go of any worry over lost sleep, there's a good chance you'll soon drift off anyway.

---

* Then again, we saw earlier that it's important to get up out of bed anytime you've been lying awake for fifteen minutes—a rule that would seem to require you to have access in bed to a visible clock. It's generally best, however, if you simply leave the bedroom when you *estimate* that fifteen minutes have passed; most people quickly get very good at guessing in this fashion, and it allows them to avoid staring at the clock all night.

THE PROBLEM OF HYPERSOMNIA

Our review of the habits of healthy sleep has focused so far on insomnia and related sleep disturbances. But about 20% of people with depression suffer from *hypersomnia*—sleeping far too much. What can be done for them?

As it turns out, many cases of depressive hypersomnia result from inefficient sleep: multiple awakenings through the night and a reduced amount of restorative slow-wave sleep. Because people with this problem get such poor quality sleep, they may find themselves in bed for twelve or fourteen hours a night, and yet still feeling tired.

Fortunately, as we've seen, several elements of Therapeutic Lifestyle Change help increase slow-wave sleep—especially exercise and sunlight exposure—and adopting the habits of healthy sleep we've covered in this chapter can also provide an enormous boost to sleep quality. I've consistently observed good outcomes among hypersomnia patients in our TLC groups as they've put these various strategies into practice, and most eventually found their sleep returning to normal.

WHEN ALL ELSE FAILS

In the great majority of cases, employing these ten habits of healthy sleep—in tandem with the other antidepressant elements of Therapeutic Lifestyle Change—will effectively put an end to the common sleep problems that characterize depression. But there are some important exceptions. Most arise from the presence of medication side effects, undiagnosed sleep disorders, or other medical conditions.

Oddly enough, some common antidepressant medications carry the potential to interfere with sleep. Often this involves repeated awakenings due to periodic limb movements. (Stimulants such as caffeine and amphetamines can have a similar effect.) In a similar vein, the frequent use of some sleep medications can lead to rebound insomnia on any night when the drugs are not used.

Sleep disorders constitute another important cause of poor quality sleep. For example, some people suffer from a serious, potentially life-threatening condition known as *sleep apnea.* It involves dozens (often hundreds) of mini-awakenings throughout the night as breathing stops temporarily—usually due to an airway obstruction in the throat. Others suffer from *periodic limb movement disorder,* in which the legs or arms twitch repeatedly throughout the night, greatly reducing sleep quality. With such sleep disorders, the patient usually has no idea anything is wrong, other than a relentless sense of sleepiness and fatigue that stems from chronically poor sleep.

Numerous other medical conditions can also interfere with sleep. Chronic pain is the biggest culprit: It's virtually impossible to sleep soundly when intense physical discomfort keeps intruding into your consciousness. Allergies, colds, and other respiratory conditions also carry the potential to disrupt sleep all night long, as do diseases like *hyperthyroidism* and *pheochromocytoma* (adrenal tumor), which are capable of keeping the body continuously revved up. The list of medical causes of sleep disturbance is a lengthy one—and the topic is so complex that it warrants a book in its own right.

Therefore, if you have sleep problems that persist even after putting into practice the strategies we've reviewed in this chapter, I strongly recommend that you see your doctor or other health care professional for help as soon as possible. Remember: Our bodies were designed to sleep rather effortlessly anytime we go to bed with a tired body and a still mind. If you can't do so, it's a sign you need medical attention.

PART THREE
MAKING THE CHANGE

10
Putting It All Together

Although we've already explored several potent strategies for fighting depression (omega-3 supplementation, anti-rumination activity, exercise, sunlight exposure, social connection, and healthy sleep), we haven't yet discussed how to put everything together into a complete package. How, in other words, can you incorporate all six antidepressant strategies into your life at the same time?

It's not a trivial challenge. When I first began describing the Therapeutic Lifestyle Change (TLC) program to my colleagues, back before we'd started recruiting any patients into our first treatment study, some warned me that the program was too ambitious. Quite simply, my colleagues thought people would find it too difficult to make so many changes all at once.

They had a point. In fact, I agreed: TLC *is* an ambitious program, and it does require a great deal of dedication. But I wasn't worried. I knew from years of experience that most depressed individuals are willing to do whatever it takes to escape the illness, to find relief from its relentless, debilitating pain. They simply need some clear, practical direction about how to make the necessary changes, as well as a bit of coaching along the way.

Still, as I put the TLC program together, my top priority was to make sure it was truly doable. That meant breaking things down into small, manageable stages—to be implemented gradually, one at a time, over the span of several weeks. It also meant starting with the easiest changes up front, and then introducing more challenging elements later in treatment, after patients had gained some momentum (and confidence). Fortunately, this week-by-week approach has proven to be highly successful—much more so than I could have predicted.

In the pages that follow, you'll find a weekly step-by-step outline of the Therapeutic Lifestyle Change program. The recommended schedule is based on the assumption that you haven't yet made any of the six core therapeutic lifestyle changes. However, if you've already made progress with some of these steps (for example, if you're currently exercising on a regular basis), you'll be able to skip past those corresponding parts of the schedule.*

BEFORE YOU BEGIN: SEE YOUR DOCTOR

Depression can be triggered by several medical conditions, including diabetes, heart disease, sleep apnea, thyroid problems, mononucleosis, and hormonal imbalance. Likewise, numerous drugs, including some psychiatric meds, can induce depressive

* The protocol is also based on the assumption that you're currently battling symptoms of depression. But you can still benefit from implementing the protocol even if you're not depressed: It will help to dramatically reduce your risk of future depression.

symptoms as a side effect.* For this reason, I believe it's crucial for every person suffering from depression to see their doctor for a complete physical exam, just to make sure the disorder isn't the direct result of another serious illness or an adverse drug reaction (either of which could require immediate medical attention.)

In fact, I advise you to schedule an appointment with a doctor†—if you haven't already done so in the recent past—as the first step toward putting the principles of Therapeutic Lifestyle Change into practice. During your appointment, you can also get your doctor's clearance to begin an aerobic exercise routine, use a light box, and take the various nutritional supplements included in the TLC protocol. And, if you don't know how to take your pulse already, your doctor can teach you during the appointment.

MEASURING YOUR PROGRESS

How can you tell, as you proceed through the protocol, if you're making any real progress—getting any better—from one week to the next?

Although you could always try to guesstimate your depression level each week, such ballpark guesses tend to be wildly inaccurate. It's much more useful to have a precise measurement. That's why you'll find a superb depression scale in Appendix A that you can use to track your symptoms each week as you adopt each change in your lifestyle. It usually takes only a few minutes

---

* Both medical and drug-related causes of depression are discussed in some detail in Chapter 11.

† You could, alternatively, see a licensed nurse practitioner.

to fill out and score this brief questionnaire, and then plot your score on the graph provided in Appendix B.

So, before you begin putting the TLC program into practice, take a moment to complete this scale. It will give you a nice baseline measurement of your depressive symptoms; this in turn will allow you to tell, during the weeks ahead, whether or not the recommended lifestyle changes are helping as they should.

THE TLC PROTOCOL

Week 1

Supplements. During your first week, I suggest starting with a simple change that takes only a minute of your day, but that still has a surprisingly potent effect on the brain: nutritional supplementation. There are five products you'll need to buy. (All can be found at a local health food store or chemist, but they're usually less expensive when purchased online.)

- Omega-3: This is best obtained in the form of high-quality fish oil capsules (or liquid). Try starting at a total omega-3 dosage of 1000 mg of EPA* each day.
- Vitamin D: If, like most Brits, you're not synthesizing enough vitamin D in your skin—through regular brief exposure to the sun's UV rays—it is important to take a

* Many fish oil capsules contain an EPA amount (in mg) that does not divide evenly into the 1000 mg target. In such cases, it's preferable to get as close to 1000 mg as you can without going under. So, in the hypothetical case of 300 mg capsules, it would be better to take 4 capsules (1200 mg) rather than 3 capsules (900 mg) daily.

supplement. I recommend a dose of 50 mcg each day, in the form of vitamin D_3.

- Antioxidants: Because omega-3s are fragile molecules, they need some help in the body to do their job. Specifically, they require the protection provided by antioxidants. If you can manage to eat five or more servings of vegetables and fruit each day, that will do nicely. Otherwise, you might consider taking a 250 mg supplement of vitamin C each day.
- Evening primrose oil: Evening primrose oil provides your brain with an essential fat called GLA, which can get depleted when you take high doses of omega-3s. You need only a little of this oil, though—just one or two 500 mg capsules each week.* It's important not to exceed this dose, because taking too much can cause unwanted inflammation.

Rumination. In addition to starting nutritional supplementation this week, you can take an important first step toward ending rumination. Specifically, I suggest that you try noticing throughout the day each time you find yourself brooding over negative thoughts. As described earlier, it's impossible to stop rumination without learning first how to detect the process when it's happening. (Most depressed individuals spend a great deal of time brooding without any real awareness that they're doing so.) Several strategies for learning how to notice rumination are discussed in Chapter 5.

Depression Scale. At the end of each week, complete the depression scale and compare the result with your baseline score to see if any changes have occurred.

---

* Each capsule provides 40 to 50 mg of GLA—a full week's supply unless you are very physically active, in which case you can bump the dosage up to two capsules per week.

Week 2

Supplements. Continue as in Week 1.

Rumination. Now that you've become more skilled at noticing your ruminative thoughts (after a week's worth of practice), begin interrupting these thoughts by redirecting your attention each time they occur. You can do this by applying the many techniques described in Chapter 5, including making a list of engaging activities to try this week; identifying and avoiding the specific situations that commonly lead you to ruminate; and scheduling at least one activity each day to take the place of those high-risk situations.

Exercise. You won't start the exercise part of the program until Week 3, but you'll need to make sure you have a few things in place by then. First, pick up a heart rate monitor, or if you can't afford one right now, make sure you can reliably take your pulse. Second, choose the form of exercise you'll be starting with, and make sure you have access to any necessary equipment. (For some people, this will mean lining up a gym membership or booking some classes.) Finally, unless you've already been working out on a regular basis, you may want to consider hiring a personal trainer for at least the first six weeks to help you get started. (You can contact any local gym or health club for referrals.)

Depression Scale. Complete the depression scale and record your score.

Week 3

Supplements. Continue as before.

Rumination. Keep working to improve your ability to notice rumination, and try to get to the point where you can catch yourself the moment it begins. Likewise, keep experimenting with different activities to interrupt it. Every time you find something that works, try other activities that seem similar. For example, if you find that playing Scrabble online is helpful, you might experiment with some other online games. Finally, continue avoiding high-risk situations and substituting more engaging activities in their place. Schedule at least one such activity each day.

Exercise. Mark off in your schedule three hour-long blocks of time for exercise this week. (Even though you won't be exercising for the full hour, this will leave enough time for you to cool down and clean up afterwards.) Each time you work out, the goal is to exercise intensely enough to get your heart rate in the target aerobic range (refer to Chapter 6, Table 6-1) and keep it there for thirty minutes. If you haven't been active in some time (or even if you have), I strongly recommend that you begin with brisk walking, because it is by far the easiest, most natural aerobic activity for most people to pick up.

Light. If you're going to be using a light box for your bright light exposure, order it this week so it will be on hand for Week 4.

Depression Scale. Complete the depression scale and record your score.

Week 4

Supplements. Continue as before.

Rumination. Continue as before.

Exercise. Continue as before. If you weren't successful last week in exercising aerobically three times, that's a good indication that hiring a personal trainer may be necessary to help you get started.

Light. Begin scheduling thirty minutes of bright light exposure each morning, as outlined in Chapter 7. (Or, if you're consistently waking up too early in the morning, begin scheduling thirty minutes of exposure roughly five hours before your planned bedtime.) Also look for other opportunities to get the benefit of natural sunlight exposure during the day (especially from 11:00 am to 3:00 pm, when vitamin D synthesis is possible).

Depression scale. Complete the depression scale and record your score.

Week 5

Supplements. Continue as before.

Rumination. Continue as before.

Exercise. Continue as before. If you aren't satisfied at this point with your chosen form of exercise, try experimenting with another type instead.

Light. Continue as before.

Social support. Schedule at least three social activities for the week ahead, writing them in your calendar. It's best to spend time with friends or loved ones whom you can see in person. When that's not possible, substitute phone calls (or video chats) with out-of-town friends and relatives. Another alternative is time spent on supportive online forums for depression (see page 191).

Depression scale. Complete the depression scale and record your score.

Week 6

Supplements. Continue as before.

Rumination. Continue as before.

Exercise. Continue as before. If you've still not been successful in exercising aerobically at least three times each week, you will almost certainly need to hire a personal trainer to help you with this part of the program.

Light. Continue as before.

Social support. Schedule at least four social activities for the week ahead, writing them in your calendar. In addition, evaluate whether or not you have any truly toxic relationships in your life; if you do, try working to improve the relationships that are open to improvement (see page 191) and limiting your contact with any irredeemably toxic individuals by at least 50% in the week ahead.

Sleep. Adopt the goal of getting adequate sleep each night: seven to nine hours, depending on your body's needs (see Chapter 9). Put into practice the first two habits of healthy sleep: use your bed only for sleeping and wake up at the same time every morning.

Depression scale. Complete the depression scale and record your score.

Week 7

Evaluation. You've now been putting the principles of Therapeutic Lifestyle Change into practice for six weeks. Most people will see at least some benefit by this point. Please take a moment to look at your weekly depression scores, going all the way back to the first score before you started the TLC program. Do you see a clear trend toward improvement, with your current level of symptoms at least 25% lower than when you began? If not, it will be important to skip ahead now to Chapter 11, which focuses on troubleshooting, and also to consider immediately contacting a licensed therapist for assistance (including help with putting the TLC program into practice), if you haven't done so already.

Supplements. Continue as before. However, if you haven't seen at least a 50% reduction in your symptoms from baseline (when you began the TLC program), consider increasing your omega-3 dose to 2000 mg each day of EPA.

Rumination. Continue as before.

Exercise. Continue as before. If you haven't seen at least a 50% decrease in your baseline depressive symptoms, consider bumping up your exercise regimen to at least five thirty-minute workouts each week.

Light. If your depression scale score is now below 10, you can decrease bright light exposure to fifteen minutes each day.

Social support. Schedule at least five social activities for the week ahead. Also, try limiting your contact with any irredeemably toxic individuals by an additional 50% in the week ahead.

Sleep. Continue as before. Also, work to incorporate the remaining habits of healthy sleep (habits 3 through 10, outlined in Chapter 9).

Depression scale. Complete the depression scale and record your score.

Week 8

Supplements. Continue as before.

Rumination. Continue as before.

Exercise. Continue as before.

Light. If your depression scale score is now below 10, you can decrease morning/evening bright light exposure to fifteen minutes each day.

Social support. Schedule at least one social activity each day. In addition, target at least one form of community involvement to participate in during the upcoming week. Finally, try keeping your contact with any irredeemably toxic individuals to a minimum.

Sleep. Continue as before.

Depression scale. Complete the depression scale and record your score.

Weeks 9 through 12

Supplements. Continue as before.

Rumination. Continue as before.

Exercise. Continue as before.

Light. When your depression scale score drops below 10, you can decrease bright light exposure to fifteen minutes each day. Continue adding another fifteen to thirty minutes' worth of sunlight exposure (when it's available) during the day.

Social support. Continue as before, and increase your community involvement to at least two forms of activity each week.

Sleep. Continue as before.

Depression scale. Complete the depression scale and record your score.

Evaluation. By the end of twelve weeks (roughly three months), the great majority of our TLC patients at the University of Kansas have experienced significant improvement in depressive symptoms. At a minimum, we expect to observe at least a 50% decrease in severity from pretreatment, at which point most people no longer meet the full diagnostic criteria for major depression, and the overall trajectory points toward recovery. If you don't see such improvement* when looking at your own depression scores, please turn to Chapter 11, which focuses on troubleshooting, and consider contacting a licensed therapist for assistance.

OVERCOMING DEPRESSION FOR LIFE

If you've successfully applied the six major elements of Therapeutic Lifestyle Change as outlined in the preceding section, you've taken an important step toward the goal of long-term freedom from depression. However, even after you've experienced relief from the acute agony of depressive illness, there's never room for complacency when battling such a relentless foe. As we've seen, the rate of relapse in depression is very high: Over half of those who recover from depression will face the disorder again at some point.

Fortunately, you can reduce this risk dramatically. There's abundant evidence that each of the major lifestyle changes we've

* In other words, you should see at least a 50% reduction in your initial depression score (the one obtained before you began putting these lifestyle changes into practice).

outlined can protect against the return of depression. The key is to make sure you stay at it—that you continue living the depression cure every day in the months and years ahead.

The best analogy might be that of adult-onset (Type II) diabetes, a serious illness that can often be controlled through a strict regimen of diet and exercise. If a diabetic fails to follow the appropriate lifestyle regimen, however, blood sugar skyrockets, and damage to the body's major organs (heart, kidneys, brain, eyes) usually follows. That's why doctors tell those afflicted by the disease, in no uncertain terms, that diabetes is a lifelong illness—they will always have it—but it can be successfully managed; they can remain healthy if they work on it each and every day.

Depression is very much the same. You can eliminate the symptoms, but the disorder's enduring imprint on the brain, with its corresponding risk of relapse, is always there.* Still, you're largely in control of your own fate. You have a superb chance of remaining healthy if you're willing to work at it—to make the antidepressant lifestyle regimen a nonnegotiable priority in your life.

In addition, there are two general principles of relapse prevention that will help ensure your depression remains a thing of the past:

Stress management. Depression can be triggered by the brain's runaway stress response, and the illness often follows closely on the heels of taxing life events. So, even though the regimen

* That sounds depressing, so let me sound a more hopeful note: With each passing month of recovery, depression's imprint on the brain grows more and more faint.

we've outlined is effective in putting the brakes on the brain's stress response circuits, it's best—when possible—to eliminate the major sources of stress from your life.

In Chapter 8, for example, we discussed the importance of identifying and limiting so-called *toxic relationships*, which can stand in the way of a full recovery from depression. Likewise, it's crucial to avoid the strain of such unhelpful social ties after the illness has receded. Here's a good rule of thumb to keep in mind: Any relationship that consistently provokes a high level of stress is one that adds to your risk of future depression.

Another particularly disruptive social stressor is the decision to relocate geographically. We've become such a transient society that most people barely think twice about moving halfway across the country, even if it means severing all of their important social bonds in the process. But we're simply not designed to be uprooted like that. It takes a huge toll on our mental health, kicking the brain's stress circuits into high gear. Not surprisingly, relocation is a common trigger of depression. This is not to say that one should never consider moving away from friends and family, but the anticipated benefits of such a move (such as a good job or educational opportunity) should be carefully weighed against the costs—the increased stress and the temporary lack of social support the move will entail.

It's also important to limit stress in the workplace. For example, a few years ago one of my patients found herself in a hostile, unsupportive work environment. Her boss was prone to harsh, critical outbursts (even though he greatly valued her as an employee), and her coworkers treated her as an outcast because of her political views. (She was an outspoken liberal in an office filled with conservatives.) Rather than quit her job, which would have brought its own set of stresses, she began exploring ways to improve things at work. A frank, open conversation with her boss led him to apologize for his occasional outbursts: He also pledged to treat her with greater consideration in the future. And she was successful in connecting with two coworkers around common interests that had nothing to do with politics. (At my suggestion, she also found noise-cancelling headphones a great benefit when conservative talk shows were blaring on the office radio.)

Vigilance. When it comes to staying healthy and depression-free, it's crucial to stay ever attuned to the possible emergence of new symptoms, and to do whatever it takes to nip them in the bud. Preventing the onset of depression is a lot like stopping a snowball that's rolling down a hill. If you catch it quickly, before it has a chance to build up much size or momentum, it's easy to halt it in its tracks. But if you wait too long, it becomes an unstoppable juggernaut that crushes everything in its path.

Some situations are particularly likely to trigger the return of some depressive symptoms, and you'll need to be especially attentive when you face them. Common high-risk situations to watch out for include the death of a loved one, the experience of divorce (or other romantic breakup), bouts of physical illness, caring for a sick relative, geographic relocation (or the loss of a close friend due to relocation), the loss of employment, an unexpected financial setback, and even extended periods of gloomy weather (and corresponding low sunlight exposure).

As soon as you begin to notice the return of any depressive symptoms, even if they're relatively mild, it's important to address them immediately. The following three principles can be helpful in that respect:

- First, it's often possible to render obvious triggering events less stressful. For example, when overwhelmed by the task of caring for her elderly mother, one of my patients was able to reduce her stress load by hiring a home-health nurse. I've observed, though, that people often resist opportunities to lighten their burdens like this. Many times it's because they feel they don't deserve the help, and sometimes they're simply unwilling to ask for it. But such help can make an enormous difference in keeping stress at a manageable level.
- It's also important to evaluate, with complete honesty, how effectively you've been putting the six principles of Therapeutic Lifestyle Change (TLC) into practice every day. Have you slacked off in any areas? If so, it will be helpful to renew your commitment to implementing each one—to make certain you're getting the full antidepressant benefit of the TLC protocol each day.
- If, on the other hand, you've experienced some breakthrough symptoms of depression despite sticking to the entire TLC regimen, it's usually a good idea to check in with your doctor if the symptoms last more than a few days. (I'd advise you to check in *immediately*, however, if you're having suicidal thoughts.) In addition, you can try turning things up a notch on the therapeutic lifestyle front for a few weeks—taking advantage of the potent ability of these simple strategies to clamp down on the brain's runaway stress response (and corresponding depressive symptoms). For example, you might consider immersing yourself in your

social support network, spending as much face time as possible with those who can love and nurture you through your time of distress.

A complete set of strategies for enhancing the antidepressant effect of the TLC regimen is outlined in the following chapter, along with a detailed troubleshooting guide.

11
When Roadblocks Emerge: A Troubleshooting Guide

The Depression Cure. Admittedly, this is a bold title—inspired by the promise of reclaiming the protective legacy of an antidepressant way of life. But not everyone who picks up this book will find the cure they've been looking for, at least not right away. Some will still find themselves battling depressive symptoms, even after attempting to make all the recommended changes. What if you happen to be one of them? What should you do then?

The answer hinges on how successful you've been in putting the full Therapeutic Lifestyle Change (TLC) protocol into practice. In most cases, when I've seen someone continue to struggle with depression after trying the TLC program, it's because they've run into some important roadblocks that kept them from making the necessary changes. Fortunately, several troubleshooting strategies can help address these obstacles to recovery.

Every once in a while, however, someone does a pretty good job of making the recommended lifestyle changes, and yet they still face lingering symptoms of depression.* In such cases, several additional treatment recommendations† may prove helpful. We'll cover them in some detail in the concluding section of this chapter.

THE BEST OF INTENTIONS

We are all creatures of habit. The brain's reward pathways light up with pleasure every time we indulge in one of our habitual behaviors, no matter what it happens to be—reading the paper, flossing teeth, walking the dog, making the bed, and so on. That's why we find it so hard to change our typical way of doing things. Keeping our usual m.o. is usually much more rewarding than adopting a new one. (It takes a few weeks of real effort before any new behavior turns into a full-fledged habit—after which it finally becomes rewarding and, thus, self-sustaining.)

The bottom line: Lifestyle change is much easier said than done. Think about the millions of people who resolve each year to start working out, to eat healthily, to stop smoking, to watch less TV, or to get more sleep—and how few succeed. If lifestyle change were simple, we wouldn't be facing an epidemic of obesity, with two-thirds of American adults now overweight.

Compound this difficulty with the fact that depression makes it particularly hard for someone to initiate new activity. As we've seen, the disorder shuts down circuits in the left frontal cortex,

* However, I've never seen someone utilize the entire TLC protocol without at least some improvement in their depressive symptoms.

† Some other diagnostic possibilities may also need to be considered.

the part of the brain that allows us to put our intentions into action.

By all rights, then, Therapeutic Lifestyle Change might look like some sort of cruel pipe dream—something that sounds great on paper but that proves impossible to put into practice in the real world. And yet I've watched countless depressed individuals find a lasting cure by making the TLC program a central part of their lives. How did they succeed?

In most cases, they had help. They needed help. While I've known a few dozen people over the years who've been able—completely on their own—to put the TLC protocol into practice after simply hearing about it (in a newspaper or magazine article or a talk I'd given), such individuals are the exception, not the rule. Typically, their depressive symptoms were on the milder end of the continuum, so they still had enough energy and initiative to make the necessary changes.

So, if you've failed on your own to make some of the therapeutic lifestyle changes described in *The Depression Cure*, please know that you're not alone. Among the clinically depressed, such difficulties are par for the course. But with the help of some good coaching, you're still likely to benefit from everything in the TLC protocol—omega-3 supplementation, anti-ruminative activity, aerobic exercise, sunlight exposure, increased social support, and healthy sleep habits.

You simply need to find someone who can help you translate your intentions into action. By gently encouraging you each step along the way as you put the protocol into practice, a TLC coach can, in effect, play the role of your left frontal cortex—shoring up your ability to initiate the changes you've already committed to making.

Finding a TLC Coach

Where can you find such coaching? There are two different options worth exploring: You can use either a professional therapist or an amateur coach. We discuss both options in this section.

A professional therapist. In my experience, most depressed individuals, especially those struggling with the TLC protocol, can benefit from the expert guidance of a trained therapist. But there's a bewildering array of licensed mental health practitioners to choose from: psychiatrists, clinical psychologists, counseling psychologists, social workers, nurse practitioners, and other assorted counselors and therapists. Generally speaking, those with the best, most advanced training in helping people change the way they live—the crux of the TLC protocol—are clinical psychologists. (Please keep in mind, however, that highly trained psychiatrists, counselling psychologists, nurse practitioners, and clinical social workers can be effective in this coaching role, as well.)

Over the past many years, I've been contacted by depressed individuals all over the world looking for a professional in their area to help them put the principles of TLC into practice, and I direct them to a highly skilled therapist whenever I can. But it has to be someone who is willing to work with them on implementing the antidepressant lifestyle changes outlined in *The Depression Cure* (as opposed to other traditional psychotherapy activities, such as exploring the details of childhood). In addition, I always look for a therapist who's been trained in *behavior therapy*—the type of treatment that focuses on changing what we *do*.

---

* You can find the EABCT directory at www.eabct.eu

A superb resource for finding such therapists in your area is the *European Association of Behavioural and Cognitive Therapies* (EABCT). Another option is to ask for a referral for a skilled behavior therapist from your doctor or other trusted professionals in your community.

When you contact a psychologist or other mental health professional to serve as your TLC coach, please bear in mind that all therapists are not created equal (even among those who are highly trained). There are some that you'll "click" with right away and some that you won't. According to the best research, you'll likely have a good intuitive sense of how well you're going to hit it off with a therapist within the first session or two. So, if it doesn't feel like a reasonably good fit early on, it's probably best to consider moving on to the next name on your referral list.

An amateur coach. A completely different approach to coaching, however, can sometimes be a viable option: the amateur coach. Some people are in the fortunate position of having a loved one—a spouse, parent, sibling, child, or close friend—who is both willing and able to serve as their TLC coach. Although this approach has some potential pitfalls, I've also seen it work very well, as long as the following conditions are met:

- Rapport: There has to be a strong, trusting relationship in place—with rock-solid rapport—between the coach and the person he or she is helping. This is crucial, because TLC coaches sometimes need to push their depressed charges out of their comfort zones. Even when they do this with great tact and gentleness, it will come across as nagging—and damage the underlying relationship—if the level of rapport is not high at the outset.

- Knowledge: The coach also needs to become knowledgeable about the ins and outs of the entire TLC protocol. This is not a difficult task, but it does require a significant time commitment.
- Dedication: Clearly, coaching someone through the TLC program takes a high level of dedication. It requires checking in with them on a regular basis, providing timely prompts for each major area of lifestyle change. Early in the process, this can even mean arranging for several different prompts each day—depending on how much difficulty the depressed individual has with initiating activity. (As the weeks pass and symptoms improve, much less prompting will usually be necessary.)

Troubleshooting Tips

Whether or not you choose to take advantage of a TLC coach, you can overcome some of the most common obstacles to implementing the program by attending to a set of basic troubleshooting tips. Although these are described, one lifestyle element at a time, at various places throughout the book, Table 11-1 provides a handy summary of the best strategies for addressing major TLC trouble spots.

WHEN TLC ISN'T ENOUGH

Occasionally, someone will do a good job of adopting all the major lifestyle changes recommended in the TLC program,

TABLE 11-1. *TLC Trouble Spots and Solutions*

TLC Element	*Problem*	*Potential Solution*
Omega-3 Supplement	*Trouble remembering to take supplements every day*	Give yourself an unavoidable visual reminder. For example, store the bottle on your nightstand, on your pillow, or next to your toothbrush.
	Burping up fishy taste, or indigestion or discomfort	Switch to a triglyceride-based fish oil supplement, particularly one from a trusted source like Nordic Naturals.
	Can't take fish oil (vegetarian or seafood allergy)	Use flaxseed oil, hemp seed oil, or an algae-based omega-3 supplement to get necessary EPA.
Anti-ruminative Activity	*Trouble catching rumination when it's happening (in "real time")*	Several times each day, stop whatever you're doing to monitor and observe your thoughts. If needed, use prompts, such as programmable alarms on your phone; calls from your TLC coach; or regular breaks in your schedule (such as a trip to the bathroom).
	Low motivation to stop rumination (it feels beneficial or useful)	Give yourself permission to ruminate on a specific problem, but with a strict time limit of no more than ten minutes a day. (After that, you've hit the point of diminishing returns, and no additional insights are likely to emerge.)
	Difficulty stopping rumination	Make a list of your most engaging activities (both social and solo) and experiment with each during bouts of rumination to determine which are the most effective at stopping rumination. Also, try writing down ruminative thoughts, and then walking away from them.

Aerobic Exercise	*Can't get started, or can't stick to an exercise regimen*	Hire a personal trainer or find an exercise buddy who will hold you accountable and provide appropriate prompts.
	Ruminating during exercise	Exercise to engaging music or audiobook/podcast or try a more engaging, social form of exercise.
	Not enjoying exercise	Find an exercise partner (or trainer); experiment with more game-like physical activities; try taking brisk walks immersed in the beauty of nature.
Bright Light Exposure	*No reliable natural sunlight available right now (too cloudy or cold, days too short, and so on)*	Buy a 10,000-lux light box.
	Eyes can't tolerate the light box, or feeling jittery or nauseated	Try doubling the distance from the light box for a week, and then gradually moving closer.
	Can't make time in my morning routine for light exposure	Try sitting in front of the light box (or outside on sunny mornings) during breakfast; place the light box safely on the bathroom counter while grooming; use the light box during the first fifteen to thirty minutes at work.
Social Connection	*Low motivation to socialize; feel like withdrawing*	Remind yourself that this is completely normal in depression: Your brain thinks you're physically ill and need to withdraw. But social activity helps fight depression. If needed, use a TLC coach for prompting and encouragement.

	It feels like existing relationships have been damaged by depressive withdrawal	Confide about depression to friends and loved ones, explain how it causes withdrawal, and ask for help reestablishing each relationship.
	Spending time with some friends and loved ones makes me feel worse, not better	Avoid co-rumination, focusing instead on joint activities. Also, identify any toxic relationships, and begin to limit time spent with such individuals.
	Few friends or loved ones to spend time with	Try reconnecting via phone or video chat (Skype) with friends or loved ones that live elsewhere; join an online depression forum to receive support from others struggling with the illness; become involved in a community organization.
Sleep	*No time in busy schedule for eight hours of sleep each night*	Make sleep your top priority, realizing that healthy sleep leads to greater efficiency in everything else, more than making up for any lost time spent in bed.
	Trouble falling asleep	Avoid stimulating activity and use only dim light an hour before bedtime; avoid caffeine except in the morning; turn down the thermostat at bedtime; increase morning bright light exposure and avoid late sunlight exposure; follow all the principles of healthy sleep outlined in Chapter 9.
	Trouble staying asleep	Avoid early morning bright light exposure and substitute exposure in late afternoon or early evening; use blackout curtains in the bedroom; increase exercise; follow all the principles of healthy sleep outlined in Chapter 9.

but will still suffer from serious depressive symptoms. Such a dilemma has several potential causes—mostly due to various medical conditions or other co-occurring forms of mental illness—and these need to be addressed with the help of a trained clinical professional.

Medical Complications

Because depression is literally a form of physical illness, it makes sense that the disorder can sometimes be caused by another serious medical condition. Many different types of medical illness can, under some circumstances, trigger the onset of clinical depression; they can also make the disorder very difficult (sometimes impossible) to treat effectively until the underlying medical issue is addressed.

Therefore, if you've found the TLC protocol ineffective in clearing up your depression, it's absolutely essential that you see a physician right away for a complete medical evaluation—to rule out any number of illnesses that might be keeping you depressed. Some of the more common medical culprits are

- Diabetes
- Hypothyroidism (low thyroid function)
- Sleep apnea
- Mononucleosis
- Persistent infection
- Hormonal imbalance
- Malnutrition
- Heart disease

- Cancer
- Stroke
- Brain injury
- Parkinson's disease
- Chronic fatigue syndrome

In addition, many medications—even some of the drugs commonly used in treating mental illness—carry the potential to trigger depression, and they can also maintain the disorder once it's begun. Your physician can help you evaluate this possibility, as well. It will be especially important to bring it to your doctor's attention if you're taking any of the following types of medication:

- Benzodiazepines (Rivotril, Ativan, Valium)
- Tranquilizers/sedatives
- Beta blockers
- Antihistamines
- Birth control pills
- Steroids
- Non-steroidal anti-inflammatory drugs (NSAIDs)
- Antipsychotics
- Antihypertensives (blood pressure medications)
- Fluoroquinolone antibiotics (Cipro)

Psychiatric Complications

There is strong research evidence that the various elements of Therapeutic Lifestyle Change are effective not just in the treatment of depression, but also in the reduction of symptoms across a number of other psychological domains. TLC can reduce anxiety, soothe irritability, put the brakes on impulsive behavior, weaken addictive cravings, and tighten erratic thinking.

Nevertheless, some forms of mental illness may make it difficult to fully recover from depression until they're directly addressed in treatment by a skilled clinician. The more common such co-occurring conditions are described in this section.

Post-Traumatic Stress Disorder (PTSD). Following severe trauma, many people suffer PTSD—a painful syndrome that involves intrusive traumatic memories and nightmares, emotional numbing, relentless tension, extreme vigilance, exaggerated startle reflex, and avoidance of people and situations associated with the trauma. Because PTSD keeps the brain's stress response circuits in overdrive, it can powerfully interfere with recovery from depression. Fortunately, the disorder has a high rate of treatment response to skilled psychotherapy.

Other anxiety disorders. Despite TLC's ability to reduce overall anxiety, several specific anxiety disorders usually require a more focused intervention to bring about full recovery. These include obsessive-compulsive disorder, panic disorder, agoraphobia, social anxiety disorder, and specific phobias. All can be successfully treated in the majority of cases by behavior therapy, with a focus on gradual exposure and habituation to anxiety-producing stimuli.*

Substance abuse and dependence. Alcohol and other drugs of addiction have an array of harmful effects on brain function, and they typically also bring about high levels of depressive life stress. They also wreak havoc on the user's social support net-

* A related form of treatment, CBT, is also effective for most anxiety disorders.

harmful core beliefs, or *schemas,* about oneself and others; such schemas cause extraordinary suffering, and they can make it impossible to form satisfying relationships.

TAKING ANTIDEPRESSANT LIFESTYLE TO THE NEXT LEVEL

As we've seen, our remote hunter-gatherer ancestors were extraordinarily resilient in the face of difficult life circumstances, and largely free from the scourge of depressive illness. They were protected by a set of habits that benefit the brain more powerfully than any known antidepressant medication. The Therapeutic Lifestyle Change program is designed to help people reclaim this protective legacy from the ancestral past. It's a treatment approach based on the best research findings from clinical labs around the world, an approach that's proven effective for the great majority of depressed patients who put it into practice.

However, the TLC program was designed with an important consideration in mind: I wanted to make sure the treatment was truly doable, that depressed patients would actually be able to make the changes I was asking of them. As a result, I ended up leaving some potentially helpful things out of the basic program—despite good research support for their ability to fight depression—simply because I didn't want to overwhelm patients with too many lifestyle changes to juggle all at once.

So, while the standard TLC regimen is already highly effective for most people, some additional strategies may prove helpful if your depressive symptoms have not fully cleared up after you've made each of the treatment's recommended lifestyle changes.

It's possible, in other words, for you to *take antidepressant lifestyle change to the next level*, provided you're willing to put even more time and effort into the process of recovery. In this section I describe the several options worth considering.

Upping the Exercise Dose

Whereas our hunter-gatherer forebears engaged in vigorous physical activity for several hours each day, the TLC protocol calls for a total of only ninety minutes of aerobic exercise each week. Frankly, that's a low dose of exercise, given the robust antidepressant effect of physical activity on the brain. Although this modest amount of exercise is still potently antidepressant, many people would likely experience even greater clinical benefit from a higher level of activity.

According to fitness researchers, the beneficial effects of exercise on the body steadily increase as we ramp up our weekly workout time—yielding more energy, better cardiac and pulmonary function, improved metabolism, and so on. Remarkably, the health dividends of exercise appear to increase up to a dose of at least an hour each day.

Several years ago I decided to experiment with a more ambitious workout regimen myself, mostly so I could see firsthand if it really made any noticeable difference. I went from exercising 30 minutes every other day to working out 45 to 60 minutes each day, and the effects were immediate and compelling: My sleep quality, energy level, stamina, calmness, mental clarity, and sense of well-being all significantly improved. The benefits proved well worth the extra time investment, so I've stayed with it. Now, if I skip even a single daily workout, the next day I'll feel relatively sluggish, antsy, and just not as sharp.

Researchers have yet to study the effectiveness of such a "high dose" exercise regimen in combating depression (in part, because it's difficult to get people to volunteer for that much exercise). But I have no doubt the added activity is beneficial for the brain, just as it's already proven to be for the rest of the body. So, if you're already getting ninety minutes of aerobic activity each week (as recommended in the standard TLC protocol), you might want to consider bumping it up—experimenting with gradually higher levels of activity for the next several weeks to see if you notice a difference in your depressive symptoms (and other dimensions of well-being). I recommend adding an extra sixty minutes or so to your routine each week, until you're up to 45 minutes of exercise each day (roughly three hundred minutes a week).

Increase Omega-3

The starting omega-3 dosage recommended in the TLC protocol—1000 mg of EPA per day—is adequate for most people, but it's not high enough to get everyone's blood levels of omega-6 and omega-3 fats in balance. Even some who try doubling this standard dosage still won't achieve the proper fatty acid ratio for optimal brain function. As we saw in Chapter 4, the only way to ensure this ideal balance is with a blood test, which will allow your doctor to evaluate the ratio of omega-6 and omega-3 fats in your blood plasma. (Remember, the target ratio is 2 to 1.) Although having your blood drawn is inconvenient, it can help ensure that your brain is getting all the omega-3 fats it needs.

Decrease Dietary Sugar

As we've seen, chronic inflammation—the body's immune response running amok—is a major culprit in depressive illness. It's an insidious process that, over time, ravages both body and brain. And even though we can help get the body's inflammation response under control by increasing our intake of omega-3 fats, a dangerous pro-inflammatory villain is lurking at the heart of the modern Western diet: sugar.

The typical American now consumes a staggering eighty pounds of processed sugars* each year. That's twenty-five teaspoons of sugar—the equivalent of four hundred calories—every day. This ubiquitous sweetener now makes up an unfathomable 20% of our diets. And each little white grain carries the potential to nudge the brain a little further away from the state of healthful balance needed to break the grip of depressive illness. (Please note that the natural sugars found in fruits and vegetables pose no such hazards to the brain.)

Unfortunately, neuroscientists have discovered that sugar is potently addictive. It can light up the brain's pleasure centers in a manner similar to cocaine or heroin. This makes the "sugar habit" incredibly difficult to break. Most of us have been hooked on the stuff since childhood.

But it *is* possible to cut way back on sugar intake—enough to reduce the sweetener's potential depressive impact—with just a bit of effort. It's simply a matter of finding reasonable, satisfying substitutes for the major sources of sugar in your diet: the soft drinks, candy, ice cream, juices, snack bars, breakfast cereals, and other assorted sweets.

---

* This figure includes related sugary sweeteners like high-fructose corn syrup.

Although simply switching to soft drinks and snacks laced with artificial sweeteners might seem like an obvious strategy, I'm hesitant to recommend this approach. Instead, I recommend substituting natural, healthy alternatives to the refined sugars in your diet. For example, honey is *anti*-inflammatory, and it has an array of other health benefits. (It's antibiotic, antiviral, and even seems to help protect against adult-onset diabetes.) And while it's probably not a good idea to eat honey by the bucketful—"everything in moderation" is a great nutritional rule of thumb—using a little to sweeten your drinks, and the occasional snack, will certainly help take the sting out of eating less sugar. Other natural sweeteners to keep in mind include *stevia* (also known as *sweetleaf*), a South American herb that's actually a little sweeter than sugar, and *Xylitol*, a plant derivative now recommended by dentists to help fight cavities.

Fortunately, as you work to eliminate the major sources of refined sugar from your diet, you'll notice that fruits and other whole foods will begin to taste much sweeter. (In essence, your taste buds will quickly recalibrate, so that fruit starts to taste about as sweet as chocolate bars and cakes used to.) This happy development, in turn, will make it much easier to continue keeping refined sugar intake to a minimum.

Eat More Tryptophan

The brain makes its entire supply of serotonin, a feel-good neurotransmitter, out of a protein called *tryptophan*. Most of us get plenty of tryptophan in our diets; it's found in abundance in meats like turkey, chicken, beef, pork, and fish, as well as cheese, eggs, milk, beans, and soy products. But when we're severely strained, stress hormones can limit the amount of tryptophan available to the brain, which in turn causes serotonin activity in the brain to plummet. This can, in turn, trigger a vicious feedback loop: Depression causes elevated stress hormones, which suppress tryptophan levels in the bloodstream, which reduce serotonin activity in the brain, which deepens the depression, and so on.

One way to help break this cycle is to increase dietary tryptophan intake—to eat several servings of meat, eggs, dairy, and soy products each day. Another alternative is to take a tryptophan supplement, a strategy with some research support in fighting depression. (A typical dose in published studies is 1 to 3 grams daily.) However, because there have been alarming reports of life-threatening impurities found in over-the-counter tryptophan supplements, I'm not a huge fan of going that route. Although there is a safe, high-dose form of the protein available as a prescription "drug", a potentially better option is to take 200–300 mg daily of an over-the-counter supplement called 5-HTP. This is a modified version of tryptophan that's more easily converted to serotonin. Please note that even though 5-HTP is sold without a prescription, it should only be taken under medical supervision. It can occasionally cause serious side effects, especially when taken together with antidepressants or other medications that influence serotonin signaling.

Acetyl-L-Carnitine

Acetyl-l-carnitine (ALC), a nutrient derived from the amino acid carnitine, plays a critical role in regulating the brain's

stressors, our ability to cope with them successfully will determine whether or not we keep depression at bay.

The most effective coping strategy—by far—involves turning to loved ones, friends, and extended community for intensive social support. As we've seen, the physical and emotional presence of others provides a powerful safety cue for the brain, coaxing it to put the brakes on its stress response circuits even in the face of painful life circumstances. As a result, social support is a potent buffer against the experience of depression.

Then again, not everyone is lucky enough to have such a protective network in place. But it turns out that even *one* caring, committed individual can make all the difference—even if that person is a clinician you see for only one or two sessions a week.

In many cases, our ability to cope with difficult events also hinges on the way we interpret them. Sometimes things are not as catastrophic as we think they are. Good psychotherapists are highly trained to help their depressed patients see such stressful situations in a less dire light. But a good friend or loved one can sometimes play a similar role—pointing out the subtle and not-so-subtle ways that depression might cause a situation to look bleaker than it truly is.

I've also seen many individuals find enormous comfort and strength through participation in a faith community. And the benefit often goes far beyond the wonderful social support such communities can provide. It also comes from adopting an interpretive point of view that says, in effect, "As agonizing as this situation seems right now, there's a mysterious way in which it's not as bad as I think it is." I've also witnessed several of my patients find a similarly helpful reinterpretation of stressful circumstances through the practice of mindfulness meditation,* which helps promote a deep, radical acceptance of each moment life presents us with.

The principles of Therapeutic Lifestyle Change have proven to be extraordinarily effective in treating depression in patients of all ages. Equally important, however, is their ability to protect against the future onset of illness.

Remember, we were never designed for the sedentary, socially isolated, sleep-deprived, poorly nourished, indoor, frenetic pace of modern American life. Our brains, our bodies, our minds, our hearts, and our souls were all built for something different—for a life filled with abundant physical activity, social connection, healthful sleep, balanced nutrition, natural sunlight, and the sort of meaningful, engaging activities that leave little time for depressive rumination. By living the lives we were meant to lead, reclaiming the protective features of the past and integrating them into the present, we can overcome depression for the long haul. We can vanquish that treacherous foe once and for all. We can live the depression cure.

* An increasingly popular technique now taught around the world. There are also several superb instructional books on mindfulness meditation, including classics such as Jon Kabat-Zinn's *Full Catastrophe Living* and *Wherever You Go, There You Are*, and Thich Nhat Hahn's *The Miracle of Mindfulness*. Likewise, some popular mobile phone apps, such as Calm and Headspace, are available to guide you through mindfulness meditation exercises.

Appendix A: Depression Scale

Following is a list of some ways you may have felt or behaved. Please make a copy and indicate how often you experienced these things *during the past week* (circle one number on each line):

During the past week . . .	Rarely or none of the time (< 1 day)	Some (a little of the time) (1–2 days)	At least half the time (3–4 days)	Just about all the time (5–7 days)
1. I was bothered by things that usually don't bother me.	0	1	2	3
2. I did not feel like eating; my appetite was poor.	0	1	2	3
3. I could not shake off the blues, even with others' help.	0	1	2	3
4. I felt that I was just as good as other people.	3	2	1	0
5. I had trouble keeping my mind on what I was doing.	0	1	2	3
6. I felt depressed.	0	1	2	3
7. I felt that everything I did was an effort.	0	1	2	3
8. I felt hopeful about the future.	3	2	1	0
9. I thought my life had been a failure.	0	1	2	3

10. I felt fearful.	0	1	2	3
11. My sleep was restless.	0	1	2	3
12. I was happy.	3	2	1	0
13. I talked less than usual.	0	1	2	3
14. I felt lonely.	0	1	2	3
15. People were unfriendly.	0	1	2	3
16. I enjoyed life.	3	2	1	0
17. I had crying spells.	0	1	2	3
18. I felt sad.	0	1	2	3
19. I felt that people disliked me.	0	1	2	3
20. I could not "get going."	0	1	2	3

Scoring: Your score is the sum of all 20 circled numbers.

Center for Epidemiological Studies Depression Scale (CES-D). Radloff, LS (1977). The CES-D scale is a self-report depression scale for research in the general population. *Applied Psychological Measurement, 1,* 385–401.

Appendix B. Tracking Chart for Depression Symptoms

Please make a copy of the following grid, and then record your depression scale score (from Appendix A) on the grid to help track your symptoms through each week of the Therapeutic Lifestyle Change program.

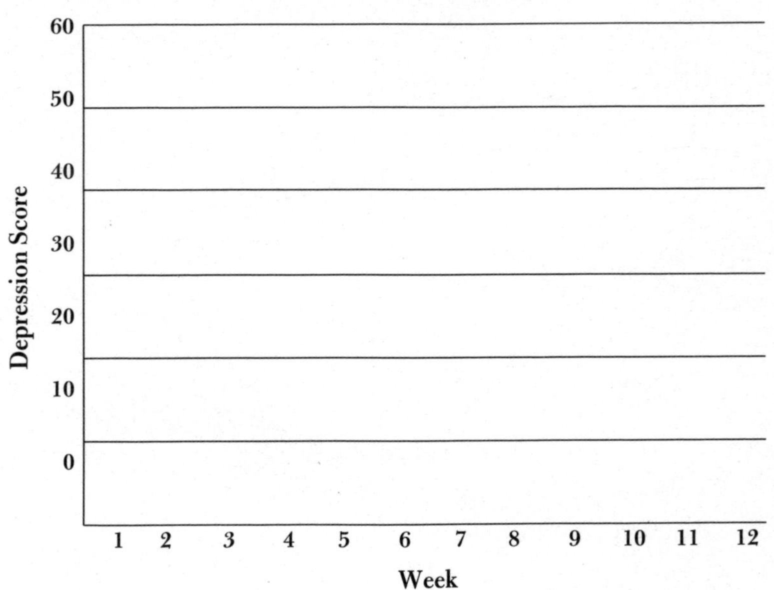

Notes

CHAPTER 1: THE EPIDEMIC AND THE CURE

4 **They work for fewer than half.** Nierenberg et al., 2008. Boren et al., 2009.

4 **The US and UK hasn't declined: It's increased.** Mojtabai & Jorn, 2015.

4 **Nearly one in three Americans.** Kessler et al., 2012.

4 **Roughly ten times higher today.** Seligman, 1990.

5 **Amish communities have a rate of depression.** Egeland and Hostetter, 1983. More recent evidence comes from the work of Miller et al., 2007.

5 **Across the entire industrialized world.** Hidaka, 2012.

5 **Fraction of that observed in the West.** Weissman et al., 1996.

5 **Anthropologist Edward Schieffelin.** Schieffelin, 1985.

6 **Until about twelve thousand years ago.** Diamond, 1997.

6 **They've changed very little.** Tooby and Cosmides, 1990.

6 **A staggering 70%.** Fryar et al., 2016.

7 **A mere 4%.** Rampersaud et al., 2008.

9 **Over three times higher.** Karwoski, 2008; Ilardi et al., 2007; Ilardi et al., 2009.

10 **More omega-3 fat than we do.** Simopoulos, 2006.

10 **Countries with the highest levels.** Peet, 2004.

11 **British researchers recently studied.** Peet and Horrobin, 2002

13 **Remarkably good shape.** Cordain et al., 1998.

14 **Compared aerobic exercise and Lustral.** Blumenthal et al., 1999. The finding was later replicated by Blumenthal et al., 2007.

14 **To become depressed again.** Babyak et al., 2000.

17 **Winter daylight is scarce.** Mersch et al., 1999.

18 **The typical village.** Dunbar, 1996.

21 **Lack a supportive social network.** Harris, 2001.

21 **Disrupted sleep is one.** Thase, 2005.

21 **80% of depressed patients.** Armitage, 2000.

22 **About 10 hours a night.** Bower, 1999.

22 **American adults clock in.** Sleep in America Foundation, 2008.
25 **Our clinical trials.** Ilardi et al., 2007; Karwoski, 2008; Ilardi et al., 2009.

CHAPTER 2: MAKING SENSE OF DEPRESSION

33 **Brain's runaway stress response.** Nemeroff and Vale, 2005.
34 **When the stress response lasts.** Steiger, 2007.
35 **The illness is most often triggered.** Hammen, 2005.
36 **Left frontal hemisphere.** Henriques and Davidson, 1991; Coan & Allen, 2003.
37 **Actually start shrinking.** Frodl et al., 2008.
38 **Rats are experimentally deprived.** Rechtschaffen et al., 2002.
39 **The best studies.** Hamet and Tremblay, 2005, for example.
40 **A large landmark study of New Zealanders.** Caspi et al., 2003.
40 **Social support networks.** Harris, 2001.
40 **British team of researchers.** Brown and Harris, 1978.
41 **Emotionally abusive spouse.** Harris, 2001.
41 **Prone to depression.** Nolen-Hoeksema et al., 2008.
41 **Researchers have found that estrogen.** MacQueen and Chokka, 2004.
42 **Testosterone has been strongly linked.** Seidman, 2003.
43 **Exercise changes the brain.** Ploughman, 2008.
44 **It rises to well over 50%.** Mueller et al., 1999.
44 **Toxic imprint on the brain.** Post, 1992.

CHAPTER 3: TREATING DEPRESSION

48 **Over 300 million antidepressant prescriptions.** Stagnitti, 2008.
49 **Only 23% were depression-free.** Corey-Lisle et al., 2004.
49 **Only 28% of study patients.** Trivedi et al., 2006. This was the remission rate observed with a widely used clinician-based rating scale; the rate with a patient self-report scale was similar, but slightly higher.
50 **He found that in 56%.** Kirsch et al., 2002.
51 **Among severely depressed patients.** Khan et al., 2002.
52 **Roughly half of all depressed patients.** Trivedi et al., 2006 (NEJM—augmentation article).
53 **Up to 50%.** Mueller et al., 1999.
53 **Goes off his or her prescribed medications.** Olfson et al., 2006.
54 **Combed through their database.** www.fda.gov/cder/drug/antidepressants
55 **It may afflict the majority.** Opbroek et al., 2002.

56 **Many people taking SSRIs.** Werneke et al., 2006.
56 **Potential to cause insomnia.** Mayers and Baldwin, 2005.
59 **CBT is every bit as effective.** Parker et al., 2008.
59 **Leads to complete recovery.** DeRubeis et al., 2005; Keller et al., 2000.
60 **A group of clinicians** Dimidjian et al., 2006.
63 **A definitive set of studies.** Svartberg and Stiles, 1991.
64 **As high as 65%.** Husain et al., 2004.
64 **Most ECT patients.** Odeberg et al., 2008.
65 **Permanent brain damage.** Reviewed in Breggin, 1999.
65 **Up to 70%.** Freeman & Kendell, 1986. More recently, Sackeim et al., 2007, observed compelling evidence of enduring memory deficits following ECT in the most rigorous study of the issue to date.
65 **Drop in IQ.** Lipman et al., 1993.
66 **Sales of antidepressant drugs.** IMS MIDAS®, MAT December 2006.

CHAPTER 4: BRAIN FOOD

72 **Insanely high doses.** Page et al., 1999.
72 **Supplementing their diets.** Carzelon et al., 2005.
73 **Our hunter-gatherer ancestors.** Simopoulos, 2006.
73 **A staggering 16 to 1.** Simopoulos, 2002.
74 **"Civilized" early farmers.** Cohen, 1989.
74 **Brains even grew smaller.** Ruff et al., 1997.
75 **Consumption of omega-6 fats.** Pollan, 2008.
76 **Depression tends to be less common.** Peet, 2004.
76 **Lower omega-3 blood levels.** Peet et al., 1998.
77 **The message of serotonin.** Chalon, 2006; McNamara and Carlson, 2006.
77 **Scramble dopamine signals.** McNamara and Carlson, 2006; Chalon, 2006.
78 **Inflammation is also one.** Miller, 2009 (in press).
80 **Published research so far.** Reviewed in Ross et al., 2007.
82 **Help stabilize heart rhythm.** Masuelli et al., 2008.
82 **The best supported daily dosage.** Ross et al., 2007.
87 **Cut back its production of GLA.** Sears, 2007.
89 **Help suppress some allergic reactions.** Miyake et al., 2007.
89 **Ratio on this blood test.** www.drsears.com/tabid/399/itemid/68/AAEPA-Blood-Test-Services
91 **Ratios barely budged.** Young et al., 2005.
91 **Their rates of depression.** Hibbeln, 1989.

CHAPTER 5: DON'T THINK, DO

101 **Amplify negative emotions.** Ciesla and Roberts, 2007.
101 **When we ruminate.** Moulds et al., 2007.
102 **Link between depression and rumination.** Nolen-Hoeksema et al., 2008.
103 **Some surprising quirks.** Marcus, 2008.
103 **Brain uses our mood.** Duncan and Barrett, 2007.
108 **Study of depressed teenagers.** Rose et al., 2007.

CHAPTER 6: ANTIDEPRESSANT EXERCISE

125 **Several hours each day.** Cordain et al., 1998.
126 **Long list of health benefits.** Penedo and Dahn, 2005.
127 **Ambitious study of exercise.** Blumenthal et al., 1999.
127 **Stimulates the brain's release.** Vaynman and Gomez-Pinilla, 2006.
130 **Researchers have looked.** Barbour et al., 2007.
137 **Exercising with others.** Blumenthal et al., 2007. Those exercising in a group setting had better outcomes than those working out alone, but the difference between the two groups was not statistically significant.

CHAPTER 7: LET THERE BE LIGHT

148 **Over one hundred times brighter.** Eastman, 1990.
149 **The production of serotonin.** Praschak-Rieder et al., 2008.
150 **More social contact.** Aan Het Rot et al., 2008. This study also observed an effect of bright light in rendering people less quarrelsome and less prone to fighting.
151 **Study of Montreal residents.** Guillemette et al., 1998.
152 **The average American.** Rosen and Rosenthal, 1991.
153 **It's been evaluated.** Golden et al., 2005.
153 **Yields even better results.** Lam et al., 2006.
157 **Blue light turns out.** Wu et al., 2006.
168 **The mood-elevating effects.** Goel and Etwaroo, 2006.
169 **Hundreds of genes.** Marhsall, 2008.
170 **Low blood levels.** Health News, 2008.
170 **Intruiging clinical trial.** Gloth et al., 1999.
171 **Vitamin D deficient.** Holick, 2009.
172 **Canadian medical researchers.** Vieth et al., 2001.
172 **Patients taking 1000 mcg.** Kimball et al., 2007.

CHAPTER 8: GET CONNECTED

177 **They're exquisitely attuned.** Newton, 2008.
178 **"Alone time" is virtually unknown.** For example, Chagnon, 1996.
178 **Nearly 25% of Americans.** McPherson et al., 2006.
180 **Enhances social connectedness.** Harris, 2001.
181 **Compared with our counterparts.** Putnam, 2000.
181 **Recent landmark study.** McPherson et al., 2006.
191 **Psychologists have documented.** Leiberg and Anders, 2006.
192 **Joint rumination is.** Byrd-Craven et al., 2008.
200 **Science of Well-Being.** New York Times, January 7, 2007.
203 **Interesting line of research.** Dunbar, 1996.

CHAPTER 9: HABITS OF HEALTHY SLEEP

208 **Adverse effects start.** See, for example, Chee and Chuah, 2008.
208 **Physical exercise profoundly improves.** Dworak et al., 2008.
209 **Most adults need.** Dement, 2000.
209 **The average American.** Sleep in America Foundation, 2008.
209 **Over 90% of Americans.** Lovett, 2005.
216 **A sleep meter.** Dement, 2000.
227 **Some common antidepressant medications.** Mayers and Baldwin, 2005.

CHAPTER 10: PUTTING IT ALL TOGETHER

242 **Our TLC patients.** Ilardi et al., 2007; 2009.
242 **Rate of relapse.** Mueller et al., 1999.

CHAPTER 11: WHEN ROADBLOCKS EMERGE

250 **Left frontal cortex.** Henriques and Davidson, 1991.
258 **Medical illness can.** Gill and Hatcher, 2007.
259 **Drugs commonly used.** Dhondt et al., 1999.
260 **Reduce anxiety.** Knapen et al., in press.
260 **Soothe irritability.** Sagduyu et al., 2005.
260 **Impulsive behavior.** Hallahan et al., 2007.
260 **Addictive cravings.** Hosseini et al., in press.
260 **Erratic thinking.** Wu et al., 2008.
261 **Depression in bipolar disorder.** Stoll et al., 1999.
264 **According to fitness researchers.** Blair et al., 2004.

266 **Sugar is potently addictive.** Lenoir et al., 2007.
268 **Amount of tryptophan.** Russo et al., 2003.
269 **One study.** Vieth et al., 2001.

Bibliography

Aan Het Rot, M., D. S. Moskowitz, and S. N Young. "Exposure to bright light is associated with positive social interaction and good mood over short time periods: A naturalistic study in mildly seasonal people." *Journal of Psychiatric Research,* 42 (2008): 311–319.

American Psychiatric Association. *Diagnostic and statistical manual of mental disorders: DSM-IV-TR. 4th ed., text revision.* Washington, DC (2000).

Andrade, L., J. J. Caraveo-Anduaga, P. Berglund, R. V. Bijl, R. De Graaf, W. Vollebergh, E. Dragomirecka, R. Kohn, M. Keller, R. C. Kessler, N. Kawakami, C. Kilic, D. Offord, T. B. Ustun, and H. U. Wittchen. "The epidemiology of major depressive episodes: Results from the International Consortium of Psychiatric Epidemiology (ICPE) Surveys." *International Journal of Methods in Psychiatric Research,* 12 (2003): 3–21.

Armitage, R. *Canadian Journal of Psychiatry,* 45 (2000): 803–809.

Babyak M., J. A. Blumenthal, S. Herman, P. Khatri, M. Doraiswamy, K. Moore, W. E. Craighead, T. T. Baldewicz, and K. R. Krishnan. "Exercise Treatment for Major Depression: Maintenance of Therapeutic Benefit at 10 Months." *Psychosomatic Medicine,* 62 (2000): 633–638.

Barbour K. A., T. M. Edenfield, and J. A. Blumenthal. "Exercise as a Treatment for Depression and Other Psychiatric Disorders: A Review." *Journal of Cardiopulmonary Rehabilitation and Prevention,* 27 (2007): 359–367.

Blair S. N., M. J. LaMonte, and M. Z. Nichaman. "The Evolution of Physical Activity Recommendations: How Much Is Enough?" *American Journal of Clinical Nutrition,* 79 (2004): 913S–920S.

Blumenthal J. A., M. A. Babyak, P. M. Doraiswamy, L. Watkins, B. M. Hoffman, K. A. Barbour, S. Herman, W. E. Craighead, A. L. Brosse, R. Waugh, A. Hinderliter, and A. Sherwood. "Exercise and Pharmacotherapy in the Treatment of Major Depressive Disorder." *Psychosomatic Medicine,* 69 (2007): 587–596.

Blumenthal J. A., M. A. Babyak, K. A. Moore, W. E. Craighead, S. Herman, P. Khatri, R. Waugh, M. A. Napolitano, L. M. Forman, M. Appelbaum, P. M. Doraiswamy, and K. R. Krishnan. "Effects of Exercise Training on Older Patients with Major Depression." *Archives of Internal Medicine,* 159 (1999): 2349–2356.

Bower, B. "Slumber's Unexplored Landscape." *Science News, 156* (1999): 205.

Brown, G. W. and T. O. Harris. *Social Origins of Depression*. London: Tavistock, 1978.

Breggin, P. R. "Electroshock: Scientific, Ethical, and Political Issues." *International Journal of Risk & Safety in Medicine*, 11 (1999):5–40.

Byrd-Craven, J., D. C. Geary, A. J. Rose, and D. Ponzi. "Co-ruminating Increases Stress Hormone Levels in Women." *Hormones and Behavior,* 53 (2008): 489–492.

Carlezon, W. A. Jr, S. D. Mague, A. M. Parow, A. L. Stoll, B. M. Cohen, and P. F. Renshaw. "Antidepressant-like Effects of Uridine and Omega-3 Fatty Acids Are Potentiated by Combined Treatment in Rats." *Biological Psychiatry,* 57 (2005): 343–350.

Caspi, A., K. Sugden, T. E. Moffitt, A. Taylor, I. W. Craig, H. Harrington, J. McClay, J. Mill, J. Martin, A. Braithwaite, and R. Poulton. "Influence of Life Stress on Depression: Moderation by a Polymorphism in the 5-HTT Gene." *Science,* 301 (2003): 386–389.

Chagnon, N. A. *Yanomamo*. New York: Harcourt Brace, 1996.

Chalon, S. "Omega-3 Fatty Acids and Monoamine Neurotransmission." *Prostaglandins, Leukotrienes, and Essential Fatty Acids,* 75 (2006): 259–269.

Chee, M. W. and L. Y. Chuah. "Functional Neuroimaging Insights into How Sleep and Sleep Deprivation Affect Memory and Cognition." *Current Opinions in Neurology,* 21 (2008): 417–423.

Ciesla, J. A. and J. E. Roberts. "Rumination, Negative Cognition, and Their Interactive Effects on Depressed Mood." *Emotion,* 7 (2007): 555–565.

Coan J. A.and J. J. Allen. "Frontal EEG Asymmetry and the Behavioral Activation and Inhibition Systems." *Psychophysiology*, 40 (2003):106–114.

Cohen, M. N. *Health and the Rise of Civilization*. New Haven: Yale University Press, 1989.

Compton, W. M., K. P. Conway, F. S. Stinson, and B. F. Grant. "Changes in the Prevalence of Major Depression and Comorbid Substance Use Disorders in the United States between 1991–1992 and 2001–2002." *American Journal of Psychiatry,* 163 (2006): 2141–2147.

Cordain L., R. W. Gotshall, S. B. Eaton, and S. B. Eaton 3rd. "Physical Activity, Energy Expenditure and Fitness: An Evolutionary Perspective." *International Journal of Sports Medicine,* 19 (1998): 328–335.

Corey-Lisle, P. K., R. Nash, P. Stang, and R. Swindle. "Response, Partial Response, and Nonresponse in Primary Care Treatment of Depression." *Archives of Internal Medicine,* 164 (2004): 1197–1204.

Dement, W. C. *The Promise of Sleep*. New York: Dell, 2000.

DeRubeis, R. J., S. D. Hollon, J. D. Amsterdam, R. C. Shelton, P. R. Young, R. M. Salomon, J. P. O'Reardon, M. L. Lovett, M. M. Gladis, L. L. Brown, and R. Gallop. "Cognitive Therapy versus Medications in the Treatment of Moderate to Severe Depression." *Archives of General Psychiatry,* 62 (2005): 409–416.

Dhondt, T., P. Derksen, C. Hooijer, B. Van Heycop Ten Ham, P. P. Van Gen, and T. Heeren. "Depressogenic Medication as an Aetiological Factor in Major Depression: An Analysis in a Clinical Population of Depressed Elderly People." *International Journal of Geriatric Psychiatry,* 14 (1999): 875–881.

Diamond J. *Guns, Germs and Steel: The Fates of Human Societies*. New York: Random House, 1997.

Dimidjian, S., S. D. Hollon, K. S. Dobson, K. B. Schmaling, R. J. Kohlenberg, M. E. Addis, R. Gallop, J. B. McGlinchey, D. K. Markley, J. K. Gollan, D. C. Atkins, D. L. Dunner, and N. S. Jacobson. "Randomized Trial of Behavioral Activation, Cognitive Therapy, and Antidepressant Medication in the Acute Treatment of Adults with Major Depression." *Journal of Consulting and Clinical Psychology*, 74 (2006): 658–670.

Duncan, S. and L. F. Barrett. "Affect Is a Form of Cognition: A Neurobiological Analysis." *Cognition and Emotion,* 21 (2007):1184–1211.

Dworak, M., A. Wiater, D. Alfer, E. Stephan, W. Hollmann, and H. K. Strüder. "Increased Slow Wave Sleep and Reduced Stage 2 Sleep in Children Depending on Exercise Intensity." *Sleep Medicine,* 9 (2008):266–272.

Eastman, C. I. "Natural Summer and Winter Sunlight Exposure Patterns in Seasonal Affective Disorder." *Physiology and Behavior,* 48 (1990): 611–616.

Egeland, J. A. and A. M. Hostetter. "Amish Study, I: Affective disorders among the Amish, 1976–1980." *American Journal of Psychiatry,* 140 (1983): 56–61.

Freeman C. and R. Kendell. Patients' experience of and attitudes to electroconvulsive therapy. *Annals of the New York Academy of Sciences*, 462 (1986): 341–352.

Frodl, T. S., N. Koutsouleris, R. Bottlender, C. Born, M. Jäger, I. Scupin, M. Reiser, H. J. Möller, and E. M. Meisenzahl. "Depression-Related Variation in Brain Morphology over Three Years: Effects of Stress?" *Archives of General Psychiatry,* 65 (2008): 1156–1165.

Gill, D. and S. Hatcher. "Withdrawn: Antidepressants for Depression in Medical Illness." *Cochrane Database of Systematic Reviews,* Jul 18;(4) (2007): CD001312.

Gloth, F. M. 3rd, W. Alam, and B. Hollis. "Vitamin D versus Broad Spectrum Phototherapy in the Treatment of Seasonal Affective Disorder." *Journal of Nutrition, Health, and Aging,* 3 (1999): 5–7.

Goel, N. and G. R. Etwaroo. "Bright Light, Negative Air Ions and Auditory Stimuli Produce Rapid Mood Changes in a Student Population: A Placebo-Controlled Study." *Psychological Medicine,* 36 (2006): 1253–1263.

Golden, R. N., B. N. Gaynes, R. D. Ekstrom, R. M. Hamer, F. M. Jacobsen, T. Suppes, K. L. Wisner, and C. B. Nemeroff. "The Efficacy of Light Therapy in the Treatment of Mood Disorders: A Review and Meta-analysis of the Evidence." American *Journal of Psychiatry,* 162 (2005): 656–662.

Guillemette, J., M. Hébert, J. Paquet, and M. Dumont. "Natural Bright Light Exposure in the Summer and Winter in Subjects with and without Complaints of Seasonal Mood Variations." *Biological Psychiatry,* 44 (1998): 622–628.

Hallahan, B., J. R. Hibbeln, J. M. Davis, and M. R. Garland. "Omega-3 Fatty Acid Supplementation in Patients with Recurrent Self-Harm. Single-Centre Double-Blind Randomised Controlled Trial." *British Journal of Psychiatry,* 190 (2007): 118–122.

Hamet, P. and J. Tremblay. "Genetics and Genomics of Depression." *Metabolism,* 54 (5 Suppl 1) (2005): 10–15.

Hammen, C. "Stress and Depression." *Annual Review of Clinical Psychology,* 1 (2005): 293–319.

Harris, T. "Recent Developments in Understanding the Psychosocial Aspects of Depression." *British Medical Bulletin,* 57 (2001): 17–32.

Health News. "Check Your Vitamin D Intake to Avoid Multiple Health Consequences. Three 2008 Studies Link Low Vitamin D Levels to Depression, Hip Fractures, and Increased Risk of Death." Volume 14 (2008): 9–10.

Henriques, J. B. and R. J. Davidson. "Left Frontal Hypoactivation in Depression." *Journal of Abnormal Psychology,* 100 (1991): 535–545.

Hibbeln, J. R. "Fish Consumption and Major Depression." *Lancet,* 351 (1998): 1213.

Holick, M. F. "Vitamin D Status: Measurement, Interpretation, and Clinical Application." *Annals of Epidemiology,* 19 (2009): 73–78.

Hosseini, M., H. A. Alaei, A. Naderi, M. R. Sharifi, and R. Zahed. "Treadmill Exercise Reduces Self-Administration of Morphine in Male Rats. *Pathophysiology* (in press).

Howland, R. H, B. Lebowitz, P. J. McGrath, K. Shores-Wilson, M. M. Biggs, G. K. Balasubramani, and M. Fava; STAR*D Study Team. "Evaluation of Outcomes with Citalopram for Depression Using Measurement-based Care in STAR*D: Implications for Clinical Practice." *American Journal of Psychiatry,* 163 (2006): 28–40.

Husain M.M., A. J. Rush, M. Fink, R. Knapp, G. Petrides, T. Rummans, M. M. Biggs, K. O'Connor, K. Rasmussen, M. Litle, W. Zhao, H. J. Bernstein, G. Smith, M. Mueller, S. M. McClintock, S. H. Bailine, C. H. Kellner. "Speed of Response and Remission in Major Depressive Disorder with Acute Electroconvulsive Therapy (ECT): A Consortium for Research in ECT (CORE) Report." *Journal of Clinical Psychiatry*, 65 (2004):485–91.

Ilardi, S. S., J. D. Jacobson, K. A. Lehman, B. A. Stites, L. Karwoski, N. N. Stroupe, D. K. Steidtmann, A. K. Hirani, J. A. Prohaska, B. Sampat, and C. Young. "Therapeutic Lifestyle Change for Depression: Results from a Randomized Controlled Trial." Presented at the annual meeting of the Association for Behavioral and Cognitive Therapy, Philadelphia (November 2007).

Ilardi, S. S., L. Karwoski, K. A. Lehman, B. A. Stites, and D. Steidtmann. "We Were Never Designed for This: The Depression Epidemic and the Promise of Therapeutic Lifestyle Change." Manuscript under review (2009).

Karwoski, L. "Therapeutic Lifestyle Change: Piloting a Novel Group-Based Intervention for Depression." Doctoral dissertation, University of Kansas (2008).

Keller, M., J. McCullough, D. Klein, B. Arnow, D. Dunner, A. Gelenberg, et al. "A Comparison of Nefazodone, the Cognitive Behavioral Analysis System of Psychotherapy, and Their Combination for the Treatment of Chronic Depression." *New England Journal of Medicine,* 342 (2000): 162–171.

Kessler, R. C., P. Berglund, O. Demler, R. Jin, and E. E. Walters. "Lifetime Prevalence and Age-of-Onset Distributions of DSM-IV Disorders in the National Comorbidity Survey Replication." *Archives of General Psychiatry,* 62 (2005): 593–602.

Khan, A., R. M. Leventhal, S. R. Khan, and W. A. Brown. "Severity of Depression and Response to Antidepressants and Placebo: An analysis of the Food and Drug Administration Database." *Journal of Clinical Psychopharmacology,* 22: 40–45.

Kimball, S. M., M. R. Ursell, P. O'Connor, and R. Vieth. "Safety of Vitamin D3 in Adults with Multiple Sclerosis." *American Journal of Clinical Nutrition,* 86 (2007): 645–651.

Kirsch, I., T. J. Moore, A. Scoboria, and S. S. Nicholls. "The Emperor's New Drugs: An Analysis of Antidepressant Medication Data Submitted to the U.S. Food and Drug Administration." *Prevention & Treatment,* 5, Article 23 (2002).

Knapen, J., E. Sommerijns, D. Vancampfort, P. Sienaert, G. Pieters, P. Haake, M. Probst, and J. Peuskens. "State Anxiety and Subjective Well-Being Responses to Acute Bouts of Aerobic Exercise in Patients with Depressive and Anxiety Disorders." *British Journal of Sports Medicine* (in press).

Lam, R. W., A. J. Levitt, R. D. Levitan, M. W. Enns, R. Morehouse, E. E. Michalak, and E. M. Tam. "The Can-SAD Study: A Randomized Controlled Trial of the Effectiveness of Light Therapy and Fluoxetine in Patients with Winter Seasonal Affective Disorder." *American Journal of Psychiatry,* 163 (2006): 805–812.

Leiberg, S. and S. Anders. "The Multiple Facets of Empathy: A Survey of Theory and Evidence." *Progress in Brain Research,* 156 (2006): 419–440.

Lenoir, M., F. Serre, L. Cantin, and S. H. Ahmed. "Intense Sweetness Surpasses Cocaine Reward." *PLoS ONE,* Aug 1; 2(1) (2007): e698.

Lipman R. S., E. A. Brown, G. A. Silbert, D. G. Rains, D. A. Grady. "Cognitive Performance as Modified by Age and ECT History." *Progress in Neuropsychopharmacology and Biological Psychiatry,* 17 (1993):581–594.

Lovett, R. "Coffee: The Demon Drink?" *New Scientist,* 2518 (24 September 2005).

MacQueen, G. and P. Chokka. "Special Issues in the Management of Depression in Women." *Canadian Journal of Psychiatry,* 49 (3 Suppl 1) (2004): 27S–40S.

Marcus, G. *Kluge: The Haphazard Construction of the Human Mind.* New York: Houghton Mifflin Company, 2008.

Marshall, T. G. "Vitamin D Discovery Outpaces FDA Decision Making." *Bioessays,* 30 (2008): 173–182.

Masuelli, L., P. Trono, L. Marzocchella, M. A. Mrozek, C. Palumbo, M. Minieri, F. Carotenuto, R. Fiaccavento, A. Nardi, F. Galvano, P. Di Nardo, A.

Modesti, and R. Bei. "Intercalated Disk Remodeling in Delta-Sarcoglycan-Deficient Hamsters Fed with an Alpha-Linolenic Acid-Enriched Diet." *International Journal of Molecular Medicine,* 21 (2008): 41–48.

Max, D. T. "Happiness 101." *New York Times* (7 January 2007).

Mayers, A. G. and D. S. Baldwin. "Antidepressants and Their Effect on Sleep." *Human Psychopharmacology,* 20 (2005): 533–559.

McNamara, R. K. and S. E. Carlson. "Role of Omega-3 Fatty Acids in Brain Development and Function: Potential Implications for the Pathogenesis and Prevention of Psychopathology." *Prostaglandins, Leukotrienes, and Essential Fatty Acids,* 75 (2006): 329–349.

McPherson, J. M., L. Smith-Lovin, and M. B. Brashears. "Social Isolation in America: Changes in Core Discussion Networks over Two Decades." *American Sociological Review,* 71 (2006): 353–375.

Mersch, P. P., H. M. Middendorp, A. L. Bouhuys, D. G. Beersma, and R. H. van den Hoofdakker. "Seasonal Affective Disorder and Latitude: A Review of the Literature." *Journal of Affective Disorders,* 53 (1999): 35–48.

Miller, A. H., V. Maletic, and C. L. Raison. "Inflammation and Its Discontents: The Role of Cytokines in the Pathophysiology of Major Depression." *Biological Psychiatry* (in press).

Miller, K. B., B. Yost, A. Flaherty, M. M. Hillemeier, G. A. Chase, C. S. Weisman, and A. M. Dyer. "Health Status, Health Conditions, and Health Behaviors among Amish Women: Results from the Central Pennsylvania Women's Health Study (CePAWHS)." *Women's Health Issues,* 17 (2007): 162–171.

Miyake, Y., S. Sasaki, K. Tanaka, Y. Ohya, S. Miyamoto, I. Matsunaga, T. Yoshida, Y. Hirota, H. Oda; Osaka Maternal and Child Health Study Group. "Fish and Fat Intake and Prevalence of Allergic Rhinitis in Japanese Females: The Osaka Maternal and Child Health Study." *Journal of the American College of Nutrition,* 26 (2007): 279–287.

Moulds, M. L., E. Kandris, S. Starr, and A. C. Wong. "The Relationship between Rumination, Avoidance and Depression in a Non-Clinical Sample." *Behavioral Research and Therapy,* 45 (2007): 251–261.

Mueller, T. I., A. C. Leon, M. B. Keller, D. A. Solomon, J. Endicott, W. Coryell, M. Warshaw, and J. D. Maser. "Recurrence after Recovery from Major Depressive Disorder during 15 Years of Observational Follow-up." *American Journal of Psychiatry,* 156 (1999): 1000–1006.

National Sleep Foundation. *2008 Sleep in America Poll* (2008).

Nemeroff, C. B. and W. W. Vale. "The Neurobiology of Depression: Inroads to Treatment and New Drug Discovery." *Journal of Clinical Psychiatry,* 66 Suppl 7 (2005): 5–13.

Newton, R. P. "The Attachment Connection: Parenting a Secure and Confident Child Using the Science of Attachment Theory." Oakland, CA: New Harbinger, 2008.

Nierenberg, A. A., M. J. Ostacher, J. C. Huffman, R. M. Ametrano, M. Fava, and R. H. Perlis. "A Brief Review of Antidepressant Efficacy, Effectiveness, Indications, and Usage for Major Depressive Disorder." *Journal of Occupational and Environmental Medicine,* 50 (2008): 428–436.

Nolen-Hoeksema, S., B. E. Wisco, and S. Lyubomirsky. "Rethinking Rumination." *Perspectives on Psychological Science,* 3 (2008): 400–424.

Odeberg, H., B. Rodriguez-Silva, P. Salander, B. Mårtensson. "Individualized Continuation Electroconvulsive Therapy and Medication as a Bridge to Relapse Prevention after an Index Course of Electroconvulsive Therapy in Severe Mood Disorders: A Naturalistic 3-Year Cohort Study." *Journal of ECT*, 24 (2008):183–90.

Ogden, C. L., M. D. Carroll, L. R. Curtin, M. A. McDowell, C. J. Tabak, and K. M. Flegal. "Prevalence of Overweight and Obesity in the United States, 1999–2004." *JAMA,* 295 (2006): 1549–1555.

Olfson, M., S. C. Marcus, M. Tedeschi, and G. J. Wan. "Continuity of Antidepressant Treatment for Adults with Depression in the United States." *American Journal of Psychiatry,* 163 (2006): 101–108.

Opbroek, A., P. L. Delgado, C. Laukes, C. McGahuey, J. Katsanis, F. A. Moreno, and R. Manber. "Do SSRIs Inhibit Emotional Responses?" *International Journal of Neuropsychopharmacology,* 5 (2002): 147–151.

Page, M. E., M. J. Detke, A. Dalvi, L. G. Kirby, and I. Lucki. "Serotonergic Mediation of the Effects of Fluoxetine, but not Desipramine, in the Rat Forced Swimming Test." *Psychopharmacology,* 147 (1999): 162–167.

Parker, G. B., J. Crawford, and D. Hadzi-Pavlovic. "Quantified Superiority of Cognitive Behaviour Therapy to Antidepressant Drugs: A Challenge to an Earlier Meta-Analysis." *Acta Psychiatrica Scandinavica,* 118 (2008): 91–97.

Peet, M. "International Variations in the Outcome of Schizophrenia and the Prevalence of Depression in Relation to National Dietary Practices: An Ecological Analysis." *British Journal of Psychiatry,* 184 (2004): 404–408.

Peet, M. and D. F. Horrobin. "A Dose-Ranging Study of the Effects of Ethyl-Eicosapentaenoate in Patients with Ongoing Depression Despite Apparently Adequate Treatment with Standard Drugs." *Archives of General Psychiatry,* 59 (2002): 913–919.

Peet, M., B. Murphy, J. Shay, and D. Horrobin. "Depletion of Omega-3 Fatty Acid Levels in Red Blood Cell Membranes of Depressive Patients." *Biological Psychiatry,* 43 (1998): 315–319.

Penedo, F. J. and J. R. Dahn. "Exercise and Well-Being: A Review of Mental and Physical Health Benefits Associated with Physical Activity." *Current Opinion in Psychiatry,* 18 (2005): 189–193.

Ploughman, M. "Exercise Is Brain Food: The Effects of Physical Activity on Cognitive Function." *Developmental Neurorehabilitation,* 11 (2008): 236–240.

Pollan, M. *In Defense of Food: An Eater's Manifesto.* New York: Penguin Press, 2008.

Post, R. "Transduction of Psychosocial Stress into the Neurobiology of Recurrent Affective Disorder." *American Journal of Psychiatry*, 149 (1992):999–1010.

Praschak-Rieder, N., M. Willeit, A. A. Wilson, S. Houle, and J. H. Meyer. "Seasonal Variation in Human Brain Serotonin Transporter Binding." *Archives of General Psychiatry,* 65 (2008): 1072–1078.

Putnam, R. D. *Bowling Alone: The Collapse and Revival of American Community*. New York: Simon & Schuster, 2000.

Rampersaud, E., B. D. Mitchell, T. I. Pollin, M. Fu, H. Shen, J. R. O'Connell, J. L. Ducharme, S. Hines, P. Sack, R. Naglieri, A. R. Shuldiner, and S. Snitker. "Physical Activity and the Association of Common *FTO* Gene Variants with Body Mass Index and Obesity." *Archives of Internal Medicine,* 168 (2008): 1791–1797.

Rechtschaffen, A., B. M. Bergmann, C. A. Everson, C. A. Kushida, and M. A. Gilliland. "Sleep Deprivation in the Rat: X. Integration and Discussion of the Findings. 1989." *Sleep*, 25 (2002): 68–87.

Rose A. J., W. Carlson, E. M. Waller. "Prospective Associations of Co-Rumination with Friendship and Emotional Adjustment: Considering the Socioemotional Trade-Offs of Co-Rumination." *Developmental Psychology*, 43 (2007):1019–1031.

Rosen, L. N. and N. E. Rosenthal. "Seasonal Variations in Mood and Behavior in the General Population: A Factor-Analytic Approach." *Psychiatry Research,* 38 (1991): 271–283.

Ross, B. M., J. Seguin, and L. E. Sieswerda. "Omega-3 Fatty Acids as Treatments for Mental Illness: Which Disorder and Which Fatty Acid?" *Lipids, Health, and Disease,* 18 (2007): 6–27.

Ruff, C. R., E. Trinkhaus, and T. W. Holliday. "Body Mass and Encephalization in Pleistocene Homo." *Nature,* 387: 173–176.

Russo, S., I. P. Kema, M. R. Fokkema, J. C. Boon, P. H. Willemse, E. G. de Vries, J. A. den Boer, and J. Korf. "Tryptophan as a Link between Psychopathology and Somatic States." *Psychosomatic Medicine,* 65 (2003): 665–671.

Sackeim H. A., J. Prudic, R. Fuller, J. Keilp, P. W. Lavori, M. Olfson. "The Cognitive Effects of Electroconvulsive Therapy in Community Settings." *Neuropsychopharmacology,* 32 (2007):244–254.

Sagduyu, K., M. E. Dokucu, B. A. EddyA, G. Craigen, C. F. Baldassano, and A. Yildiz. "Omega-3 Fatty Acids Decreased Irritability of Patients with Bipolar Disorder in an Add-on, Open Label Study." *Nutrition Journal,* 4 (2005): 6.

Schieffelin, E. L.. "The Cultural Analysis of Depressive Affect: An Example from Papua New Guinea." In A. M. Kleinman and B. Good (Eds.), *Culture and Depression* (pp. 101–133). Berkeley: University of California Press, 1985.

Sears, B. *The Omega Rx Zone: The Miracle of the New High-Dose Fish Oil.* New York: Collins Living, 2002.

Seidman, S. N. "Testosterone Deficiency and Mood in Aging Men: Pathogenic and Therapeutic Interactions." *World Journal of Biological Psychiatry,* 4 (2003): 14–20.

Seligman, M. "Why Is There So Much Depression Today? The Waxing of the Individual and the Waning of the Commons." In Rex Ingram (ed.), *Contemporary Psychological Approaches to Depression* (pp. 1–9). New York: Plenum, 1990.

Simopoulos, A. P. "Omega-3 Fatty Acids in Inflammation and Autoimmune Diseases." *Journal of the American College of Nutrition,* 21 (2002): 495–505.

Simopoulos, A. P. "Evolutionary Aspects of Diet, the Omega-6: Omega-3 Ratio, and Gene Expression." In M. S. Meskin, W. R. Bidlack, & R. K. Randolph: *Phytochemicals: Nutrient-Gene Interactions* (pp. 137–160). CRC Press: 2006.

Stagnitti, M. N. *Statistical Brief #206: Antidepressants Prescribed by Medical Doctors in Office Based and Outpatient Settings by Specialty for the U.S. Civilian Noninstitutionalized Population, 2002 and 2005.* Agency for Healthcare Research and Quality: Medical Expenditure Panel Survey, June 2008.

Steiger, A. "Neurochemical Regulation of Sleep." *Journal of Psychiatric Research,* 41 (2007): 537–552.

Stoll, A. L., W. E. Severus, M. P. Freeman, S. Rueter, H. A. Zboyan, E. Diamond, K. K. Cress, and L. B. Marangell. "Omega-3 Fatty Acids in Bipolar Disorder: A Preliminary Double-Blind, Placebo-Controlled Trial." *Archives of General Psychiatry,* 56 (1999): 407–412.

Svartberg, M. and T. C. Stiles. "Comparative Effects of Short-Term Psychodynamic Psychotherapy: A Meta-Analysis." *Journal of Consulting and Clinical Psychology,* 59 (1991): 704–714.

Thase, M. E. "Correlates and Consequences of Chronic Insomnia." *General Hospital Psychiatry,* 2 (2005): 100–112.

Tooby, J. and L. Cosmides. "On the Universality of Human Nature and the Uniqueness of the Individual: The Role of Genetics and Adaptation." *Journal of Personality,* 58 (1990): 17–67.

Trivedi, M. H., M. Fava, S. R. Wisniewski, M. E. Thase, F. Quitkin, D. Warden, L. Ritz, A. A. Nierenberg, B. D. Lebowitz, M. M. Biggs, J. F. Luther, K. Shores-Wilson, A. J. Rush; STAR*D Study Team. "Medication Augmentation after the Failure of SSRIs for Depression." *New England Journal of Medicine,* 354 (2006): 1243–1252.

Trivedi, M. H., A. J. Rush, S. R. Wisniewski, N. N. Nierenberg, D. Warden, L. Ritz, G. Norquist, R. H. Howland, B. Lebowitz, P. J. McGrath, K. Shores-Wilson, M. M. Biggs, G. H. Balasubramani, and M. Fava for the STAR*D Study Team. "Evaluation of Outcomes with Citalopram for Depression Using Measurement-based Sare in STAR*D: Implications for Clinical Practice." *American Journal of Psychiatry,* 163 (2006): 28–40.

U.S. Department of Health and Human Services. *Physical Activity and Health: A Report of the Surgeon General.* Atlanta: U.S. Department of Health and Human Services, Centers for Disease Control and Prevention National Center for Chronic Disease Prevention and Health Promotion, 1999.

Vaynman, S. and F. Gomez-Pinilla. "Revenge of the 'Sit': How Lifestyle Impacts Neuronal and Cognitive Health through Molecular Systems that Interface Energy Metabolism with Neuronal Plasticity." *Journal of Neuroscience Research,* 84 (2006): 699–715.

Vieth, R., P. C. Chan, and G. D. MacFarlane. "Efficacy and Safety of Vitamin D3 Intake Exceeding the Lowest Observed Adverse Effect Level." *American Journal of Clinical Nutrition,* 73 (2001): 288–294.

Weissman, M. M., R. C. Bland, G. J. Canino, C. Faravelli, S. Greenwald, H. G. Hwu, P. R. Joyce, E. G. Karam, C. K. Lee, J. Lellouch, J. P. Lepine, S. C.

Newman, M. Rubio-Stipec, J. E. Wells, P. J. Wickramaratne, H. Wittchen, and E. K. Yeh. "Cross-National Epidemiology of Major Depression and Bipolar Disorder." *Journal of the American Medical Association,* 276 (1996): 293–299.

Werneke, U., S. Northey, and D. Bhugra. "Antidepressants and Sexual Dysfunction." *Acta Psychiatrica Scandinavica,* 114 (2006): 384–397.

Wu, J., S. Seregard, and P. V. Algvere. "Photochemical Damage of the Retina." *Survey of Ophthalmology,* 51 (2006): 461–481.

Wu, A., Z. Ying, and F. Gomez-Pinilla. "Docosahexaenoic Acid Dietary Supplementation Enhances the Effects of Exercise on Synaptic Plasticity and Cognition." *Neuroscience,* 155 (2008): 751–759.

Young, G. S., J. A. Conquer, and R. Thomas. "Effect of Randomized Supplementation with High Dose Olive, Flax or Fish Oil on Serum Phospholipid Fatty Acid Levels in Adults with Attention Deficit Hyperactivity Disorder." *Reproduction Nutrition Development,* 45 (2005): 549–558.

Acknowledgments

Most of what I know about depression I have learned from my patients. Their courage and determination in fighting the illness have inspired me more than words can express.

Because clinical research is a collaborative process, I am deeply indebted to the many talented students who helped make the Therapeutic Lifestyle Change (TLC) program a reality. First and foremost, I am grateful to Leslie Karwoski for her boundless dedication, intellectual creativity, and administrative skill as the first project coordinator for the TLC Lab; without her heroic contributions, the TLC program could not have come to fruition. I also want to thank Andy Lehman—our longtime lab coordinator—for his rare gift of bringing order to chaos, and Brian Stites for his energetic efforts on every conceivable front. Likewise, I want to express my gratitude to Dana Steidtmann for her steady willingness to step up at every turn and for coining the name of the protocol itself. Thanks are also due to the student cotherapists who served so skillfully on the project—Amyn Hirani, Chantal Young, Jenny Prohaska, Susan Reneau, and Brenda Sampat—and to the other key members of our research team, including April Minatrea, Natalie Stroupe, Eugene Botanov, Matt Gallagher, Brandon Hikaka, Jenny Wurtz, Chris Heath, John Jacobson, Adam Brazil, Sarah Thompson, Mark Brehm, Adrienne Belk, Adriann Farrell, and Christina Williams.

I owe a profound debt of gratitude to Ed Craighead, my mentor in graduate school and beyond, for his unwavering support, and for teaching me much of what I know about clinical research. Additionally, the feedback of my colleagues has served as an invaluable catalyst for improving the TLC program. I am especially grateful to Rick Ingram, Omri Gillath, Nancy Hamilton, John Colombo, Paul Atchley, Ray Higgins, Ruthann Atchley, and Sarah Kirk at the University of Kansas, and to David Miklowitz (University of Colorado), David Buss (University of Texas), and Scott Lilienfeld (Emory University).

My heartfelt appreciation as well to Harriet Lerner for her generous friendship and insightful guidance regarding the writing process, and for recommending *The Depression Cure* to Jo-Lynne Worley—agent extraordinaire—and her partner, Joanie Shoemaker. I also want to thank Matthew Lohr, my first editor at Da Capo, for believing in the project, and Wendy Francis for her wise editorial role in shepherding the book to completion. Additionally, Christine Marra helped improve the manuscript in countless ways with her editorial production team.

Many dear friends and loved ones—especially my parents—were also kind enough to read early drafts of the manuscript and provide superb feedback, and I cannot thank them enough. Likewise, my beloved daughter, Abby, has shown a maturity and understanding far beyond her years in putting up with my relentless work schedule this past year; her *joie de vivre* has sustained me through many moments of flagging stamina, and I thank God for her every day of my life.

Finally, I am eternally grateful to my wife, Maria, for her love, support, friendship, encouragement, and clinical wisdom, and for serving as such a valuable sounding board during the writing process. Her contributions are reflected on each page of *The Depression Cure*.

Index

Index references in bold refer to text graphics.

About the Author

Stephen S. Ilardi, PhD, is associate professor of clinical psychology at the University of Kansas and the author of over forty professional articles on mental illness. Through his active clinical practice, Dr. Ilardi has treated several hundred depressed patients. He lives with his family in Lawrence, Kansas.